W9-ABM-906

SOME FAMOUS
SEA FIGHTS

Some Famous Sea Fights

BY

FITZHUGH GREEN

AND

HOLLOWAY FROST

Essay Index Reprint Series

BOOKS FOR LIBRARIES PRESS
FREEPORT, NEW YORK

Reprinted 1968 by arrangement with Appleton-Century,
affiliate of Meredith Press

LIBRARY OF CONGRESS CATALOG CARD NUMBER:
68-58792

PREFACE

In this volume we have endeavored to present eight pictures of sea warfare at widely separated periods by describing great naval battles in their historical settings.

We have attempted to combine accuracy of detail with popular treatment of the subject so as to make our description interesting both to the technical and the general reader.

The campaigns and battles are clarified by numerous sketches and illustrated with prints which show the types of warship of the period.

In the selection of the actions described in this volume we have been guided by the desire to show sea-power at widely spaced epochs and to bring on the scene every great historical navy at least once, and have avoided any magnification of our own naval history.

In every chapter, except that describing the battle of Gibraltar, we have had access to the original authorities and have developed our story directly from them. We are indebted to the Navy Department Library for furnishing all the books used in the preparation of this work.

We are sincerely grateful to the Japanese Admiralty for permission to use two paintings by a famous Japanese artist and to Mr. A. G. H. Macpherson and Halton & Truscott Smith, Ltd., for their permission to use a number of very fine prints contained in "The Sea: Its History and Romance," by Frank C. Bowen.

Fitzhugh Green
Holloway Frost

CONTENTS

ILLUSTRATIONS

Macpherson Collection

H.M.S. "LONDON," SECOND-RATE, 90 GUNS, OFF RAM HEAD, NEAR PLYMOUTH
(FROM A LINE ENGRAVING PUBLISHED 1781)

SOME FAMOUS SEA FIGHTS

SOME FAMOUS SEA FIGHTS

CHAPTER I

Salamis

THE Battle of Salamis was fought in the Aegean Sea in 480 B.C., between an invading Persian horde and the desperate Greeks. It was one of the grandest sea fights in all history. In it nearly half a million men and over a thousand ships came to grips. Xerxes, the Persian leader, sat on an overlooking hill and wept when he saw his vast fleet crushed.

Herodotus, Greek poet, was five years old at the time. So when he came later to record the details of the battle he got them from eye-witnesses. Since Greece had set up man's first full literary standard, the story of Salamis is the first word-picture of a sea fight that was ever completely recorded.

Before Christ the Mediterranean and its environments comprised the known world. Crete was the England of its day; its colonies another British Empire. Then the Phoenicians, on the eastern end of the Mediterranean, grew strong at sea and smashed Crete. Next the Persians, grown rich, bought mercenaries and smothered the Phoenicians. Swollen with wealth and power, the Persians determined to acquire Greece.

At Salamis occurred the decisive clash between these two ancient civilizations—the great Persian Empire and the small group of Greek city States. Actually the struggle was not ended until Mardonius was defeated the following year at Platea. But Salamis was its turning point. This battle was as decisive as the battle of the Nile, which centuries later showed Bonaparte that, despite military successes, the permanent retention of Egypt by the French was impossible. Sea power both times counted most. For in ancient days the communications between Asia Minor and Greece depended upon water transportation almost as much as did those between France and Egypt in 1800.

Not only did great issues hang in the balance at Salamis, but the battle itself was staged on a gigantic scale. In a strait less than a mile wide, there were packed some twelve hundred vessels, manned by nearly three hundred thousand men. This number far exceeded those engaged in the great modern sea battle off Jutland. Herodotus estimates as 5,283,220 the total of Xerxes' host, including army and fleet, camp-followers, and crews of merchant vessels. "As for the number of the women who ground the corn," he adds, "of the concubines, and the eunuchs, no one can give any sure account of it; nor can the baggage horses and other sumpter-beasts, nor the Indian hounds which followed the army, be calculated, by reason of their multitude. Hence I am not at all surprised that the water of the rivers was found too scant for the army in some instances; rather it is a marvel to me how the provisions did not fail, when the numbers were so great." He couldn't add that there were no telephones, telegraphs, motor trucks, canned food, railroads, or other modern aids to feeding an army.

At this crisis of world history the Persian Empire was still young and at the height of its power. No Alexander could then have performed his feats against it. Seventy-eight years only had passed since Cyrus the Great had arrived upon the scene and made himself king over the Medes and the Persians. Four years later, in 554 B.C., he overcame Croesus, King of Lydia, in the battle of Thymbra. His lieutenants continued the conquest of Asia Minor. Cyrus went right on and overran the great territories extending to the eastward as far as India and to the northward past the present boundaries of Russia and Turkestan. Nothing now remained but mighty Babylon, with its walls seventy feet thick and 325 feet high. It took Cyrus two years to reduce this great fortress, and then only by a stratagem, as the famous handwriting appeared on the walls of Belshazzar's palace. This showed the man's resourcefulness as well as his power to lead.

During his remaining years he endeavored to extend his conquests over the Scythians, those mystic tribes of nomads on the northern fringes of civilization. After varying fortunes, the great leader and his entire army were annihilated north of the Jaxartes River in 529 B.C.

Cambyses, next to rule Persia, reigned only eight years. But even this short time gave him the opportunity to further increase the extent of his empire, notably by the conquest of Egypt in 525 B.C. It is a pity we haven't a clearer picture of this gorgeous golden age of that pagan empire. Surely her wise men must have shaken their heads.

After these great conquerors came Darius, in 521, who by his able statesmanship and military ability consolidated the wide empire during a long reign of thirty-six years. While very successful in this way, his military expeditions to extend the Persian power were not always so fortunate. He was an administrator more than soldier. In 508 he crossed the Bosporus and marched to the Danube to attack the Scythians. But his army was worn down in a protracted campaign similar to Napoleon's Russian adventure; and he was fortunate to recross the Bosporus after a loss of seventy thousand men. In the following years, however, his generals were able to seize Thrace and Macedonia.

In 500 the Ionian Greeks in Asia Minor revolted and with the assistance of the Athenians burned Sardis. This hostile mixing of Athens into Persian affairs was the primary cause of the great conflict between Persia and Greece. Having put down the revolution, Darius, in 492, sent his first fleet against Greece. But the whole force was completely wrecked off the Mont Athos promontory. Two years later he sent a second powerful fleet directly against Athens, only to have the army landed from it defeated in the battle of Marathon by the Athenians under Miltiades. Darius died in 485 while organizing another expedition. He left a country seething with desire to destroy Greece. Salamis was almost at hand.

As Xerxes came to the throne his first efforts were

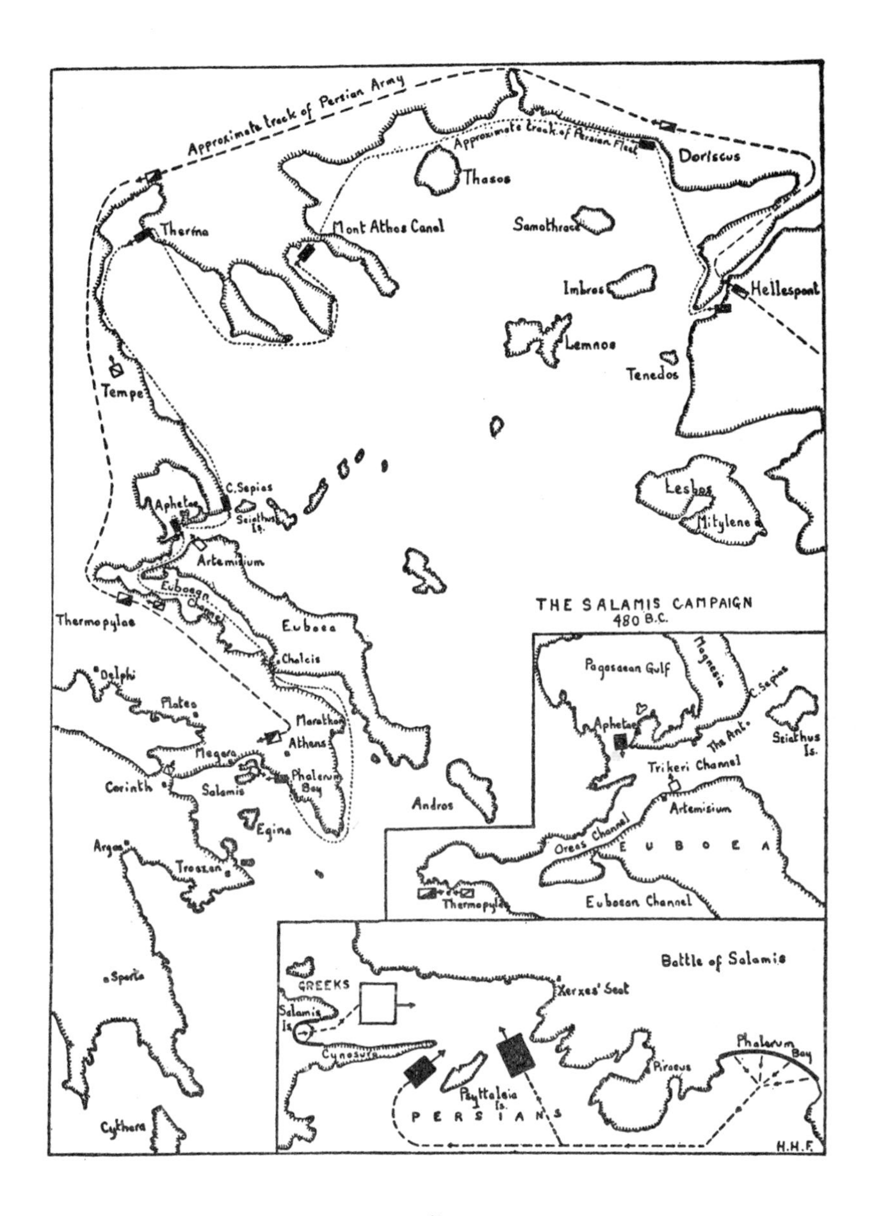

Approximate track of Persian Army
Approximate track of Persian Fleet
Doriscus
Thasos
Therma
Mont Athos Canal
Samothrace
Imbros
Hellespont
Lemnos
Tenedos
Tempe
C. Sepias
Aphetae
Sciathus Is.
Artemisium
Euboean Channel
Lesbos
Mitylene
THE SALAMIS CAMPAIGN
480 B.C.
Thermopylae
Euboea
Chalcis
Delphi
Platea
Marathon
Athens
Megara
Phalerum Bay
Corinth
Salamis
Andros
Egina
Argos
Troezen
Sparta
Cythera
Pagasaean Gulf
Magnesia
C. Sepias
Aphetae
The Ant.
Sciathus Is.
Trikeri Channel
Artemisium
Oreos Channel
E U B O E A
Thermopylae
Euboean Channel
Battle of Salamis
GREEKS
Xerxes' Seat
Salamis Is.
Cynosura
Phalerum Bay
Piraeus
Psyttaleia Is.
PERSIANS
H.H.F.

devoted to crushing an Egyptian revolt. Then, after long consultation with his advisers, he decided to attack Greece, both to avenge the defeat at Marathon and to extend the boundaries of his empire through Europe. In 484 he commenced preparations on a scale which reminds us of World War campaigns.

In addition to the bridging of rivers, the building of roads, and the collection of provisions in Asia Minor, Thrace, and Macedonia, Xerxes performed two great engineering feats. In order to prevent another disaster to the fleet off Mont Athos, he dug a canal through the peninsula. Herodotus says this gigantic task took three years to complete. It was about a mile and a half in length, some ten feet deep and wide enough for two triremes to pass with their oars out—that is, about 150 feet. The maximum depth of excavation was sixty feet.

And the Greeks knew what he was about. Picture their feelings!

The first bridges over the Hellespont were carried away in a storm. "So when Xerxes heard of it," Herodotus reports, "he was full of wrath, and straightway gave orders that the Hellespont should receive three hundred lashes and that a pair of fetters should be cast into it. * * * When the sea was thus punished by his orders, he likewise commanded that the overseers of the work should lose their heads." Such was the vainglory of the mighty emperor. No wonder divine wrath came on him later. Every day brought Salamis nearer.

Thus encouraged, the new engineers took good care that they should not suffer a similar fate. To form the foundation for the upper bridge no less than 360 large vessels, either triremes or fifty-oared galleys, were securely moored in a line abreast across the channel. These vessels supported six great cables which ran from shore to shore; two were made of white flax and four of papyrus. Across the cables were laid planks, upon which were placed brushwood covered with a thick layer of earth. On either side bulwarks were built up to such a height that the animals would not be frightened at the sight of the water as it rushed down with its three-knot current. The construction of the lower bridge was similar, except that only 314 vessels were used. Such creations and the cost in labor would be stupendous even today.

In the fall of 481 Xerxes mustered part of his army at Sardis, where he spent the winter. Early in the spring he broke up for the Hellespont, where he was joined by the other troops and his fleet. He foresaw no battle ahead: only a brush, a fleeing enemy, and triumph.

It was here that Artabanus, the soothsayer, accurately disclosed the two great dangers which most threatened the success of the expedition. "O King," he said with amazing temerity, "it is not possible that a man of understanding should find fault with the size of thy army or the number of thy ships. Yet, the more thou addest to these, the more hostile will those two things, whereof I speak, become.

"These two things are the land and the sea. In all the wide sea there is nowhere a harbor large enough to receive thy vessels, in case a storm arose, and afford them a sure protection. And thou shalt want not one such harbor only but many in succession along the entire coast by which thou art about to make thy advance. In default, then, of such harbors, it is well to bear in mind that chances rule men, and not men chances. Such is the first of the two dangers.

"Now I will speak to thee of the second: the land will also be thine enemy. For if no one resists thy advance, as thou proceedest further and further, insensibly lured onwards (for who is ever sated with success?), thou wilt find it more and more hostile. I mean that should nothing else withstand thee, the mere distance, becoming greater as time goes on, will at last produce a famine. Methinks it is best for men, when they take council, to be timorous, and imagine all possible calamities; but when the time for action comes, then to deal boldly."

The prophet's high standing with his master is evidenced by the fact that he was suffered to live after so dire a boding as this.

To the argument Xerxes made a reply which set forth the true principles of leadership. Since he later acted so at variance with its noble sentiments, it is possible that we are indebted for it to the imagination of the Greek historian.

"There is reason, O Artabanus," the king is alleged to have said, "in every peril which thou hast listed. But I pray thee, fear not all things alike, nor count up every risk. For if in each matter that comes before us thou wilt look to all possible chances, never wilt thou achieve anything. Far better it is to have a stout heart always, and suffer one's share of evils, than to be ever fearing what may happen, and never incur a mischance. * * * Success for the most part attends those who act boldly, not those who weigh everything and are slack to venture. Thou seest to how great a height the power of Persia has now reached? Never would it have grown to this point if those who sat upon the throne before me had been like-minded with thee; or even, though not like-minded, had listened to councilors of such a spirit. 'Twas by brave ventures that they extended their sway; for great empires can only be conquered by great risks. We follow, then, the example of our fathers in making this march."

It was a fine retort, worthy of a great leader.

The crossing of the Hellespont over its two bridges required seven days and nights. The vast Persian army and fleet then proceeded separately to Doriscus, where the forces were mustered. Herodotus says that the army numbered 1,700,000 infantry, 80,000 cavalry and 20,000 in the camel and chariot corps. Think of the supplies this horde must have needed! He describes in great detail the clothing and arms of the races which made up the array, including the Ethiopians and Arabians from the southern, the Indians from the eastern, and the Scythians from the northern limits of the empire.

The fleet consisted of 1207 triremes, furnished as follows:

Phoenicians	300	Egyptians	200
Cyprians	150	Cicilians	100
Pamphylians	30	Lycians	50

Dorians	30	Carians	70
Ionians	100	Islanders	17
Aeolians	60	Hellespontians	100

Each of these vessels was manned by about 200 sailors of the race furnishing the vessel. Each crew contained also about thirty soldiers, who were either Persians, Medes or Sacans. In addition to the triremes, there were some 3000 thirty-oared and fifty-oared galleys and horse transports, each manned by about eighty sailors. The entire fleet mustered about 518,000 men. Above these numbers there were many camp-followers ashore with the army and many grain ships to carry provisions for both army and fleet. The disorganized mob of camp-followers no doubt gave as much color as the armed forces.

After inspecting his army, Xerxes boarded a Sidonian galley and reviewed the fleet. "The captains took their ships," says Herodotus, "to a distance of about four hundred feet from the shore and here lay-to, with their vessels in a single row, prows facing the land. Upon the decks were the fighting men, accoutered as if for war, while the king sailed along in the open space between the ships and the shore and so reviewed the fleet."

Xerxes, filled with pride at the might of his huge army, asked Demaratus, an exiled Spartan, if he thought that the Greeks would lift a hand against such a host. To which the Spartan retorted:

"Want has at all times been a fellow-dweller with us in our land, while Valor is an ally whom we have gained by dint of wisdom and strict laws. Her aid enables us to drive out want and escape thraldom. Brave are all the Greeks who dwell in any Dorian land; but what I am about to say does not concern all, but only the Lacedaemonians. First, then: come what may, they will never accept thy terms, which would reduce Greece to slavery; and further, they are sure to join battle with thee though all the rest of the Greeks should submit to thy will. As for their numbers, do not ask how many they are, that their resistance should be a measurable thing; for if a thousand of them should take the field, they will meet thee in battle; and so will any number, be it less than this or be it more."

Xerxes' amusement at this bold statement might well seem justified; for, compared with the military and naval power of the Persian Empire, the forces which the Greek States could bring into the field was insignificant. But while these States had never extended their sway over wide territories, their military traditions had been established long before Cyrus, and their military organization probably has never in history been surpassed for thoroughness and efficiency.

Let us consider this matter for a moment:

As early as 880 B.C. Lycurgus by his strict laws made the everyday life of the Spartans such arduous preparation for war that war itself was welcomed as a relaxation. Every military virtue was bred into this noble race. Little Sparta, with its five thousand heavy infantry, for centuries enjoyed the reputation of invincibility. Its very name has come down as synonymous with stoic courage and stout spirit.

Athens was not far behind. She was able to bring

about eight thousand heavy-armed infantry into battle, although their training was not so complete nor their discipline so strict. But if the Athenian soldier was not equal to the Spartan, his leaders were more competent and worldly-wise and made up deficiency of the individual by the skilful strategy of their campaigns. There were other powerful Greek States. But due to continual internal wars, jealousy not only prevented proper cooperation but caused many to side with the Persians. Unhappily, there was no national spirit in Greece. Xerxes counted heavily upon this to assist him in his campaign.

Napoleon declared that in war men are nothing, but that one man is everything. Never was there a campaign which more clearly illustrated this epigram. So, the lowly-born Abrotonon might well say with pride:

> Let the Greek women scorn me, if they please;
> I was the mother of Themistocles.

Here, if ever, was a real *strategos*, as the Athenians called their generals. He merits being called the father of naval strategy. And to this consummate leadership mainly is due the triumphal outcome of the campaign. A man of unbounded energy and ambition, a born military leader, a skilful politician, he was resolved to stop at nothing to make Athens great or to advance his personal fortunes. At this time he had the foresight to see that these objectives were linked with the fortunes of Greece. So he was the patriot after all.

At Marathon, Themistocles with Aristides commanded the Athenian center. "When others were of opinion," says Plutarch, "that the battle of Marathon would be an end to the war, Themistocles thought that it was but the beginning of far greater conflicts. For these, to the benefit of all Greece, he kept himself in continual readiness and his city also in proper training, foreseeing from far before what would happen." So clear-cut sometimes are the workings of Fate that one cannot but suspect a sentient overlord of creation.

Themistocles' preparation took the form of naval expansion. Knowing that he could not persuade his people that they were in danger of being attacked by the Persians, who lived at a great distance and whose coming was very uncertain, he proposed that the silver from the mines of Laurium should no longer be distributed among the citizens but used to construct triremes to fight with the Eginetans, who controlled the seas off the Attic coast. By this and other means he ultimately increased the Athenian fleet from fifty to two hundred triremes. . . . And daily Salamis drew nigh.

In 481 Greece at last was aroused to its danger. A congress of leaders met at Corinth. Here resourceful Themistocles did much to compose the differences between the States. For instance, he brought to a close the war with the Eginetans. Messengers were sent to Syracuse, Crete, Corcyra, and to the Argives, asking for assistance. But all efforts to muster aid were ineffectual, principally because these nations refused to serve under Sparta's leadership. Grecian pride would not relinquish the right to command, either on land or at sea.

The Greeks, growing anxious, now sent spies to Sardis, where they were captured. With not a little wit, Xerxes had them shown all the Persian forces and sent back unmolested. His hope was that the Greeks would capitulate before he began his march. Thus would his troops be saved all the trouble of an expedition.

When the Athenians assembled to elect their general it looked as though Epicydes, an eloquent orator but a poor soldier, should win the vote. "But Themistocles," says Plutarch, "fearing that, if the command should fall into such hands, all would be lost, bought off Epicydes and his pretensions."

Themistocles was a man of enterprise. He at once proposed that the galleys set sail and meet the Persians at a great distance from Greece. But this proved too bold a course for the hesitant Athenians to adopt.

The Thessalians, who would now be the first to receive the Persian attack, sent an embassy to the congress at Corinth to point out their danger. They declared that unless they were supported by a strong force it would be necessary for them to surrender. In reply 10,000 heavy-armed infantry set forth under Themistocles and Evaenetus (the Spartan) to hold the defile of Tempe. But the former soon found that this position could be turned by another route. And believing that his command was not strong enough to hold both or to fight on the broad plains of Thessaly, he prudently returned home without having accomplished any more than causing the Persians to march by a longer route. Themistocles was not a Xenophon on this occasion.

Meanwhile Xerxes had commenced his advance from Doriscus in three columns. One followed the shore in company with the fleet, while the other two took parallel routes farther inland. The fleet passed through the Mont Athos canal and pushed ahead to Therma, where it waited until the army assembled. Here the heralds that Xerxes had sent to the Greek States returned to him. Ten of them brought the "earth and water" which indicated submission. Those sent to Sparta and Athens were cruelly killed, a grievous breach of international law even for those days.

Before examining the next moves of the Greeks to meet the Persian advance, it will be appropriate to examine the capabilities of the naval vessels then in use. It was upon these that existing strategical methods depended. The naval vessel of ancient history was the trireme, a galley with three banks of oars one above the other. It was about 150 feet in length, eighteen feet in extreme width and drew about four feet of water. In battle it was used principally for ramming. To this end a heavy pointed bronze casting was fitted to the bow below the water line. In order to ram, high speed was essential. The design of the ship was therefore long and narrow, somewhat along the lines of modern destroyers, so that two hundred rowers could be seated. In addition, there were some thirty soldiers stationed where the vessel was decked over at bow and stern, who discharged arrows, threw javelins, and at times even boarded with the sword and axe.

While the trireme was designed for battle, it was utterly unsuited for long cruises. The large number of men carried—forty men would be the crew of a vessel of the same size in these days—made living conditions on board most uncomfortable. Water and provisions could be carried for only about three days. Also the oars could not be used in rough weather. Even in smooth water the endurance of the rowers limited the distance which could be covered without a good rest to about eighty miles. Although a mast could be set up and a sail hoisted, this was useful only with a favorable wind. Due to their shallow draft, it was difficult for triremes to gain any distance to windward. In storms oars would be broken up and the sail of little value, so that ships were driven before the wind. Woe to those on a lee shore!

All these limitations made it desirable to keep under way only during daylight. Each night the ships were drawn up on the beach and the crews rested. As the crews could be organized for fighting on shore, this facilitated defense of the landing place and the seizure of provisions. In some cases triremes were left in the water with an anchor down at the bows and a line running from the stern to the shore. Where the small extent of the beach would not permit this the ships were anchored in several lines. This was fatal if caught by a storm. That such a procedure was often unavoidable is seen in the fact that a beach twelve miles long would be required for the Persian fleet to be secured in one line, assuming the small interval of fifty feet between vessels.

The Aegean Sea with its many islands was well suited for the use of the trireme, particularly when the fleets were small. It was much safer to proceed through the islands than along the coast. In a storm a lee could always be found on one side of an island; while along the coast an onshore gale was fatal unless friendly protected harbors were available. As the size of fleets increased, it became more and more difficult to find harbors and beaches of sufficient size to receive them and to secure provisions for so many men. Thus the size of the Persian fleet was not without its disadvantages.

After the failure to hold the defile at Tempe, there were but two positions where there seemed any likelihood of stopping Xerxes' advance: the Pass of Thermopylae and the Isthmus of Corinth. As the latter position would surrender Athens and all northern Greece to the enemy, it was decided to hold Thermopylae. At Artemisium there was an excellent position for the fleet; and as these places are near to one another it would be easy for the fleet and army to hold communication.

The Greek position was, in fact, an ideal one. The Pass at Thermopylae was at one place "only wide enough for a single carriage" to pass between the mountains and the sea. An old wall across the road was repaired by the defending force. Here the barbarians could make no use of their vast numbers nor of their cavalry. Surely strategy is ancient as the race.

Twenty-two miles northeast of Thermopylae was Artemisium, a fine beach on the northern shore of the island of Euboea perfectly protected against the weather and from attack on the land side by Xerxes' army. This position commanded the narrow passage between Euboea and the mainland leading to both Thermopylae and Athens. It protected, therefore, the sea flank of the Greek army; prevented the Persian army from crossing to Euboea; kept the Persian fleet from using the protected inland route to Athens and even from bringing up supplies by sea to the Persian army. Furthermore, the only sheltered base for the Persian fleet was within the Pagasaean Gulf. Therefore, its own lines of supplies would have to run through the Trikeri Channel, which also was commanded by the Greeks at Artemisium. The Greeks had only to hold their double position for a short time to compel the enemy to withdraw from lack of food, which could not be transported through the mountains in sufficient quantities for such an enormous host. On the other hand, the Greeks could obtain ample food from Euboea; or if they desired, could bring it up by either sea or land.

The tactical position at Artemisium was almost as favorable from the naval viewpoint as Thermopylae was from the military; for in its narrow passages and channels the Persians could not bring their full force to play. Triremes could not be spaced at less than sixty yards' interval abreast; a three mile channel would allow a front of but one hundred vessels. The Greeks, with their 271 ships, later reinforced to 325, could therefore form a line about three ships deep, with both their flanks protected by the land, while the Persians with their greater numbers risked locking their ships together in a confused mass.

As the Greeks took up their position they did not fail to obey the command of the Delphic Oracle to "pray to the winds, for the winds would do Greece good service."

Upon the assembly of the fleet there occurred the usual acrid discussion as to which State should nominate the commander-in-chief. This clearly shows how loose was the bond between units. As the Athenians had provided nearly half the fleet, they demanded that Themistocles be given the command; but he tactfully withdrew in favor of Eurybiades the Spartan.

This matter settled, three scouting vessels hastened to the northward of Sciathus Island. Here they were set upon by ten Persian scouts; two were captured, while the third was beached so that the crew could escape. The Persian vessels then located a sunken rock, called "the Ant," between Sciathus and the Magnesian coast, and there set up a stone pillar which they had brought with them for that purpose. Apparently this mark was a beacon to indicate the course to be followed by the fleet.

As soon as smoke signals from Sciathus told Eurybiades of the loss of his scouting vessels, he hurriedly withdrew to Chalcis to watch the narrow passage there between Euboea and the mainland. These feverish movements of the Greeks reveal the terrific anxiety under which they labored.

Xerxes soon broke out from Therma with his army and reached a position facing the Greek defenses at Thermopylae. This done, the fleet left Therma and proceeded along the coast to the southward. It consisted now of 1327 triremes, the Thracians having been compelled to furnish some 120 additional vessels when the Persian army marched through their territories.

By dark the fleet had reached the region of Cape Sepias on the Magnesian coast. Here the short beach compelled the galleys to anchor in eight rows off the shore. This proved most unfortunate. In the morning a gale rose and blew directly on the coast for three days. Some 400 triremes in addition to many small craft were wrecked among the rocks.

As a result of this favor of fortune the Greeks later built a temple to Boreas, the god of winds, for his timely intervention at this stage in the campaign. His favor was attributed to the fact that his wife was supposed to be an Athenian woman. "Whether it was owing to this," naïvely writes Herodotus, "that Boreas fell with violence on the barbarians at their anchorage I cannot say."

When the Greek admirals heard the good news from their scouts, they hastened back with all speed to Artemisium, expecting to find a very few ships left to oppose them. But when the storm ceased, the Persians, far from being dismayed by their disaster, devised a plan to surround the Greek fleet. Two hundred of the invading triremes were detached from the main force. Secretly they sailed around Sciathus Island to run down the eastern coast of Euboea and cut off the retreat of the defenders who lay in the Euboean Channel. The remainder sailed through the Trikeri Channel into the Pagasaean Gulf and established themselves at Aphetae. This was the place where Jason sent Hercules ashore to get water before sailing for the Golden Fleece. Fifteen of their ships, bringing up the rear, mistook the Greek fleet for their own and were captured.

While the Persians had still some seven hundred triremes, the Greeks had but 271. These vessels were furnished and manned as follows:

Athenians	127[1]	Corinthians	40
Megarians	20	Chalcideans	20[2]
Eginetans	18	Sicoyanians	12
Lacedaemonians ...	10	Epidaurians	8
Eretrians	7	Troezenians	5
Styreans	2	Ceans	2

The Ceans furnished two and the Locrians seven fifty-oared galleys.

When it was learned that the Persians had not lost as many vessels as had been reported, the Greeks became panicky again and began to speak of drawing back from Artemisium toward the inner parts of their country. At this distance it is difficult to realize the terrific moral effect of the gigantic Persian force.

[1] Partly manned by the Plateans.
[2] Vessels furnished by the Athenians.

The Euboeans, badly upset by this sign of weakness, sent thirty talents of silver to Themistocles to bribe the leaders to remain. Five talents went to Eurybiades and three to the Corinthian commander. There remained to win over only Architiles, captain of the Athenian sacred galley. As he had not money to buy provisions, he wished to retire. Themistocles then sent him a talent to buy food and declared that if he heard any further protests, "he would report it among the Athenians that he had received money from the enemy." Themistocles apparently did not lose money by this shrewd move. According to Herodotus, "he likewise made his own gain on the occasion; for he kept the money and no one knew of it." Such were the petty motives which ruled naval strategy in ancient days.

Scyllias, the most expert diver of his day, now deserted the Persian fleet. He brought to the Greeks at Artemisium full information of their losses and of the force despatched to encircle Euboea. How he contrived to reach his own force is still an entertaining mystery. The tale which is commonly told was that he dived into the sea at Aphetae and did not come to the surface till he reached Artemisium, a distance of nearly eighty furlongs. Evidently the fellow knew the value of publicity. Herodotus naïvely adds: "My own opinion is that on this occasion he made the passage to Artemisium in a boat."

Late in the afternoon the Greeks decided to engage the Persian fleet. They felt it was high time they made a practical test of their mode of fighting and skill in manoeuvering. In order to prevent their flanks from being turned, they brought the sterns of their ships together into a small compass and turned their prows on every side toward the barbarians: a sort of starfish effect it was. At a second signal, although enclosed within a narrow space and closely pressed upon by the foe, they fell bravely to work and captured thirty ships of the barbarians.

Night, however, soon put an end to the fight and the fleets returned to their bases. Once more the winds heard the prayers of the Greeks. A second gale completely wrecked the Persian detachment of 200 ships on the Euboean coast.

During the next day a reinforcement of fifty-three vessels arrived for the Greek fleet. Also one vessel had deserted from the enemy. As a result their total was now 325 triremes. Encouraged by this reinforcement and the news of the new Persian disaster, the Greeks again offered battle and sank several Cilician ships. We thus perceive how closely the two sides were matched when numbers were fairly equal.

At noon of the third day the Persians, ashamed that so small a number of ships should harass their fleet, and apprehensive of Xerxes' anger, forced the action. This time they advanced in crescent formation to outflank the Greeks. Both sides fought desperately but no decision was won. "The Greeks suffered much, both in ships and men," says Herodotus, "but the barbarians experienced a far greater loss of each." Nevertheless, at least five Greek ships were captured and over half the Athenian ships were damaged. So the defenders decided to withdraw. Execution of this decision was hastened by the arrival of a thirty-oared galley with startling news from Thermopylae.

Let us glance for a few moments on the heroic drama being played on that famous stage.

On the day of the first sea battle Xerxes had made his first assault upon the small defending force under Leonidas, King of Sparta, twenty-first in direct descent from Hercules. This force consisted of some 5500 heavy-armed infantry, of whom 300 were Spartans, and some light-armed troops. A much larger force was due to reinforce this advance guard as soon as the Carnean and Olympic festivals were celebrated. What a touch of characterization, to keep the gala days intact when the very life of the race was threatened!

For two days Xerxes' assaults were driven back with terrible losses. His numbers were of little value in the narrow pass, and the Greeks individually were both better armed and better fighters. On the evening of the second day a native traitor led Hydarnes with a picked force of Persians over a mountain path guarded by 1000 Phocians. While it would seem that this force was ample to hold the path, it was quickly put to flight by showers of arrows.

Hearing that his flank was turned, Leonidas called a council. He faced a glum party. His allies were unquestionably discouraged at the turn things had taken. So he ordered them to retire while there was still time. He and his 300 Spartans elected to remain. He no doubt recalled that before the war the Delphic Oracle had stated that "either Sparta must be overthrown by the barbarians, or one of her kings must perish." Herodotus concluded later that Leonidas' decision was influenced by this oracle and "the wish to secure the whole glory for the Spartans." With him seven hundred Thespians "*stayed entirely of their own accord, refusing to retreat, and declaring that they would not forsake Leonidas and his followers. So they abode with the Spartans and died with them.*" Let that sentence be their epitaph, just as fine as the famous inscription set up in honor of the Spartans:

Go, stranger, and to Lacedaemon tell
That here, obeying her behests, we fell.

This tragedy was the ill news that reached Artemisium after the third sea battle and confirmed the decision of the Greek leaders to retire down the Euboean Channel. "Though the fights between the Greeks and Persians in the Straits of Euboea," says Plutarch with keen judgment, "were not so important as to make any final decision in the war, yet the experience which the Greeks obtained in them was of great advantage; for thus, by actual trial and in real danger, they found out that neither number of ships, nor riches and ornaments, nor boasting shouts, nor barbarous songs of victory, were any way terrible to men who knew how to fight and were resolved to come hand to hand with their enemies." On one of the pillars of the temple of Diana at Artemisium they later chiseled this verse:

With numerous tribes from Asia's regions brought,
The sons of Athens on these waters fought;

Erecting, after they had quelled the Mede,
To Artemis this record of the deed.

During the retirement Themistocles resorted to a shrewd bit of propaganda. "He took notice," says Plutarch, "of the harbors and fit places for the enemies' ships to come to land at, and engraved large letters on such stones as he found there by chance. He did the same on others which he purposely set up near the landing places. In these inscriptions he called upon the Ionians to forsake the Medes, if this were possible, and come over to the Greeks; but, if this could not be done, at any rate to impede and disturb the Persians in all engagements. * * * He hoped that these writings would prevail upon the Ionians to revolt, or to raise some trouble by making their fidelity doubtful to the Persians."

The Greek fleet now assembled at Salamis; the army retired to the Isthmus of Corinth. Themistocles, by means of tricks and stratagems, finally persuaded the Athenians to desert their city and go to Salamis and other islands. By one of his customary tricks he obtained enough money to pay each seaman eight drachmas. When the Athenians were on their way down to the haven of Piraeus, the shield with the head of Medusa was suddenly reported missing. This gave Themistocles a good pretext for searching for it. He ransacked all private places, and of course found among the goods of the refugees considerable sums of money concealed. This he confiscated and applied to the public use. In consequence, his soldiers and seamen were well provided for the campaign. Rough tactic, yes; but certainly *pro bono publico.*

When Xerxes heard that there were some 8000 Spartans, all as brave as the 300 who had given him so much trouble, he was much concerned. He asked Demaratus the Spartan how he might with least trouble subdue these men.

The latter then advocated an interesting plan. "Detach three hundred vessels from the body of your fleet," he replied, "and send them to attack the shores of Laconia. There is an island called Cythera in those parts not far from the coast, concerning which the sage Chilon declared that Sparta would gain if it were sunk to the bottom of the sea. For years he has expected that it would give occasion to some project like that which I now recommend to you. Send ships to this island and threaten the Spartans. If once they have a war of their own close to their doors, you need not fear their giving any help to the rest of the Greeks so long as the danger lasts."

Achaemenes, the admiral, immediately protested. "O King, we have just lost four hundred vessels by shipwreck. If three hundred more be sent away to make a voyage around the Peloponnese, our enemies will become a match for us. Keep our whole fleet in one body and it will be dangerous for them to attack. Besides, while our sea and land forces advance together, the fleet and army can each help the other; but if they be parted, cooperation is out of the question." Good sound logic now as well as then.

Had Demaratus proposed sending fifty vessels instead of 300, we would be inclined to favor his plan; this small force would have created a diversion as well as a larger one, and would have left the fleet still a large margin of superiority over the Greeks. When we see to what means Themistocles had to resort to get his fleet to fight at Salamis, the effectiveness of such a diversion as suggested by Demaratus cannot be denied. Xerxes took the advice of his admiral.

The Persian fleet now joined its army at Thermopylae. And here it was Xerxes who resorted to a stratagem. Of the 20,000 Persian dead all were secretly buried save 1000; the 4000 Greek dead, of whom only about 1000 were fighting men, were all left on the field. The sailors were then given leave to visit the battlefield to see for themselves the completeness of the Persian victory. "It was, indeed," says Herodotus scornfully, "most truly a laughable device." That the Persian leader was successful in his deceit is a good commentary on the intellectual quality of his men.

The Persians, receiving a few deserters, asked what the Greeks were doing.

"Holding the Olympic games, watching athletic sports and chariot races," was the reply.

"And what," asked a Persian, "is the prize for which they contend?"

"An olive-wreath," said the Greek, "which is given to the man who wins." This sign of unconcern on the part of their enemies astonished the invaders.

There was little resistance as Xerxes now advanced to the southward for six days and occupied Athens with his army while the fleet drew up on the nearby beach at Phelerum. The campaign had reached its climax.

The situation was a most interesting one: The Greek fleet at Salamis held a very strong position; tactically it was almost impregnable. It could resist an attack simply by holding the narrow straits between Salamis and the coast; while a force of heavy-armed infantry, reinforced by the crews of the fleet, could easily beat off a landing attack on Salamis itself. Strategically also its position was most fortunate. If the Persian fleet or army passed Salamis, its sea communications would be cut. For while Xerxes undoubtedly could have gone on with his army, drawing his provisions from Greece itself, this hostile fleet would still have been a thorn in his side if he were held up for any time before the Corinth wall.

He had three methods of dislodging the Greeks from Salamis: first, by advancing with his army to Corinth in the hope that this would draw there the Greek fleet; second, by sending a few vessels to harry the Peloponnesian coast in order to draw there the vessels of the States attacked; third, to blockade and starve out the Greeks in Salamis by dividing his fleet so as to hold both exits. This last possibility might appear to give the Greeks an opportunity to attack half the Persian fleet. However, the narrow waters would prevent either side from bringing its full strength to bear. Hence one section of Xerxes' force would be able to hold out until the other could follow up the Greeks and attack them in the rear. Altogether this last plan was good strategy and warranted a trial.

On the day that Athens was occupied by the Persians, Eurybiades, the Spartan, called a council to decide upon what should be done by the fleet, which had been brought by reinforcements up to a strength of 379 triremes. On receipt of the bad news from ashore the council partly broke up in alarm. Even the captains who waited long enough to vote cast their ballots for a speedy return to Corinth. Upon returning to his ship Themistocles was accosted by Mnesiphilus, an Athenian, who urged that another attempt be made to fight at Salamis, stating that once the fleet reached Corinth it was certain that each contingent would depart to defend its own coasts. In our modern day of unified nations it is difficult to perceive how loosely the Greek force was hung together.

Themistocles was so impressed with this argument that he repeated it to Eurybiades and prevailed upon him to reconvene the council. Then with a fine eloquence he appealed to his people's hearts and common sense.

"Hear now," he said, "and judge between the two courses. At the isthmus thou wilt fight in an open sea, which is greatly to our disadvantage, since our ships are heavier and fewer in number than the enemy's. Further, thou wilt in any case lose Salamis, Megara and Egina, even if all the rest goes well with us. The land and sea force of the Persians will then advance together, and thy retreat will but draw them toward the Peloponnese, so bringing all Greece into peril. If, on the other hand, thou doest as I advise, these are the advantages which thou wilt so secure: In the first place, as we shall fight in a narrow sea with few ships against many, if the war follows the common course, we shall gain a great victory, for to fight in a narrow space is favorable to us; in an open sea, to them. Again, Salamis will in this case be preserved, Salamis where we have left our defenseless women and children. Thus, my friends, that very point by which ye set most store is secured as much by this course as by the other. For whether we fight here or at the isthmus, we shall equally give battle in defense of the Peloponnese. * * * If things turn out as I anticipate, and we crush our enemy on the sea, then we shall have not only kept our isthmus free from the barbarians, but the barbarians will have advanced no further than Attica, and from thence fled back in disorder. Finally, we shall, moreover, have saved Megara, Egina and Salamis itself, where an oracle has said that we are to overcome our enemies."

However, this able estimate did not convince the stubbornly apprehensive council. Whereupon Themistocles announced that the 180 Athenian vessels would take aboard the women and children and found a new city in Italy. This move proved more effective than reasoning. With promptness Eurybiades announced that the fleet would fight at Salamis.

On the same day Xerxes called a grand council. When a vote was taken, all his captains save only Artemisia, Queen of Halicarnassus, declared for battle.

"If thou art not over-hasty," said the queen, "to engage with them by sea but will keep thy fleet near the land, then whether thou abidest as thou art or marchest forward toward the Peloponnese, thou wilt easily accomplish all for which thou art come hither. The Greeks cannot hold out against thee very long; thou wilt soon part them asunder and scatter them to their several homes. In the island where they lie I hear they have no food in store; nor is it likely if thy land force begins its march toward the Peloponnese that they will remain quietly where they are—at least such as come from that region. * * * On the other hand, if thou art hasty to fight, I tremble lest the defeat of thy sea force bring disaster likewise to thy land army."

The feminine mind rarely has seen so clearly as on this occasion.

While it certainly would have been an excellent plan to try the effect of a land advance against the isthmus before fighting a sea battle under such unfavorable conditions, Xerxes agreed with the vote of the majority. As evening approached, the fleet got under way to fight at daybreak. At the same time the army advanced toward the isthmus.

One of the great decisive battles of all history was in motion.

The Persian movements caused a third Greek council. This time Themistocles, seeing in desperation that the vote would be hopelessly against him, resolved on a daring stratagem. He called to him Sicinnus, a Persian slave, and sent him to the hostile fleet with the following message:

"The Athenian commander has sent me to you privily, without the knowledge of the other Greeks. He is really sympathetic to the Persian cause and he secretly would rather success should attend on you than on his countrymen. He bids me tell you that fear has seized the Greeks and they are meditating a hasty flight. Now, then, it is up to you: if only ye will hinder the Greeks escaping, your cause is won. As they no longer agree among themselves, they will not now make any resistance—nay, 'tis likely that ye may see a fight already begun between such as favor and such as oppose your cause."

Xerxes was greatly elated at this good news. Straightway he ordered his Egyptian squadron of 200 vessels to proceed during the night around to the westward of the island so as to cut off the retreat of the Greek fleet through the channel which leads past Megara. The main body of the Persian fleet continued its advance toward the eastern entrance. This force is stated by Aeschylus, who fought in the battle, to have numbered 1000 vessels, a figure that agrees closely with Herodotus, who says that the entire fleet had been brought again to its total of 1300. Some modern authorities guess that the main fleet did not exceed 500 vessels; be that as it may, numbers were of little moment in the narrow straits.

The Greeks were still wrangling among themselves when Aristides, a famous Athenian leader and political opponent of Themistocles who had been recalled recently from his exile, reported that the enemy had occupied all lines of retreat. This report was confirmed by a Tenian trireme which had deserted the Persians, bringing the Greek total to 380 vessels. The Greeks now made ready for battle. Their fleet formed in the channel north of the Cynosura promontory. As the ships were about twenty feet wide and their oars projected about twenty feet on either side, one vessel occupied a space twenty yards wide. Assuming that adjacent vessels would require forty yards between their oar-tips, we see that vessels aligned abreast would have to be spaced at intervals of at least sixty yards. As the channel was but 1800 yards wide, the Greek front would consist of not over thirty triremes. Thus their formation would be about thirteen ships deep.

To reach the Greek formation the Persians were confronted with a problem which was well-nigh insoluble. Between the mainland and the island of Psyttaleia the channel was but 1200 yards wide. The front of a fleet passing through it could consist of but twenty vessels. It would be necessary for this force to change its front forty-five degrees to the left and, to prevent being outflanked, extend the distance between ships from sixty to ninety yards, so as to cover a front of 1800 yards as it reached the Cynosura peninsula. As an alternative to this extension of front a force with ten ships abreast could enter the passage between Cynosura and Psyttaleia, turn to the left 135 degrees and fall in on the left of the main force. It was a foregone conclusion that such complicated manoeuvers with hundreds of vessels could result in nothing but complete confusion.

Themistocles waited until the usual morning breeze was sending its heavy swell into the channel, as he believed that it would interfere with the rowing and increase the confusion evident in the Persian fleet. Then at his signal the Greeks rowed to the attack.

The picture of these mighty fleets clashing in the narrow strait was certainly one of the grandest of history. Some 1200 vessels and 300,000 men were locked in battle, ship to ship, man to man. Xerxes from his throne on high must have looked on an inspiring spectacle. A wild din reached the skies as fierce war-cries were shouted, as oars creaked in their row-locks and churned the water, as bows twanged, as arrows and javelins thudded against the ships, as rams crashed through timbers or snapped off banks of oars, and as the crews of sinking vessels cried for help.

Lycomedes, the Athenian, was the first to capture a ship. Another vessel rammed the great galley which carried the Persian admiral, and the invading leader fell, pierced by the spears of Aminas and Sosicles. "Far the greater number of the Persian ships engaged in the battle," says Herodotus, "were disabled either by the Athenians or by the Eginetans. For, as the Greeks fought in order and kept their line, while the barbarians were in confusion and had no plan in anything they did, the issue of the battle could scarce be other than it was. Yet the Persians fought far more bravely here than at Euboea, and indeed surpassed themselves. Each did his utmost through fear of Xerxes, for each thought that the king's eye was upon himself. * * * The great destruction took place when the ships which had been first engaged began to fly; for they who were stationed in the rear, anxious to display their valor before the eyes of the king, made every effort to force their way to the front, and thus became entangled with such of their own vessels as were retreating."

The battle was not completed until the evening, and the Greeks "obtained," as says Simonides, "that noble and famous victory, than which neither amongst the Greeks nor barbarians was ever known more glorious exploit on the seas; not only by the joint valor and zeal of all who fought, but by the wisdom and sagacity of Themistocles."

During the battle Aristides used the soldiers on Salamis to capture Psyttaleia from its Persian garrison.

Although Xerxes still had chances of winning the campaign, the sea fight which had occurred before his own eyes completely broke his resolution. During the night, in great distress, he ordered the fleet to proceed at full speed to the Hellespont to secure his bridges.

The Greeks prepared to renew the battle the next day, but when they found that the Persian fleet had sailed, they ceased the pursuit at Andros. Here a council was held. Themistocles urged that the fleet proceed and cut the bridges. But with fine reasoning Aristides showed that they had better not drive into a corner an army which would retreat of its own accord. "Therefore, it is noways our interest, Themistocles, to take away the bridge that is already made; but rather to build another, if it were possible, that he might make his retreat with more expedition." Cool reasoning this in the heat of triumph.

Themistocles, always ready to get good ideas from others, once more contrived a stratagem. As before, he sent Sicinnus to Xerxes with a message; it advised Xerxes to retreat as quickly as possible while Themistocles tried to keep the Greeks from pursuing. The Greek leader may have had a double purpose in sending this message for afterward, when compelled to flee from Athens to Persia, it stood him in good stead and earned him a hearty welcome.

Xerxes left behind 300,000 picked troops under Mardonius and began a terrible "retreat from Moscow," in which most of his army perished.

Themistocles received great honors throughout Greece and at Corinth, where the leaders voted as to who had contributed the most to the victory. Each leader gave his first vote for himself and his second to Themistocles!

Next year the united Greek army completely defeated Mardonius at Platea. On the same day their fleet annihilated the Persian fleet at Mycale. Thus the Persian invasions of Greece were ended. It was now Alexander's turn to invade and reduce the Persian Empire.

CHAPTER II

Svold

ABOUT 800 years after Christ the Christian Charlemagne had carried his new religion to the shores of the North and Baltic seas. The pagan northerners retaliated by expeditions against both France and England. Those from the fjords of Denmark and Norway were called vikings or "inlet-men."

Few events in history are more remarkable than the cruises and exploits of these Norse sea kings. Descriptions in their sagas read like fairy tales. Time after time they issued forth from the north in their little galleys and harried at will the coasts of the Baltic and Atlantic nations. Some penetrated even into the Mediterranean. They established permanent colonies in Scotland, England, Ireland, and Normandy. Not only did they sweep from the seas, almost without effort, all other trading and fighting vessels and plunder the coastal cities, but they followed the courses of the rivers far into the interior of great nations and stormed supposedly impregnable fortresses.

But more interesting than these cruises of the sea kings, who were usually not strong enough to stand the competition in their own country, is the history of the Norsemen at home. There it was that "Greek met

Greek," and battles were fought which were almost beyond comparison for the fierceness and feats of prowess which distinguished them.

No study of sea-power would be complete without an examination of Norse traditions. Aptitude of the British, Dutch, and northern French races for the sea has been largely due to their heritage of Norse blood. It has been estimated that at least one-third of the English people before the Norman Conquest were of Norse or Danish descent. Thus the Norse tradition lies back of all European and North American sea-power.

Not only were the Norsemen perhaps the fiercest and most fearless of all races, but they had a civilization and culture far in advance of the Saxon inhabitants of England. They were feared because of their war-like expeditions, and envied for the great volume of their sea trade and their voyages of discovery and colonization.

Finally, they had a vivid literature, couched in a native tongue, at a time when most European history was a mere record of events and dates set down in Latin. The story of this virile race, one of the greatest in history, merits much more attention than it has thus far received.

At some unknown period before the time of Christ the race—later known as Norsemen—left the then fertile valleys of central Asia and settled north of the Black Sea. From there a mythological leader, called Odin, brought them across Europe and the Baltic to the Scandinavian peninsula. Odin was reputed to be a great warrior, and brought his warriors to such a fighting pitch that they were carried away by almost uncontrollable fury in battle. "His men," says the saga, "rushed forward without armor, were as mad as dogs or wolves, bit their shields, were strong as bears or wild bulls, and killed people at a blow. And neither fire nor iron told upon them. This was called *berserksgangr.*"

When about to die, Odin, so the story goes, hit upon an idea which was to perpetuate this fighting spirit after his death. "When he was near his death," according to the saga, "he made himself be marked with the point of a spear, and said he was going to Godheim, would give welcome there to all his friends; and all brave warriors should be dedicated to him. To some he gave victory; others he invited to himself; and they reckoned both of them to be well off in their fate."

This idea was worked into the Norse religion. "Odin," says Professor Boyesen, "dwells with all the other gods in Asgard, where he receives in his shining hall, Valhalla, all those who have died by the sword. He is therefore called Valfather. Those fallen warriors whom he chooses to be his guests are known as *einheriar*—i.e., great champions. Valhalla is splendidly decorated with burnished weapons. The ceiling is made of spears, the roof is covered with shining shields, and the walls are adorned with armor and coats of mail. Hence the champions issue forth every day and fight great battles, killing and maiming each other. But every night they wake up whole and unscathed and return to Odin's hall, where they spend the night in merry carousing. The maidens of Odin, the valkyries, who, before every battle, select those who are to be slain, wait upon the warriors, fill their great horns with mead, and give them the flesh of swine to eat."

This was a fine and tonic idea to instill into the hearts of fighting men. Believing it implicitly, the Norsemen fought with Odin's eye ever upon them, endeavoring to show themselves worthy to be selected among his champions and almost eager for death, from which the bright picture of Valhalla had removed all the fears.

Odin had a grandson, Frey. Another of his names was Yngve, and he established the great Yngling race. One of the most famous of the first chieftains of this line was Hake, who invaded Svithiod (Sweden), won a great battle on the Frisvols and established himself at Upsala. Later he won another great battle on the same field over two mighty sea kings, but was himself mortally wounded. "He saw," says the saga, "that his days could not be long. So he ordered a warship loaded with his dead men and their weapons to be taken out to sea, with tiller shipped and sails hoisted. Then he set fire to some tarwood and ordered a pyre to be made over it in the ship. Hake was almost if not quite dead when he was laid upon this pyre. The wind was blowing off the land. The ship flew burning in clear flame out between the islet and into the ocean. Great was the fame of this deed in after time." Thus the legend of the "Viking's Funeral."

CRUISES AND BATTLES OF THE NORTHMEN
✚ Scenes of the forays of Olaf Tryggveson
✗ Battles of earlier kings.
Faeroe Is
Shetland Is
Orkney Is.
Hebrides
NORWAY
Fraedo (955)
Hiorungavag (986)
Stord (860)
Karmt (953)
Jadar (868)
SVITHIOD
Upsala
Frisvols
GAUTLAND
Harald Harfanger 868
Hakon
Hakon
JUTLAND
DENMARK
Svold
NORDMANNIA
Jomsborg
WENDLAND or VINDLAND
Bornholm Is.
ESTLAND
Yngvar
Norgorod
Dnieper R.
Kiev
862-Rurik
Hamburg
845-Eirik
SAXLAND
Elbe R.
Oder R.
FRIESLAND
Nimwegen & Dorestad
862-Rorek
Rhine R.
FLANDERS
Rouen-841-Asgeir
Paris-845-Ragnar Lodbrok
Seine R.
Tours-841-Hastings
Loire R.
NORMANDY
VALLAND
SCOTLAND
IRELAND
Isle of Man
CUMBERLAND
NORTHUMBERLAND
ENGLAND
London
Dublin 852
Limerick 852
Waterford 852
BRETLAND
Scilly Is.
H.H.F.

King Yngvar's written history is merely a beautiful verse of song by Thiodolf, commemorating his death on an expedition to Esthonia:

> Certain it is the Estland foe
> The fair-haired Swedish king laid low.
> On Estland's strand, o'er Swedish graves,
> The East Sea sings her song of waves;
> King Yngvar's dirge is ocean's roar
> Resounding on the rock-ribbed shore.

Another, King Ingiald, was ultimately surrounded by such superior numbers of his enemies that neither battle nor flight gave him any hope. So he held a great drinking-bout for his men. When all were drunk he burned the castle that held them. All perished together. Thiodolf sings the tale:

> With fiery feet, devouring flame
> Has hunted down a royal game
> At Raning, where King Ingiald gave
> To all his men a glowing grave.
> On his own hearth the fire he raised—
> A deed his foemen even praised.

We next hear of the Yngling kings moving from Sweden into Norway, where Halfdan Whiteleg about the middle of the eighth century established himself on Oslo fjord. His descendants, while still holding Norway, extended their conquests into Schleswig, then called Nordmannia. There we hear of Siegfried assisting the Saxons against Charlemagne in 777; and of Gudrod the Hunter combating the great emperor from 799 to 810. Both Norsemen were vindictive pagans.

Upon Gudrod's death in the latter year, it appears that an elder son, Eirik, remained in Nordmannia, while Halfdan the Black, then only one year old, was brought to Norway. When he reached the age of eighteen, Halfdan commenced reducing that country to his sway, and by 840 he had successfully accomplished his purpose. His second wife, Ragnhild, was the daughter of Sigurd Hiort, a famous champion of whom fabulous tales of prowess are told. Ragnhild bore a son, Harald Harfanger (Fairhaired), who was to prove himself worthy of his distinguished lineage.

In 860 Halfdan died, and Harald being but ten years old, the nobles threw off their allegiance. But the young king vowed to reconquer his father's dominions. In this he was ably assisted by his uncle Guthorm, who was leader of the Hird, as the body of paid men-at-arms at the court was called. After winning ten battles on land, in 867 Harald built a fleet to protect his own coasts and extend his conquests. First at Solskel he defeated a great fleet led by three sea kings. That winter he ravaged the Swedish coast, vividly described by the skald Thorbiorn Hornklofe:

> The Norsemen's king is on the sea;
> Tho' bitter wintry cold it be,
> On the wild waves his Yule keeps he.

In the last part of the eighth century the Norsemen won Gautland from the Swedes. Leaving Guthorm to hold the conquered territory, he sailed out through the Skagerrak. On the Norse coast off Jadar he defeated seven sea kings in a fierce battle. Later he cruised to the Hebrides, Orkneys, Shetlands, and Scotland to clear out the nests of the sea kings who harried his coasts. In his methods he was a combination of Paul Jones and Captain Kidd.

In the last part of the eighth century the Norsemen and Danes commenced their great sea-king cruises. Increase of population made it necessary that they spread to other countries. Superiority in fighting over southern nations indicated the proper direction for their migrations. Development of their galley, particularly its use as a sailing ship, gave them the means of executing their plans.

The typical Norse galley of this period was about seventy-five feet long, fifteen feet in extreme width, drew about one and a half feet of water and had two feet freeboard. Usually there were about sixteen rowing benches extending across the ship, on which six men could sit, three pulling on a starboard, three on a port oar. Over the rowers awnings were spread; the ends of the ship were decked across and sometimes connected by a passageway down the center line over the rowers. At the bow was a gayly painted serpent's head and at the stern a tail. In describing Harald's flagship the saga reads: "The forecastle men were picked men, for they had the king's banner. From the stem to the midhold was called *rausn* or the fore-defense; and there were the berserks." The poop was called the *lypting*, and there the captain took his station. On the starboard side of the lypting was the great steering-oar, and this side of the ship came to be named steer-board or starboard. Over the gunwales hung the shields, painted red, black, or white. Originally the Norsemen did not have sails, but about the sixth century their use was learned from the more southern races. A mast was stepped amidships, and a long yard, secured well up toward its truck, supported a large square sail painted in bright colors, often in stripes, to suit the fancy of the captain.

At first the forays of the sea kings were made with small expeditions and at random. In 789 the first parties of Danes ravaged the English coast. Ten years later Gudrod's squadrons harried Friesland, as Holland was then called. In 810 Ireland was first attacked by the Norsemen. For the next twenty years these countries were continually harried by small bands on their summer cruises.

When Halfdan the Black brought Norway under his sway, great expeditions of Norsemen left with the object of permanently establishing themselves in southern countries. The usual plan was to seize an island or easily defended promontory and from that as a base to obtain a foothold on the coasts and then proceed up the rivers. Thus in 838 Thorgisl, with 120 ships, captured Dublin and for eight years occupied half of Ireland. When he was killed by treachery the Irish regained their power. In 852, however, Olaf the White, of the Yngling race, permanently established himself in Dublin, as did Sigtrygg in Waterford and Ivar in Limerick. From these bases the energetic Olaf led great expeditions against the west coast of England and founded colonies in Northumberland. These Norsemen are said to have continued their rule in Dublin for over three centuries.

Meanwhile France and Germany were also suffering from the forays of the sea kings. In 841 the viking Hastings, according to French histories, besieged Tours on the Loire, and Asgeir burned Rouen on the Seine. Four years later the famous Ragnar Lodbrok burned Paris; and Eirik, son of Gudrod, plundered the rich commercial city of Hamburg. In 851 Asgeir sailed up the Seine and burned Fontenelle and Beauvois.

While Harald Harfanger was pacifying Norway for a second time and driving out the vikings, new migrations of both Norsemen and Danes on a large scale commenced. The Hebrides, Shetlands, Orkneys and Faeroe Islands were colonized. In 861 Iceland was discovered and soon afterward Greenland. A year later Rorek ravaged Dorestad and Nimwegen, centers of trade on the Rhine. In 866 a great expedition of Danes overran northern England. About the same time the famous Rolf Ganger, or Rollo, as he was called by the Franks, effected a permanent settlement of Normandy and founded the line of dukes leading to William the Conqueror. In 878 Alfred was glad to make peace with the Danes on the basis that they should have half of England; in 885 Paris was again attacked.

The Swedes confined their explorations mostly to the Baltic and Russia. They early founded Novgorod, and in 862 under Rurik founded the Russian State at Kiev. From there they followed the Dnieper down to the Black Sea and passed through the Bosporus out into the Mediterranean, where their expeditions mingled with those of the Norse sea kings which had come through the Straits of Gibraltar.

Strange to say, these various expeditions are seldom mentioned in the sagas. Our information concerning them comes almost entirely from the countries they attacked. Could the sagas have told the stories, we should probably look on the Norsemen in a more favorable light. Let us, however, now return to Norway, where the detailed histories of the country are contained in its own literature.

As Harald grew old the lesser kings and jarls (earls) got out of hand. This condition was aggravated by vicious fighting between the king's sons. One of them, Hakon the Good, was sent to Athelstan's court and there brought up. Another, the terrible Eirik Blood-Axe, was sent on his Grand Tour of Europe with five long-ships. He first cruised for four years in the Baltic, ravaging the coasts of Denmark, Friesland, and Saxland. For the next four years he visited Scotland, Bretland (Wales and Cornwall), Ireland, and Valland (France). Finally he cruised to Finmark (the North Cape) and Biarmaland (Archangel). Here he married Gunhild, one of the famous—or possibly infamous—characters of Norse history. Upon his return he engaged in constant fighting with his brothers, killing no less than four of them and barely escaping death in turn. In 930 Harald resigned the throne to Eirik and three years later died. "Eirik was," according to the saga, "a stout, handsome man, strong and very manly—a great and fortunate man of war; but bad-minded, gruff, unfriendly, and silent. Gunhild, his wife, was the most beautiful of women—clever, with very much knowledge, and lively; but a very false person and very cruel in disposition."

Eirik's cruelty made him so unpopular that in 934 Hakon the Good, returning from England, had little difficulty in driving him from the land. He was assisted in this by Sigurd Jarl, one of the most powerful and successful chieftains in Norway. In the next year Eirik, undaunted by his defeat and spurred on by Gunhild, assembled a fleet in the Orkneys. There he received Northumberland as a fief from Athelstan. He used this as a base for his summer cruises about the British Isles. When Athelstan died in 940, his successor, Edmund, broke with Eirik, who commenced a great cruise along the English coast. Not satisfied with this, he penetrated far into the interior, where his army was destroyed in a great battle in which he and five other kings lost their lives. Gunhild composed a poem describing his reception into Valhalla:

> Odin wakes in the morning and cries, as he opens his eyes, with his dream still fresh in his mind: What dreams are these? I thought I arose before daybreak to make Valhal ready for a host of slain. I woke up the host of the chosen. I bade them rise up to strew the benches, and to fill up the beer-vats, and I bade valkyries to bear the wine, as if a king were coming. I look for the coming of some noble chiefs from the earth, wherefore my heart is glad.
>
> Brage, Odin's counselor, now wakes as a great din is heard without, and calls out: What is that thundering, as if a thousand men or some great host were tramping on? The walls and benches are creaking

withal, as if Balder were coming back to the hall of Odin.

Odin answers: Surely thou speakest foolishly, good Brage, although thou art very wise. It thunders for Eirik the king, that is coming to the hall of Odin.

Nothing daunted by Eirik's death, Gunhild proceeded with her fierce brood to the Orkneys and assembled forces for new enterprises. We shall soon hear of her again.

After Eirik's departure from Norway, Hakon soon reduced the country and drove the Danish vikings from the coast:

> Furrowing the deep-blue sea with oars,
> The king pursues to Jutland's shores.

Here, near the scene of our great modern sea fight, Hakon won a complete victory. Incidentally, he added to his reputation by fighting without helmet or armor after the custom of the berserks.

The skald Guthorm Sindre gives a vivid picture of his next exploit:

> Hakon the brave, whose skill all know
> To bend in battle-storm the bow,
> Rushed o'er the waves of Seeland's tongue,
> His two warships with gilt shields hung,
> And cleared the decks with his blue sword,
> That rules the fate of war, on board
> Eleven ships of the Vindland men—
> Famous is Hakon's name since then.

The sword mentioned in this verse was called Kvernbite. It had been given to Hakon by Athelstan and with it he had cut a millstone to the center eye. Next the king drove the vikings from the Vindland coast and gained great booty in the southern Swedish provinces.

For many centuries the Norsemen had celebrated the festival of Yule on midwinter's night, on that day starting a drinking and eating bout which lasted three days. "First Odin's goblet," says the saga, "was emptied for victory and power to the king; thereafter Niord's and Freyja's for peace and a good season. Then it was the custom of many to drink the brage-goblet over which vows were made; finally the guests emptied a goblet to the memory of departed friends, called the remembrance goblet." Hakon had been converted to Christianity by Athelstan and he endeavored to win his people over to the new religion, but had little success. "He made a law," according to the saga, "that the festival of Yule should begin at the same time as Christian people held it and that every man, under penalty, should brew a meal of malt into ale, and therewith keep the Yule holy as long as it lasted." But the people were not enthusiastic over the change.

While Hakon was losing his popularity in religious controversies, Gunhild established herself in Denmark and her sons began to ravage the Norse coasts. Tryggve, a subordinate king, was able to keep them in check for a time; but finally Hakon and Sigurd had to come south with a fleet; they killed Guthorm Eirikson, leader of the invaders, in a great battle in Karmt Sound.

In 954 Gamle, now the senior of Gunhild's sons, made another attack on the coast. So many false alarms had been reported that this time the beacon fires were not lighted. Hakon was taken by surprise. Unfortunately, he had but a small force with him. Promptly he called a council of war; this was attended by a landowner, Egil Ulserk, who for many years had carried the banner of Harald Harfanger. The king proposed that he should withdraw until a larger force could be assembled. To this Egil, a man of spirit, replied:

"I was in several battles with thy father Harald the king, and he gave battle sometimes with many, sometimes with few; but he always came off victorious. Never did I hear him ask counsel from us, as to whether he should flee from an enemy." Egil then advised instant battle.

The council agreed with Egil. Whereupon the king split up a war-arrow and sent it off in all directions as a token for men to join him.

Then said Egil contentedly: "Our peace has lasted so long I have been afraid I might die the death of old age, within doors upon a bed of straw. Always I have preferred to fall in battle following my chief. Now it begins to look as if I shall have my wish!"

In the desperately fought battle which followed, Gamle was killed and the other sons were glad to escape to Denmark, "ill satisfied with their expedition."

In 960 Eirik's sons made another attempt. Again Hakon was taken by surprise and fought with a force only one-sixth the strength of the invaders. As a sign of their defiance of the enemy, the king and many of his men took off their armor before the battle. Hakon killed with his own hand a famous berserk, Eyvind Skreyja, and utterly routed the Danes. But in the very minute of victory he was wounded by an arrow. He died at the foot of a little hill on the shore where, by a queer coincidence of fate, he had first seen the light of day. Great was the sorrow over Hakon's death. He was lamented both by friends and enemies; and all said that never again would Norway see such a king. His friends removed his body to Seaheim and made a great mound in which they laid the king in full armor. Eyvind Skaldspiller composed a wonderful poem, of which the following is the first verse:

> In Odin's hall an empty place
> Stands for a king of Yngve's race.
> "Go, my valkyries," Odin said,
> "Go forth, my angels of the dead,
> Godul and Skogul, to the plain
> Drenched with the battle's bloody rain,
> And to the dying Hakon tell,
> Here in Valhal shall he dwell."

According to Hakon's wish, Harald, the senior of Gunhild's sons, became king; but his mother was the real power in Norway. Harald and his five brothers were engaged in constant fighting with nobles who would not recognize his right to the throne, but had little success in subduing the country. He killed Sigurd Jarl and King Tryggve by treachery. But the former's son, Hakon Jarl, survived. The latter's wife escaped with her infant son, who was destined to be the greatest Norseman of all. In 964 Harald was killed in a plot devised by Hakon Jarl and the king of Denmark.

Norway then came under the nominal sway of the Danish king, who divided the territory between Hakon Jarl and a great chief, Harald Grenske. In 965 Gunhild withdrew to the Orkneys; but the next year she returned with the two remaining sons, Ragnfred and Gudrod, and gained a foothold in the country. In 967, however, Hakon, after a battle at Thingness, drove this fierce brood from Norway for many years. Doubtless they harried many a foreign coast before finally joining Eirik Blood-Axe in Valhal. Hakon Jarl now became the ruler and threw off his allegiance to the king of Denmark, though the latter had assisted him to the throne. Endless wars followed between the two countries.

In 985 Svein, who later conquered England, came to the throne of Denmark. Wishing to devote his energies toward England, he called upon his allies, the Jomsvikings, to capture Norway. These were a celebrated union of vikings who lived at Jomsborg, on Wollin Island, at the mouth of the Oder. They lived entirely by fighting and were bound together by the strictest discipline and loyalty to each other. Unfortunately at this time their leader, Sigvald Jarl, was of a treacherous and false disposition.

Early the next year the fleet of the Jomsvikings arrived on the Norse coast. It consisted of sixty large vessels manned by about 8000 warriors. At Hiorungavag they were met by Hakon Jarl and his sons, Eirik, Svein, Sigurd, and Erling, with a fleet of 180 smaller vessels, manned by about 11,000 warriors. In the center Hakon Jarl, with Thorer Hiort and Styrkar of Gimsar, was opposed to Sigvald of the Jomsvikings. Eirik Jarl, with Gudbrand Hvite and Thorkel Leira, commanded the right wing against the famous Jomsviking Bue the Big. Svein Jarl, with Skegge and Ragnvald, commanded the left wing against the celebrated Vagn Akason.

As the battle commenced all along the line, Vagn drove back Svein Jarl. His brother, Eirik Jarl, seeing his danger, rowed around with some vessels from the other wing and re-established the fight. He then returned just in time to save his own wing, which was giving way before Bue. At this point a terrific hailstorm broke over the battle and the wind blew the rain and hail into the faces of the Jomsvikings. Apparently discouraged by this disaster, which superstitiously was attributed to the gods, Sigvald in the most cowardly manner flew from the battle, followed by thirty-five of his ships. So incensed was brave Vagn at this treachery that he endeavored to kill Sigvald with a spear, which pierced the man whom he mistook for the jarl.

Vagn and Bue, with about twenty-five vessels, remained to fight to the end. Hakon Jarl ran alongside the latter's galley and an epic combat commenced. Two Jomsviking berserks, Havard Hogvande and Aslak Holmskalle, boarded the jarl's flagship and carried all before them. Finally an Icelander, Vigfus, hurled an anvil at Aslak and split his skull. Havard's feet were cut off; though even then he is said to have continued to fight standing on his knees. In the very nick of time Eirik Jarl boarded Bue's ship from the other side. The viking was wounded in the face; and seeing that further resistance was useless, he threw overboard two chests of gold and with all his men leaped into the sea, where nearly all perished. Vagn's ship was then taken after a desperate struggle and he and twenty-nine men were made prisoners. After eighteen had been beheaded, Eirik Jarl was so impressed with the heroic bearing of his captives that he pardoned Vagn and the others. Just then Gissur the White, who was sitting next to Hakon Jarl, was killed by an arrow. A wild rush ensued to board the ship whence came the arrow. Havard was found on his knees with bow in hand. "Tell me, lads," he said, "did any one fall over there at the tree?" When told whom he had killed with his last arrow, he replied: "Then I was not so much in luck as I had hoped, for that arrow was meant for the jarl."

In the same year as the battle with the Jomsvikings occurred the first voyage to the American continent. Biarne Heriulfson sailed from Iceland for Greenland. Neither he nor any of his crew had made the cruise before. After three days, apparently of unfavorable winds, they lost sight of Iceland. "A north wind with fog set in," according to the saga, "and they knew not where they were sailing to. This lasted many days. So they hoisted sail again and sailed a whole day and night. Finally they made land." They sailed in close to it and saw that it consisted of low wooded hills. Keeping it on the port hand, they turned northward and sailed for two days. Again they saw land, which was flat and covered with trees. They continued on before a southwesterly breeze for still three days and a third time saw land, this time snowy mountains. They proved that this land was an island. Then, driven before a gale for three days, they arrived at Greenland. It is supposed that the first land seen was the New England coast, the second Nova Scotia and the third Newfoundland. Biarne reported his discovery in Norway, thus leading to the later cruises of Leif the Lucky and Eric the Red.

While Norway was prosperous under Hakon Jarl, his personal habits stirred up such resentment that in 995 the people rose against him and he was murdered by one of his own men. Just at this time there arrived in Norway the celebrated Olaf Tryggveson, the beau-ideal of the Norse tradition. His early adventures are worth recounting.

When King Tryggve was treacherously killed by Gunhild's sons in 963, his wife, Astrid, fled with some of his men. After many narrow escapes they hid on an island in a lake and there Olaf Tryggveson was born. As the winter came on, Astrid was forced to seek shelter. After many dangers she reached her father's house. Next spring Gunhild sent a picked troop to find Astrid and her son. She was forced to flee in the night for Sweden. A landowner named Thorstein managed to hide her on an islet and directed the pursuers in a false direction. Astrid finally reached Sweden. Gunhild soon sent an embassy demanding that she be given up; but this was refused. Later an attempt to seize her by force also proved futile. Astrid then set out on a voyage over the Baltic to her brother Sigurd, who held an important post at the court of King Valdemar of Russia at Novgorod.

One of the sagas tells of an unusual incident at the court of this king: "It was always the custom that at Yuletime, when the guests assembled in the hall of the king, the king's mother was borne in thither and placed in the king's high seat. There she prophesied touching any danger overhanging the country or similar thing, according to the questions which were put to her. Now it happened one winter that when the king's mother had been borne in after this fashion, King Valdemar asked her whether any foreign prince or warrior would turn his arms against, or come to, his kingdom the following year. 'I discern no token of any disastrous war or other misfortune,' she answered; 'but one wonderful thing I see. In the land of Norway there has been born lately a child who will be bred up here in Russia until he grows to be a famous prince. He will not do any hurt to this kingdom; on the contrary, he will in every way increase thy fame. He will return to his native land while he is still in the flower of his age, and will reign with great glory in this northern part of the world; but not for long. Now carry me away.' "

On the passage to Russia, Astrid was seized by Esthonian vikings. Olaf, only three years old, was sold into slavery and did not see his mother for many years. For six years the boy lived in slavery and was well treated. One day Sigurd, traveling through Esthonia, saw Olaf in the market-place, bought his freedom and took him to Novgorod. There Olaf saw the man who had killed his foster-father while in slavery. Though the lad was but ten years old, he killed the assassin immediately with an axe. To save Olaf's life from the mob which gathered, Sigurd took him to the queen's house. Seeing that the stranger was a fine-looking boy, she ordered her soldiers to protect him and herself paid the fine for the murder. Sigurd then told of Olaf's parentage and descent from Harald Harfanger. He was received at court and soon became chief of the king's men-at-arms. Later he won several battles and ultimately became the most important noble in the country. "Olaf," says the saga, "was the handsomest of men, very stout and strong; and in all bodily exercises he excelled every Northman that ever was heard of."

By the time he reached the age of eighteen Olaf saw that he was arousing jealousy. Securing permission to leave, he set out into the Baltic with a few ships. But after collecting booty at Bornholm he was forced by foul weather to seek shelter in Vindland, where King Burislav invited him to spend the winter. During the winter of 982 he married Geira, the king's sister, and reduced much of the surrounding country. In the following summer he won three battles on the Swedish coast and seized great plunder. He then assisted Emperor Otto in his campaign against the kings of Denmark and Norway.

After three years Geira died and Olaf set out on a distant cruise. Passing out of the Baltic, he harried the coasts of Friesland, Saxland, and Flanders; then he went up the east coast of England and Scotland and down the west coast through Ireland and Wales, and finally came to France. This four years' cruise is related in a verse by Halfred:

> The brave young king, who ne er retreats,
> The Englishman in England beats.
> Death through Northumberland is spread
> From battle-axe and broad spearhead.
> Through Scotland with his spears he rides;
> To Man his glancing ships he guides.
> Feeding the wolves where'er he came,
> The young king drove a bloody game.
> The Irish fled at Olaf's name,
> Fled from a young king seeking fame.
> In Bretland, and in Cumberland,
> People against him could not stand.
> Thick on the fields their corpses lay,
> To ravens and howling wolves a prey.

In the Scilly Islands a Christian priest so impressed Olaf with his fortune-telling that he allowed himself to be baptized. In 988 an English queen called Gyda called a council of people to select a husband. Alfvine, a great Saxon champion, arrived about the same time to pay court. Olaf had come there also, but had on his bad-weather clothes and coarse overgarments. He stood with his people apart from the crowd. Nevertheless, Gyda, with keen eye, selected him. Whereupon a duel was staged and he killed Alfvine in single combat.

Olaf lived for seven years in England and Ireland. It was during this time that he was given a famous dog, Vige, who was with him in all his fights.

In 995 Hakon Jarl, the ruler of Norway, sent Thorer Klakka to England to betray Olaf into his power. But Thorer was so impressed with Olaf that he took his side and urged him to make a stroke for the crown of Norway. Finally Olaf set forth with a squadron of five ships. Luckily he arrived just as Hakon Jarl was killed in a revolt, so he had no difficulty in being elected king.

Olaf the conqueror was the beau-ideal of a warrior. He was tall, strong and handsome, with the fair hair of the Yngve race. Moreover, he was a noted swimmer and an excellent archer. He threw spears with both hands at the same time; juggled three swords so that one was always in the air; and climbed the steep Hornelen mountain, placing his shield upon the summit. He could also perform the unusual feat of running along the oars outside the ship while the men were rowing. Added to this was a most winning personality, which raised him to the height of popularity.

Upon becoming king, he commenced to convert the country to Christianity, using rough-and-ready methods. As an example, we find that he sent to Iceland as a missionary Thangbrand, "a passionate, headstrong man, and a great man-slayer," and that his method of conversion was to challenge to deadly combat every man who would not accept the new faith.

Meanwhile, however, Olaf's troubles were piling up. Eirik Jarl, the hero of the battle with the Jomsvikings, went first to Sweden and then on viking cruises. Finally he married the daughter of Svein, King of Denmark and later conqueror of England. When Olaf refused to marry Sigrid the Haughty of Sweden, she married Svein, and with Eirik Jarl plotted to bring war between Denmark and Norway. Olaf married Thyra, sister of Svein, who claimed that her brother had taken her properties, and constantly urged Olaf to fight him for their recovery. A clash becoming inevitable, Svein won over King Olaf of Sweden, son of Sigrid, as an ally, and also the false Sigvald, leader of the Jomsvikings. Not daring to declare war openly, the allies decided to make a treacherous attack on the Norse king. An opportunity soon came.

Urged on by his wife, Olaf made a great expedition to Vindland with sixty men-of-war in the year 1000. Entering the Oder River, he was kindly received by the King Burishar, and his demands for his wife's property were readily met. The treacherous Sigvald went with him to the court and offered to escort his fleet on the return with eleven ships of the Jomsvikings. Sigvald delayed sailing until the allies had gathered a fleet of some seventy vessels in a harbor in the Isle of Rugen. When the trap was set, he led out Olaf's fleet through the channel between Rugen and the mainland, past the hiding-place of the hostile fleet.

King Svein, King Olaf and Eirik Jarl mounted a hill from which they sighted in the fine clear weather the Norse fleet approaching in irregular order and entirely unprepared for attack. First came a large ship owned by Styrkar of Gimsar; then one belonging to Thorkel Nefja, the king's brother; next two long-ships of the king's brothers-in-law; and finally the splendid ship of Erling Skjalgsson of Jadar. These five great ships with many smaller ones were allowed to pass without being attacked. Eirik Jarl's shrewd advice was:

"Let them sail on, for I tell you truly that there are warriors on board whom, if we go into battle with Olaf Tryggveson, it is better not to have but to miss in his fleet."

After these vessels had passed, other large ships were sighted. Sure that Olaf's famous flagship, the *Long Serpent*, would be among them, the allies manned their ships and prepared to leave the harbor. As they were to have such overwhelming numbers, it was clear that all the ships of the allies could not be brought into action against the *Long Serpent* at the same time. Lots were therefore cast to determine who would first attack the flagship. It fell to Svein of Denmark to attack first; then Olaf of Sweden; and finally, if necessary, Eirik Jarl with his Norsemen. As the vessels of Olaf Tryggveson drew near, the *Long Serpent* was easily distinguished, and fear crept into the heart of many a brave man. The noble Eirik Jarl spoke out in open admiration of his enemy: "This famous ship is befitting such a king as Olaf Tryggveson; for it is true of him that he excels other kings as much as the *Long Serpent* does other ships."

By this time all but eleven ships had passed the ambush. Thorkel Dyril, commanding the *Crane*, led the remainder. Sighting the hostile fleet in the harbor, he lowered his sails to wait for the other ships of his fleet near the part of the channel then called Svold. The ships of his division followed his motions. Soon Thorkel Nefja came up in the *Short Serpent* and ordered his division to lower their sails also. When the king arrived with the *Long Serpent*, his division commanders informed him of the overwhelming force lying in wait and advised that a retreat be made while there was yet time. At that the gallant Olaf sprang to the lypting and shouted his orders: "Let down the sail quickly as possible and some of you put out the oars to take the speed off the ship! I will rather fight than flee. For never yet have I fled from battle. My life is in God's power, but never will I take to flight; for he is not a true king who in fear flies from his foes!"

As the great host of the allies rowed out from their anchorage and started to form for battle, it was apparent to all that the Norsemen were hopelessly outnumbered and that there was no chance of victory. The brave commander of the *Crane* called over to Olaf: "Lord, here is an overwhelming force to fight against. Let us hoist our sails and follow our men out to sea. We can still do so while our foes prepare for battle, since it is not looked upon as cowardly by any one for a man to use forethought for himself and his men."

But the king shouted back: "Tie together the ships and let the men prepare for battle and draw their swords. My men shall not think of flight!"

A horn was then blown as the signal to lash the ships together. This was done with chains so that there was enough water between the ships for them to use their oars. The *Long Serpent* was placed in the center of the eleven ships. It was the largest vessel of this period of Norse history. There is some conflict as to its characteristics, but the most reliable information seems to give it a length of 180 feet; about fifty-two rowing benches, with that number of oars on each side, and a crew numbering 600 men, all specially selected for strength and courage. These men were between the ages of twenty and sixty, save Einar Thambarskelver, who, though but eighteen, was the best archer in Norway. With his bow *Thamb* he could shoot a blunt arrow through a raw oxhide hanging from a pole. In the post of honor on the forecastle were Ulf the Red, who carried the standard; Kolbjorn Stallari, Thorstein Oxafot and Vikar of Tiundaland. Two brothers-in-law of the king, Thorgeir and Hyrning, were among the chieftains on board.

On either side of the *Long Serpent* were the *Short Serpent* and the *Crane;* four smaller ships were made fast outside the *Crane* and an equal number outside the *Short Serpent,* forming a line of eleven ships abreast.

As the ships were being secured the king noticed that his ship was not far enough to the front, and shouted to his men: "Bring forward the long-ship; I will not be the hindmost of my men when the battle begins." Then spake Ulf the Red, who bore the standard: "If the *Serpent* shall be put as much forward as it is large and longer than the other ships, the men in the bows will have a hard time of it."

The hot-tempered king, incensed at this insubordination, aimed an arrow at his standard-bearer and replied: "I had the *Serpent* made longer than other ships so that it should be put forward more boldly in battle and be well known in fighting and sailing. But I did not know that I had a stem-defender who was both red- and faint-headed."

Ulf stood up bravely and answered: "Do not shoot

me, Lord, but rather where it is more needed—that is, at our foes. For what I win I win for thee. Maybe you will think your men not over-many before the evening comes." Whereat the king controlled his temper and lowered his bow.

King Olaf wore a coat of mail, covered with a red kirtle; a splendid gilt helmet was on his head and he carried a gilt shield. He stood proudly upon his lypting and, pointing to the numerous squadron of the Danes, addressed his followers: "We are not afraid of those cowards, for no more courage is in the Danes than in wood-goats. Never were Danes victorious over Northmen. They will not conquer us today." Still these Danes were a worthy foe, even for Olaf Tryggveson, for it was only some dozen years later that under Svein, their leader in this battle, they overran England.

Seeing the standard of the Swedes, King Olaf added: "Easier and pleasanter will the Swedes think it to sit at home and lick their sacrifice bowls than to board the *Long Serpent* under your weapons; but who owns those large ships to the left of the Danes?"

"It is," they answered, "Eirik Jarl Hakonson." "Then," said the king gravely, "that host is full of high-born men whom they have ranged against us. Eirik Jarl thinks he has just cause for fighting us. It is likely we shall have a hard struggle with him and his men, for they are Northmen like ourselves."

Now both fleets rowed at full speed toward each other, shouting their battle-cries. As shooting range was reached, the air was filled with clouds of arrows from bows and crossbows. When throwing range was reached, hundreds of javelins and spears were thrown.

In accordance with the plan, King Svein first attacked the Norse battle-line hand to hand, many of his ships pushing their bows up against those of the *Short Serpent, Long Serpent* and *Crane.* The rest of his ships and the Swedes remained at shooting range and kept an arrow-storm flying. In the *Long Serpent* the stem-defenders fought hand to hand; the men further aft used throwing weapons most of the time, but sometimes also used the sword. Many a man fell on both sides, "King Olaf made the bravest defense with his men, but still they fell. He fought most boldly; he shot chiefly with bows and spears, but when the chief attack was made on the *Serpent,* he went forward in hand-to-hand fight and cleft many a man's skull with his sword."

The men in the stems of the three center ships, which were larger and had a higher freeboard than the Danish galleys, dropped anchors and grapnels upon the ships opposed to them and held them fast; then, throwing weapons from their higher stations, they cleared the decks; thus Svein was forced to fall back, leaving many of his best ships in the hands of the Norsemen.

Next the Swedes attacked the center of the line. But after a long and fierce struggle they also were forced to withdraw with great losses in men and of their larger ships.

While these two prolonged contests in the center were progressing, Eirik Jarl was pursuing different tactics. With his large *Jarnbardi,* or *Ironbeard,* so named because of its great iron ram in the bow, he had run alongside one of the outer ships of Olaf's formation. After a hard fight this small vessel was captured and cut adrift from the rest of the line. In this way, always attacking the outer ships, he continued to make progress, capturing ship after ship, while the defenders retreated to the vessels in the center of the formation.

After their defeats the Danes and Swedes returned to the attack; this time they did not attempt to board, but remained at shooting and throwing range. Eirik Jarl kept at his work; as his men fell he replaced them with Swedes and Danes and continued the fight. Olaf's men also lost heavily, and there were no fresh men to take their places. At last all the ships but the *Long Serpent* were taken, their survivors having retired to the flagship. This great vessel now stood alone amid the innumerable host of the enemy. The noble king, still confident of victory, constantly encouraged his men.

After a short lull, Eirik Jarl rammed the *Long Serpent* with five of his best galleys. The saga thus describes this fight, which is almost without a parallel in history:

"Eirik Jarl laid the *Jarnbardi* alongside the *Serpent*, after which there ensued the fiercest fight and most terrible hand-to-hand struggle that could be. Eirik Jarl was in the foreroom of his ship, where a shield-burgh was drawn up. There was both hand-to-hand fighting and spear-throwing, and every kind of weapon was thrown, and whatever could be seized by the hand. Some shot with bows and some threw spears. Indeed, such a shower of weapons was thrown upon the *Serpent* that the men could hardly protect themselves against it.

"Spears and arrows flew thickly, for on all sides of the *Serpent* lay warships. King Olaf's men now became so furious that they jumped over the gunwales in order to reach their foes and kill them; but many did not lay their ships so close to the *Serpent* as to get into hand-to-hand fight. Most of them concluded it hard to deal with Olaf's champions. The Northmen thought of nothing but continually going forward to slay their foes; and many went straight overboard. For out of eagerness and daring they forgot that they were not fighting on dry land, and many sank with their weapons between the ships. King Olaf Tryggveson stood on the lypting of the *Serpent*, and chiefly used during the day his bow and javelins; always two javelins at a time. It was agreed by all, both friends and foes who were present and those who have heard these tidings told with the greatest truth, that they have known no man fight more valiantly than King Olaf Tryggveson. King Olaf surpassed most other kings, in that he made himself so easily known in battle that men knew no example of any other king having shown himself so openly to his foes, especially as he had to fight such an overwhelming force."

During this fighting, Einar Thambarskelver stood by the mast and used his bow with deadly effect. Seeing Eirik Jarl in the shield-burgh, he aimed an arrow at him, but it pierced the tiller just above the jarl's head; as the latter was asking the men about him who it was that had shot, a second arrow passed between his arm and his side; then seeing the archer, he said to Fin, a famous archer of his ship, "Shoot that tall man by the mast."

Fin shot and the arrow hit Einar's bow in the middle just as he was about to shoot his third arrow at the jarl. The great bow broke in half. "What is it that broke," cried King Olaf, "with such a noise?"

"Norway, King, from thy hands," answered the bowman.

"No! not quite so much as that," said the king; "take my bow and shoot."

Einar took the bow and drew it back over the head of the arrow. "Too weak, too weak," he said, "for the bow of a mighty king!" He then threw the bow aside and took sword and shield.

Seeing that the weapons of his men were becoming broken, the king sprang down from the lypting, unlocked the high-seat chest and carried out new swords. In the forward part of the ship had been stationed the greatest champions, and there the deck and bulwarks were highest, so that there were still enough men in this part of the ship to make boarding impossible. But amidships the decks were lower and there were only a few men left. Seeing this, Eirik Jarl sprang aboard, followed by fourteen picked men. The king's brother-in-law Hyrning ran aft to fight the boarders, and a Homeric struggle occurred between the champions of the two ships. Hyrning fought with the utmost bravery, and Eirik was forced to withdraw to the *Jarnbardi* after nearly all the boarding party had been killed or wounded.

The allied fleets then drew off for a time so that fresh crews of Danes and Swedes could be put in Eirik's ships. During this interlude he asked an old chieftain, Thorkel the High, for his advice. "Often have I been in battles," he said, "and never have I found men equally brave and so skilled in fighting as those on the *Serpent,* nor have I seen a ship so hard to win. Now as thou art one of the wisest of men, give me the best advice thou knowest how the *Serpent* may be won."

Thorkel answered: "Thou must take heavy timbers and let them fall from thy ship upon the gunwale of the *Serpent,* so it will list over; you will then find it easier to board the *Serpent* if its gunwale is no higher than those of the other ships."

When all was ready the allied forces made a combined attack upon the *Serpent.* Again the fighting was furious, but despite the heavy odds against them and the hopelessness of victory, the men of King Olaf repulsed all attacks. Then Eirik Jarl, according to Thorkel's advice, threw over heavy beams on the *Serpent's* bulwarks. This gave him an advantage, and as the Norsemen began finally to tire, the masses of the enemy poured over the side. The forecastle men again came aft and made their last stand with their beloved king. Many were the almost incredible deeds which these berserks performed. Thorstein Uxafot killed one man with a blow of his bare fist and then swung the sailyard as a club. From his raised position on the lypting, Olaf threw javelins and never once missed his aim until he threw at Eirik Jarl. As he missed his enemy with three spears, he said: "Never before did I thus miss a man. Great is the jarl's luck. It must be God's will that he now shall rule in Norway!"

Now the fight was at last drawing to a close. One by one the tiring champions, heroes of many fights, fell to the deck; first Hyrning and Thorgeir; then Vikar of Tiundaland; and last of all the valiant standard-bearer, Ulf the Red. Of the stem-defenders there remained only the valiant Kolbjorn Stallari.

"When the most valiant of the king's men in the foreroom began to fall, Kolbjorn went up on the lypting to the king. It was not easy to tell them apart, for Kolbjorn was a very large and handsome man. There was then such a thick shower of weapons in the lypting that the shields of King Olaf and Kolbjorn were covered all over with arrows. But when the jarl's men came up to the lypting, it seemed to them that so much light came over the king that they could not see through it; yet, when the light vanished they saw King Olaf nowhere."

This pretty myth was not far from true, for other accounts tell us that when the king saw that there were but nine men remaining of his crew, he raised his shield over his head, sprang overboard and disappeared beneath the waters. There is another pretty legend that Astrid, the noble wife of treacherous Sigvald Jarl of the Jomsvikings, picked him up in her galley, and that he went to the Holy Land, where he lived as a hermit for many years. Unfortunately, there is no basis of truth for this story. His dog Vige, who was on the *Serpent* during the battle, starved himself to death because of grief for his master.

Thus died King Olaf at the height of his fame. He was but thirty-six years of age, and his romantic life and glorious death have endeared his memory to the Norsemen. His heroic conduct in his last battle showed that he must have been moved by the same thought as that in the Japanese verse which Oda Nobunaga loved to quote:

> Man has to die once and once only;
> He should make his death glorious.

CHAPTER III

The Spanish Armada

DURING the last half of the sixteenth century two great movements brought Spain and England face to face for a fight to the death.

One movement was the struggle for world trade and colonial expansion. Spain and Portugal, due to their early discoveries, were the first to establish themselves in both the East and West Indies, China, the Malay Peninsula, Florida, Mexico, Central and South America. The Pope divided these colonial possessions and their surrounding seas between Spain and Portugal. Access to them was denied to other nations.

England was just beginning to realize that her future lay on the seas, resented this arbitrary disposal of the rich territories of the Orient and the New World, and demanded the right to trade with them. Refused this privilege, the hardy English mariners organized private expeditions into the forbidden waters to attack Spanish and Portuguese shipping, and finally to attack and plunder their towns. Sir Francis Drake led the way with a wonderful three years' voyage around the world from which he brought enough treasure to pay back forty-seven pounds for every pound invested in the cruise; in addition he paid enormous contributions to the Queen, who knighted the bold pirate on his famous ship, the *Golden Hind.*

Coincident with this movement was the struggle for religious freedom which was being fought with unparalleled ferocity in the Netherlands. Until the assassination of William the Silent in 1584 the desperate resistance of the Dutch burghers had been able to hold in check the finest troops of Spain, led by Alva, Requesens, Don Juan of Austria, and Alexander, Duke of Parma. While unable to withstand the Spanish veterans in the open field, the Dutch defended their cities with unheard-of devotion, while their hardy seamen controlled the seas and river mouths. In fact, William's consummate statesmanship and unfaltering resolution were finally bringing the Spanish party to complete defeat. His death, however, resulted in dissensions among his own followers and allowed Parma to seize one city after another by a skilful combination of strategy and intrigue. Alexander, the first general of Europe and probably the cleverest politician, finally completed the conquest of what is now Belgium by the capture of Antwerp, after one of the most renowned sieges of history.

One incident of this siege was to have a decisive though indirect effect upon the Armada three years later and merits a brief description. In order to prevent the inhabitants from receiving food by the Scheldt River, Alexander built, in the face of apparently insuperable difficulties, a great fortified bridge across the river, there 2400 feet wide and even to-day unbridged. An Italian resident of Antwerp, Gianibelli by name, with the help of Bory, a clockmaker, and Timmerman, a mechanician, developed an unusual plan to destroy the bridge by means of two ships loaded with explosives. In the hold of each vessel was laid a brick floor, upon which was constructed a large chamber of masonry, with marble walls five feet thick. The chamber was loaded with 7000 pounds of specially prepared powder and covered with a roof, no less than six feet thick, of tombstones laid edgeways. Over the chamber and on either side were placed marble slabs, millstones, blocks of marble, chain-shot, paving stones, and other suitable missiles. One of the ships, the *Fortune*, was to be exploded by means of a slow match, while on the *Hope* an ingenious clockwork was to strike flint and steel and ignite the magazine.

The two vessels, together with thirty-two fireships, were sent down with the tide on a dark night; false fires were lighted on both vessels so that they would be mistaken for ordinary fireships. The fireships mostly ran against a floating barrage of rafts anchored above the bridge and had no effect. The *Fortune* grounded and her explosion was so slight as not even to destroy the ship. The *Hope*, however, avoided the barrage and came up against the bridge, which was crowded with troops watching the fireships and laughing at their failure. A number of men jumped down to extinguish the slight fires on her deck. Alexander, who had been directing the proceedings, fortunately agreed to the appeals of his staff to retire to a safer place until the investigations were completed. No sooner had he left than the clockwork ignited the magazine. "The *Hope* disappeared," writes Motley, "together with the men who had boarded her, and the blockhouse against which she had struck, with all its garrison; while a large portion of the bridge, with all the troops stationed upon it, had vanished into the air. It was the work of a single instant. The Scheldt yawned to its lowest depth, and then cast its waters across the dykes, deep into the forts, and far over the land. The earth shook as with the throb of a volcano. A wild glare lighted up the scene for a moment and was then succeeded by pitchy darkness. Houses were toppled down miles away, and not a living thing, even in remote places, could keep its feet. The air was filled with a rain of plowshares, gravestones, and marble balls, intermixed with heads, limbs, and bodies of what had been human beings. Slabs of granite, vomited by the flaming ship, were found afterward at a league's distance and buried deep in the earth. A thousand soldiers were destroyed in a second of time, many of them being torn to shreds beyond even the semblance of humanity."

But great as was its material effect against the bridge at Antwerp, this could not compare with the moral effect which the cry of "Antwerp fireships" was to have three years later in Calais Roads.

In 1585, after the King of France had refused the sovereignty of the Netherlands, Elizabeth decided to intervene directly in the war. The decision of the British Council sums up clearly her reasons: "Although her Majesty should hereby enter into a war presently, yet were she better to do it now, while she may make the same out of her realm, having the help of the people of Holland, and before the King of Spain shall have consummated his conquests in those countries, whereby he shall be so provoked by pride, solicited by the Pope, and tempted by the queen's own subjects, and shall be so strong by sea, and so free from all other actions and quarrels—yea, shall be so formidable to all the rest of Christendom, as that her Majesty shall nowise be able, with her own power, nor with the aid of any other, neither by land nor by sea, to withstand his attempts, but shall be forced to give place to his insatiable malice, which is most terrible to be thought of, but miserable to suffer."

A strong military force was sent into the Low Countries under the Earl of Leicester, with such noted chieftains as Sir John Norris, Sir Philip Sydney and

> The brave Lord Willoughby,
> Of courage fierce and fell,
> Who would not give one inch of way
> For all the devils in hell.

Leicester's leadership, both military and political, left much to be desired, and he received little financial support from the queen. Under these conditions Alexander continued his successes during the campaigns of 1586 and 1587, assisted by the treachery of English leaders.

Drake's cruise into the West Indies during 1585 and 1586 was more successful. In addition to attacking Spanish trade, he stormed both San Domingo and Carthagena and burned St. Augustine, becoming, as Burghley said, "a fearful man to the King of Spain."

Meanwhile great preparations for a combined naval and military attack on England were being made by

THE ENGLISH FLEET AND THE SPANISH ARMADA

Santa Cruz in Spain and Parma in the Netherlands. Drake, "hating nothing so much as idleness," determined to "singe the beard" of the king of Spain by an attack upon his own harbors. With a fleet of sixteen ships and seven pinnaces he sailed from Plymouth on April 2, 1587. His orders were to prevent the assembly of the Armada in Lisbon and "to distress the ships within the havens themselves." Later his orders were modified by a prohibition against entering Spanish ports or committing "any act of hostility upon the land," but fortunately for Drake the pinnace carrying the orders never reached him.

Coming into the outer harbor at Cadiz, Drake beat off twelve war galleys and attacked the merchant vessels at anchor, under the fire of the shore batteries. Pinnaces and boats even attacked certain ships in the inner harbor. Provisioning his fleet from captured vessels and loading six prizes with supplies, he destroyed a number of vessels, variously stated to be between eighteen and thirty-one, of which one was a war galley and four were large vessels intended to join the Armada, and withdrew "with very little loss not worth the mentioning." Drake next appeared off Cape St. Vincent, at the southwestern point of Portugal, stormed the castle covering the anchorage, destroyed all the small craft along the coast and watered his fleet. A storm having then scattered his ships, the admiral with nine vessels made for the Azores and captured the great carrick *San Felipe,* loaded with a cargo valued at 114,000 pounds. On June 26 he came into

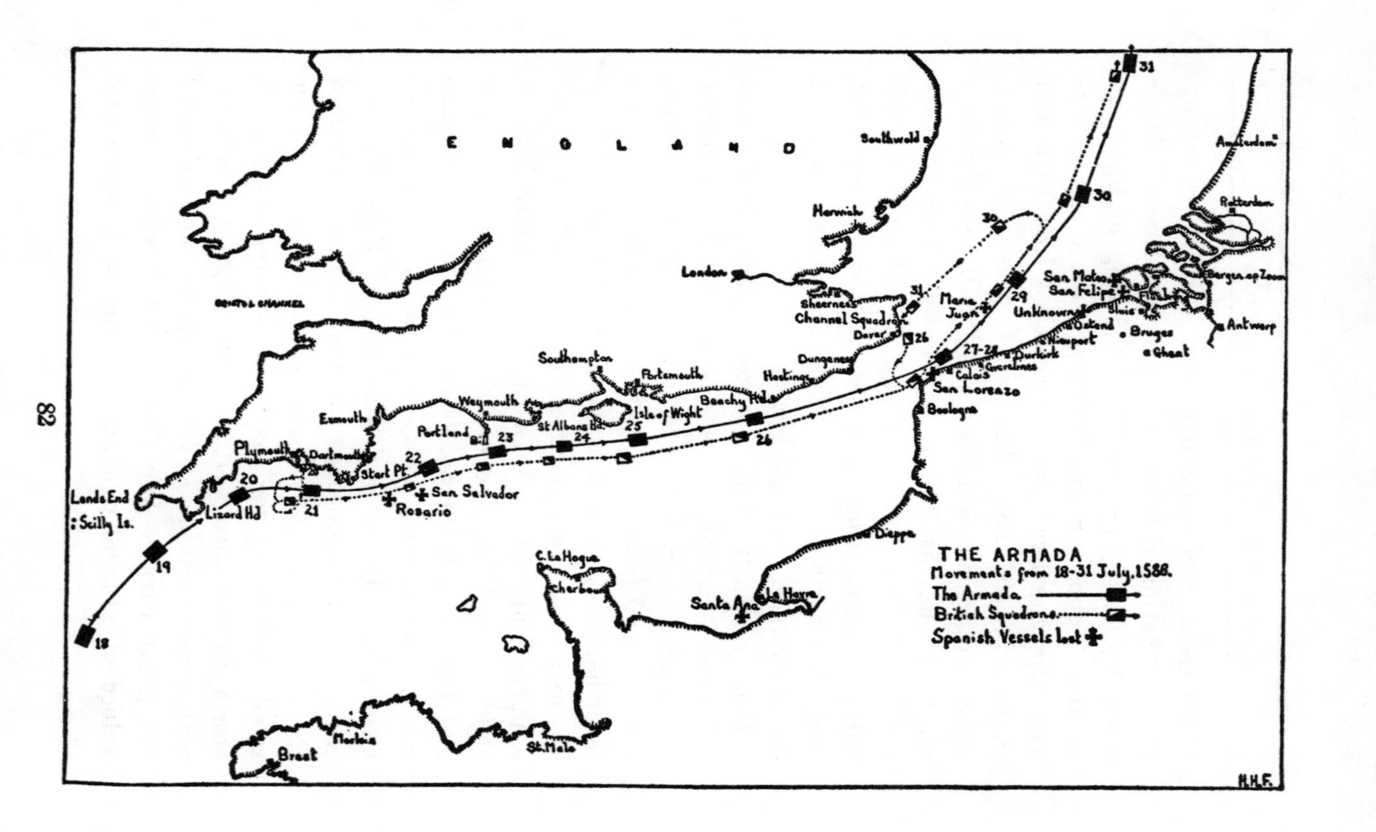
ENGLAND
BRISTOL CHANNEL
Southwold
Harwich
London
Sheerness
Channel Squadron
Dover
Dungeness
Hastings
Beachy Hd.
Southampton
Portsmouth
Isle of Wight
St Albans Hd.
Weymouth
Portland
Bill
Exmouth
Dartmouth
Plymouth
Start Pt.
Lizard Hd.
Lands End
Scilly Is.
San Salvador
Rosario
Amsterdam
Rotterdam
Bergen op Zoom
Antwerp
San Mateo
San Felipe
Flushing
Sluis
Unknown
Ostend
Bruges
Ghent
Nieuport
Dunkirk
Gravelines
Calais
San Lorenzo
Boulogne
Maria Juan
Dieppe
Le Havre
Santa Ana
C. La Hogue
Cherbourg
St. Malo
Morlaix
Brest
18
19
20
21
22
23
24
25
26
27-28
29
30
31
THE ARMADA
Movements from 18-31 July, 1588.
The Armada
British Squadrons
Spanish Vessels lost
H.H.F.

Plymouth. "God make us all thankful again and again," he said, "that we have, although it be little, made a beginning upon the coast of Spain."

Despite the brilliance of Drake's campaign, Philip II of Spain redoubled his exertions to prepare the Armada at Lisbon. Alexander, in addition to pressing his operations in Flanders, used his special fund of five million ducats to assemble a splendid expeditionary force to join the Armada and invade England. At Dunkirk and Nieuport he assembled seventy-four ships, 150 flat-bottomed boats and seventy river craft to transport a picked force of 17,000 troops, to be reinforced by 6000 landed directly from the Armada. Brilliant uniforms were provided for the *élite* regiments with which Alexander expected to make his triumphant entry into London. In the famous Tercio of Naples, 3500 strong, every man had an engraved corselet and musket barrel.

To cover these preparations Philip instructed Alexander to commence an intrigue. He was to ask a disavowal for Drake's cruises. "When you have got such a disavowal," wrote Philip, "you are to act as if entirely taken in and imposed upon by them, and, pretending to believe everything they tell you, you must renew the negotiations, proceed to name commissioners, and propose a meeting in neutral territory. * * * But to you only do I declare that my intention is that this shall never lead to any result, whatever conditions may be offered by them. On the contrary all this is done, just as they do, to deceive them, and to cool them in their preparations for defense, by inducing them to believe that such preparations will be unnecessary. You are well aware that the reverse of all this is the truth, and that on our part there is to be no slackness, but the greatest diligence in our efforts for the invasion of England, for which we have already made the most abundant provision in men, ships, and money, of which you are well aware."

So cleverly did Alexander play his cards that Elizabeth completely disavowed Drake's last expedition and sent commissioners to treat for peace. The intrigues of Burghley and Croft, of the Spanish party, eclipsed the prudent statesmanship of Walsingham. Still, some naval preparations were made. Drake retained a nucleus of his fleet at Plymouth, while Sir Henry Palmer cruised in the Narrow Seas, as the Straits of Dover were then called, with a small squadron. On December 21, 1587, Lord Howard of Effingham's commission as Lord High Admiral of England was signed, and the mobilization of his squadron in the Thames was commenced. Drake was made Vice-Admiral and ordered to prepare his squadron for an offensive movement; the Dover squadron was reinforced.

Meanwhile the fleets of Holland and Zeeland, composed of no less than ninety warships and fifty merchant vessels, cruised off Alexander's bases. One Dutch squadron carried a force of 1200 picked musketeers for landing operations. Small craft kept close off the ports and commanded the Scheldt.

After these initial preparations of the British fleet came a period of inaction. Drake was refused his ships and stores and condemned to a term of "watchful waiting," during which he spent his own money for provisions. Howard was ordered to reduce his crews to half their war strength. So disgusted was he with such inactivity that he asked for leave of absence. Hawkyns did his best to send raiding forces to the Spanish coast; while Drake expressed a correct principle of naval strategy when he said that "with fifty sail of shipping we shall do more good upon their own coast than a great many more will do here at home." He protested that his ammunition allowance would be sufficient for but one and a half days' fighting and demanded its increase threefold. It would seem that his target practice was not encouraged, for we find Howard writing to Walsingham: "There happened a mischance in one of his ships at Portsmouth, that a piece broke and killed a man, with some other hurt. If you would write a word or two unto him to spare his powder, it would do well."

But Drake's aggressive ideas were not to the liking of his queen, in whom the negotiations with Alexander had inspired great hopes of peace. In April, Lord Henry Seymour was placed in command of the squadron in the Narrow Seas, with twenty ships, nineteen pinnaces and one galley to watch Alexander, while Howard on May 23 joined Drake at Plymouth. The Dutch fleets were more than a match for Alexander's transports and Seymour could probably have been employed more profitably with the main fleet at Plymouth. This force, after Howard's arrival, was raised to about sixty-nine ships and thirty-three pinnaces, of which sixteen ships and five pinnaces belonged to the royal navy.

The preparation of the Armada was delayed by the death of Santa Cruz, its commander-in-chief. The Duke of Medina-Sidonia was appointed in his place and recommended that additional vessels be added. As their stores were lacking, it was not until May 20 that the Armada could leave Lisbon. It took three weeks to round Cape Finisterre, at the northwestern point of Spain, where a storm scattered the ships over the face of the ocean, so that they were glad to collect in the port of Corunna. Some twenty vessels reached their rendezvous off the Lizard before they could be recalled, and narrowly escaped capture. So discouraged was Sidonia that he advised that the enterprise be abandoned. Philip, however, ordered the fleet to be made ready again, and this was accomplished in a month's time, principally by the exertions of Don Pedro de Valdes.

Drake and Howard both desired to go for the Spanish coast, but were prevented by their lack of provisions. "There is here," wrote the latter, "the gallantest company of captains, soldiers, and mariners that I think was ever seen in England. It were a pity they should lack meat, when they are so desirous to spend their lives in her Majesty's service."

When provisions enough could be scraped together, the fleet put to sea, only to be held up by a storm for seven days and forced back into port. There despatches from London were found, prohibiting a cruise to the

Spanish coast, to which Lord Howard responded with spirit that he was glad that there were those at court "as are able to judge what is fitter for us to do than we here." On June 19, when the fleet put out a second time, it was again driven in by a gale, narrowly missing the Spanish ships which through error had gone on to the Lizard. Howard's men fell sick by hundreds and had to be replaced with recruits. On July 7, however, he finally got headed for Corunna to attack the Armada in port, but the wind failing two days later, and provisions being almost exhausted, he had to turn back. On the 12th he re-entered Plymouth.

As Howard began to renew his supplies for another cast to the southward, he received the remarkable news from the court that the Armada was not likely to make its appearance that year, and was ordered to decommission his four largest vessels. Such a proceeding well justified Howard's statement of last January: "If her Majesty would have spent but a thousand crowns to have had some intelligence, it would have saved her twenty times as much." Although Howard did not obey the order, he did have to discharge four or five vessels to bring up the crews of the others.

On the 19th, while the admirals were playing bowls, Captain Fleming of the *Golden Hind* brought the astonishing word that the Armada was off the Lizard. According to the story, Drake in a characteristic manner quietly said that there was time to finish the game "and beat the Spaniards after."

The Armada had sailed from Corunna on the 12th; all that is known for certain of Sidonia's orders is that he was to rendezvous at the Lizard, proceed up the channel to the Flemish coast, where he was to be joined by Alexander, who would personally direct the invasion of England and its covering operations. Some reports say that Drake was known to be at Plymouth, and that Sidonia was to attack him; others state that he was to refuse battle until Parma joined the Armada. Some accounts say that he was to seize the Isle of Wight before attempting to join Parma; others that this was to be done after Parma had landed in England.

After several days of fair weather the Armada, during the 16th and 17th, was scattered by a storm, and four galleys were forced to seek shelter in French ports, one being wrecked at Bayonne. On the 19th the Lizard was sighted, and by evening the fleet was assembled.

The English fleet was composed about as follows:

Squadron		*Vessels of Royal Navy*		*Private Men-of-war*		*Converted Merchant Vessels*	
		Ships	*Pinnaces*	*Ships*	*Pinnaces*	*Ships*	*Pinnaces*
Howard		11	8	4	3	24	16
Drake		5	2	..	..	20	13
Seymour		8	4	..	..	14	4
Totals	136	24	14	4	3	58	33

The Armada as it arrived off the British coast was composed about as follows:

Squadron	*Commander*	*Vessels of Royal Navy*			*Converted Merchant Vessels*	
		Ships	*Galle-asses*	*Pin-naces*	*Ships*	*Pin-naces*
Portugal	Medina-Sidonia	9	..	2	..	..
Castile	Diego de Valdes	13	..	2	..	..
Naples	Moncada	..	4	..	..	..
Biscaya	Recalde	..	..	..	9	2
Andalusia	Pedro de Valdes	..	..	..	10	2
Guipuscoa	Oquendo	..	..	..	10	2
Levant	Bertendona	..	..	..	9	2
Light	Mendoza	..	..	..	..	19
Storeships	Medina	..	..	..	19	16
Totals	130	22	4	4	57	43

A comparison of the two fleets is difficult, because, while the numbers are fairly well known, different methods of measuring tonnage were used, and little is known as to the number and size of the guns carried. The English had an advantage in numbers, particularly if we remember that thirty-five Spanish vessels were absolutely non-combatant and a hindrance rather than an advantage. Numbers, however, mean very little. In the first place, the pinnaces were of no value in battle. Second, the converted merchant vessels were of little use. "If you had seen the simple service done by the merchants and coast ships," wrote Wynter, "you would have said we had been little holpen by them, otherwise than that they did make a show." The Spanish merchant vessels were in most cases of even less value. Nearly all the actual fighting was done by the royal and private men-of-war, twenty-six Spanish ships against twenty-eight English.

The Spanish ships had the advantage in size, even if we subtract 35 per cent. of their tonnage to allow for the difference in their methods of determining it. But, on the other hand, the English vessels carried from 25 to 50 per cent. more guns than did Spanish vessels of equal size, and they were much faster and more easily handled. While the Armada carried some 24,000 men to 14,000 for the English fleet, the former included some 17,000 soldiers, of whom 6000 were intended for a landing force, while many others were mere peasants impressed into service. "In the kingdom of Portugal there was no preparation of men," writes Gregorio de Sotomayor, "but when they embarked themselves, they commanded 2000 Portingals to go aboard upon pain of death." On the other hand, practically all the English personnel were seamen.

The English had the further advantage of fighting in their own waters. At the time of contact they were rested by a week's stay in port, while the Armada had been under way for the same time and through a storm. The English had many safe harbors into which their ships could proceed, while there was not a single port available to Sidonia. Even while fighting, vessels were constantly coming out with reinforcements of men and supplies of food and ammunition for the English, and their sick and wounded could be sent ashore for treatment. Except for a little food bought at Calais, the Armada received no assistance whatever from the shore.

The Spanish plan, moreover, required the junction of Sidonia and Parma, and from the start this was virtually an impossibility. The Armada was prevented by shoals from entering or even approaching Parma's ports, and the currents were too strong to anchor off them. Alexander's transports, flat-bottomed boats and river craft, upon which his troops would have to be crowded like sardines, could not force their way out against the Dutch fleets, which were specially designed for sailing the shoals off Dunkirk and Nieuport; furthermore, these Spanish vessels required perfectly calm weather. "The preposterous notion," writes Motley, "that he should come out with his flotilla to make a junction with Medina off Calais was over and over again denounced by Parma with vehemence and bitterness, and most boding expressions were used by him as to the probable result were such a delusion persisted in." Nevertheless, this was the plan insisted upon by Philip, and Parma made ready his 17,000 troops so they could be embarked in one day as soon as news of the Armada's arrival was received.

One advantage the Armada had, that of surprise. So many wild reports had been spread as to the losses it had suffered that when it actually arrived at the Lizard it took the English completely by surprise. One-third of the fleet was in the Narrow Seas watching Parma; their vessels were poorly supplied with food and ammunition, and typhus was decimating their crews. Only a part of the total strength tabulated above was actually ready to put to sea. The army was in a deplorable condition. On July 27, when the Armada arrived at Calais, there were available but 4000 completely untrained militia, and Leicester wrote to the queen: "So soon as your army is assembled, let them by and by be exercised, every man to know his weapon, and that there be all other things prepared in readiness for your army, as if they should march upon a day's warning, especially carriages, and a commissary of victuals, and a master of ordnance." This was the very day upon which a landing might have been made, had the British and Dutch fleets been defeated, and rather late in the game to suggest such elementary preparations.

Furthermore, despite the nonchalance of Drake at his game of bowls, he and Howard were caught in rather an awkward position in Plymouth. Only fifty-four vessels were ready for sea, and the wind was blowing directly up the channel. These vessels commenced beating out during the night and, "through the great travail used by our men," they were assembled outside by 3 P.M. of the next day, the 20th.

"The 20th at dawn," writes Sidonia, "the Armada was near with the land, so as we were seen therefrom, whereupon they made fires and smokes." During the forenoon a council of war met on the *San Martin*. The reports of its decisions are conflicting; the Armada stood to the eastward along the coast toward Plymouth. In the mist at sundown it sighted the English ships in the distance, and at midnight a pinnace brought in prisoners who reported the combined squadrons of Howard and Drake at sea. The Armada then anchored and prepared for action at daybreak.

Howard, having available less than half his full strength, decided not to force a fight to a decision, but to harass the Armada until he could bring his own and Drake's squadrons to full strength and unite with Seymour. His tactics were to gain the weather-gage and then attack the nearest ships, in the hope that they might be disabled and fall behind; or that others, tacking to come to their assistance, might create confusion or possibly collisions in the enemy's closely-packed formation.

As Howard cleared Plymouth on the afternoon of the 20th, he found himself to leeward of the Armada, the wind being from the southwest. His first task was to gain the weather-gage—i.e., to get to windward of the Armada. With some forty-six ships he stood to the southward, close-hauled on the starboard tack. Eight vessels hugged the coast and endeavored to beat to windward, inshore of the Armada.

Early on the 21st (Sunday) Sidonia proceeded toward Plymouth on an easterly course, the wind having shifted to W.N.W. The old sketches show the Armada forming a crescent, about four ships deep in the center and two at the wings. The inside of the crescent was to the rear or westward. The Biscayan and Andalusian squadrons were on the left or northern wing, the Guipuscoan and Levant squadrons on the right or southern wing; one galleasse was on the tip of each wing. In the center were the *San Martin*, the Castilian and Portuguese squadrons, the two remaining galleasses, the light squadron and the storeships. As Sidonia, by his own admission, knew little either of war or the sea, the operations of the fleet were principally directed by Don Diego de Valdes, who, in addition to commanding the Castilian squadron, sailed in the *San Martin* as chief of staff.

During the night Howard with his forty-six ships gained a position well to the southeastward of the Armada. In the early morning he headed to the westward, passing around its southern flank. The eight ships inshore succeeded in passing its northern tip. There was slight skirmishing at long range. The battle sketches show the English fleet either in one compact mass or in groups of ships, led by the admirals; in a few cases vessels are in single column.

It was probably about noon when Howard united the two English detachments west of the Armada and attacked the rear of the crescent, his principal objective being the Biscayan squadron, under Recalde, on the tip of the northern wing. The Andalusian squadron, under Pedro de Valdes, next to the southward, was engaged only at long range. A panic ensued and many Biscayan ships pressed into the center. Recalde, however, in the *Santa Ana*, gallantly stood his ground and was attacked by Drake in the *Revenge*, Hawkyns in the *Victory*, Frobisher in the *Triumph* and other vessels. Supporting Recalde were the *Gran Grin*, a galleon of his own squadron, Don Diego Enriquez in the *San Juan*, of the Castilian squadron, and Don Diego de Pimentel in the Portuguese galleon *San Mateo*.

Describing the attack on Recalde, Sidonia reports: "The enemy assailed him with great discharging of ordnance, without closing, whereby his ship suffered much in her rigging, her forestay was cut, and her foremast had two great shot therein." The admiral then himself with the *San Martin* and other vessels hove-to and "awaited the rear to gather it into the main body of the fleet." The English then drew off, "for the Lord Admiral," says their detailed account, "considering there were forty sail of his fleet as yet to come from Plymouth, thought good to stay [i.e., await] their coming before he would hazard the rest too far."

As the Spanish vessels manoeuvered "to recover the wind," Don Pedro de Valdes, commanding the Andalusian squadron, in the *N. S. del Rosario*, collided with the *Santa Catalina* and carried away his foresail and bowsprit. At about 4 P.M. some powder barrels on the *San Salvador*, of the Guipuscoan squadron, caught fire and both decks and poop were blown out. Sidonia turned the Armada and rescued her from a threatened attack. In coming about to resume the easterly course the *Rosario's* foremast went by the board and fell over the main yard. The *San Martin* and a few other vessels stood by, but the rest of the fleet kept on. The state of the sea prevented Sidonia from getting a hawser to the injured ship, and Diego de Valdes advised him to rejoin the fleet lest he become separated from it during the night. Before so doing, Sidonia ordered the *San Francisco*, the *San Cristobal*, one galleasse and four pinnaces to stand by the *Rosario*, either to take her in tow or to save the crew, "but neither the one nor the other was found possible, owing to the heavy sea, the darkness, and the weather."

The first day's fighting had, therefore, resulted in

serious damage to three Spanish vessels, one by gunfire and two by accident. The English leaders were little pleased at this result. "The majesty of the enemy's fleet, the good order they held, and the private consideration of our own wants did cause, in mine opinion," writes Henry Whyte, "our first onset to be more coldly done than became the valour of our nation and the credit of the English Navy."

During the evening Howard held a council on the *Ark* and delivered orders "unto each captain how to pursue the fleet of Spain." Drake was appointed to lead the fleet, which proceeded about midnight. Some strange vessels were sighted, and Drake, ordering his light extinguished, tacked toward them, followed only by the *Roebuck* and two pinnaces. Howard continued his course with the *Ark*, *Bear*, and *Mary Rose*. The rest of the fleet hove-to. Drake in the early morning came on the *Rosario*, and Don Pedro de Valdes, seeing that no resistance was possible, surrendered at discretion. This incident occasioned much ill-feeling in both fleets. Valdes accused Sidonia of having deserted him, and after the return to Spain Don Diego de Valdes was thrown into prison for the advice he had given his commander-in-chief. Drake was accused by Frobisher of being a "cowardly knave and traitor," and of trying "to cozen us of our share of 15,000 ducats." The *Roebuck* took the prize into Dartmouth.

Lord Howard found himself within culverin-shot of the Armada; he could see but the topmasts of his fleet on the horizon and so continued on after the enemy until his fleet rejoined in the evening.

Macpherson Collection

THE "ARK"

This ship was Admiral Howard's flag-ship during the battles with the Armada

Sidonia on this day reorganized his fleet into two squadrons. Don Alonzo de Leyva was placed in command of the rear squadron. He had the Biscayan, Andalusian, Guipuscoan and Levant squadrons, originally thirty-eight strong, now thirty-six. To these were added the galleons *San Mateo, San Luis, Florencia,* and *Santiago,* of the Portuguese squadron, and three galleasses, "numbering," says Sidonia, "forty-three of the best ships of the Armada." With these de Leyva was "to confront the enemy," and presumably he formed them in a crescent formation, with the inside to the rear. Sidonia, with the remaining vessels of the Portuguese squadron, the complete Castilian squadron and one galleasse—nineteen ships in all—was to continue in the van, probably ahead of the crescent. With him also were the light squadron and the storeships. The duke, not satisfied with the conduct of his captains, "called to him all the sergeant majors and commanded them to go in a pinnace and range the fleet according to the prescribed order, giving it to each of them in writing that they should put every ship in her appointed place, and also that any ship which did not keep that order, or left her appointed place, that without further stay they should hang the captain of the said ship."

At 11 A.M. the *San Salvador* was abandoned; Lord Thomas Howard and Sir John Hawkyns, who occupied it, found "the deck of the ship fallen down, the steerage broken, the stern blown out and about fifty poor creatures burnt with powder in most miserable sort." The pinnace *Golden Hind* took her into Weymouth.

Early the next morning, Tuesday the 23d, the fleets were off the Portland Bill, when the wind came from the northeast. This gave the Armada the weather-gage; both fleets headed northwest for the land. Howard then tacked to the eastward to try to pass south of the Armada. A detachment from the southern wing of the Armada also came about and stood down on a southerly course for the center of the English fleet. Howard, with the *Ark*, *Victory*, *Elizabeth Jones*, and *Nonpareil*, and eight other vessels, "stood fast and abode their coming," and the leading Spaniards eased off to pass in rear of this squadron and separate it from the rest of the fleet. Other Spanish ships, however, charged in upon Howard; Captain Bertendona in the *Regazona* "very gallantly assaulted their admiral, offering to board her; but as he came near her, she bare room and stood out to sea." Following their leader came the Levant ships *Rata*, *Valencera*, and *San Juan de Sicilia*, while the Guipuscoan ship *Santa Ana*, and the Portuguese galleons *San Luis*, *San Mateo*, *Florencia*, and *Santiago* were in the thick of the fight. The van squadron also assisted in the action, as the Portuguese galleons *San Marcos* and *San Felipe* and the Castilian ship *San Juan* are mentioned as playing a prominent part. Thus Howard's squadron was forced off to the southward and the Armada was free to attack other parts of his fleet.

Northwest of the Armada lay Sir Martin Frobisher, who had with him only the *Triumph*, *Merchant Royal*, *Centurion*, *Margret and John*, *Mary Rose* and *Golden*

Lion. Sidonia directed the *San Martin* against him, followed by the Castilian galleons *Bogoña* and *San Juan Bautista;* later he was supported by the *Florencia, Valencera,* and *Santa Ana,* which had taken part in the earlier fight. A very heavy but indecisive battle then ensued, Frobisher using his guns to effect but keeping off to avoid boarding.

Now the wind shifted to S.S.W., again giving the English the weather-gage. A large English squadron between Howard and Frobisher, and apparently led by Drake, now "assailed the Spanish fleet so sharply from the westward that they were all forced to give way and bare room." The damaged *Santa Ana* being in peril, Sidonia sent a staff officer in a boat "to command the ships which were near at hand to succour Juan Martinez de Recalde." This was accomplished after a sharp fight, but now Howard in turn "called unto certain of her Majesty's ships then near at hand and charged them straitly to follow him, and to set freshly upon the Spaniards, and to go within musket-shot of the enemy before they should discharge any one piece of ordnance." The *Elizabeth Jonas,* the *Galleon of Leicester,* the *Golden Lion, Victory, Mary Rose, Dreadnaught,* and *Swallow* followed his flag in the *Ark.*

"Our capitana" (i.e., flagship), reports Sidonia, "seeing the enemy's admiral in the van, turned towards her, and lowered her topsails; and the enemy's admiral and all the fleet passed her, shot at her, ship by ship, whilst she, on her part, fired her ordnance very well and fast, so as half the enemy's fleet did not approach, but shot at her from afar." Sixteen galleons followed Sidonia, and he says that after heavy fighting, "the enemy bare room and stood out to sea."

This fighting ended at 5 P.M., having lasted for three hours; no ships were lost on either side, but the Spanish admit a loss of 110 killed and wounded. According to Howard, it had been a "wonderful sharp conflict," and he adds that "the Spaniards were forced to give way and to flock together like sheep." The truth appears to be that both fleets were glad to "call it a day." Toward evening another combat broke out in which the *Mayflower* "discharged some pieces very valiantly." While possibly the tactical honors remained with the Armada in this day's battle, its effects were favorable to the English, for it tended to wear down the Spaniards and expend their ammunition. On the other hand, the English were constantly receiving fresh men and ships, while Seymour's squadron was still available as a final reinforcement.

On Wednesday the English attempted little fighting. "Much of our munition," says their account, "had been spent, and therefore the Lord Admiral sent divers barks and pinnaces unto the shore for a new store of such provisions." Some fourteen fresh vessels joined Howard this day, bringing his total to about one hundred vessels. Because of the confusion of the previous fighting, Howard organized his forces into four squadrons, commanded by himself, Drake, Hawkyns, and Frobisher. The Spaniards also regrouped their ships. Recalde shifted his flag to the *San Juan*, and he with de Leyva now held the command of the forty or more vessels which composed the rear squadron. Early in the morning an English squadron, probably Drake's, engaged the Armada's rearguard and inflicted a loss of 140 men before Sidonia could drive it clear. The *Gran Grifon*, flagship of the storeships, received forty hits.

By Thursday morning the fleets had almost reached the Isle of Wight. The damaged *Santa Ana* and the Portuguese galleon *San Luis* were in the rear. The English squadrons were disposed in the following order from north to south: Frobisher, Howard, Hawkyns, and Drake. There was no wind.

Hawkyns lowered his boats and towed his ships toward the *Santa Ana* and *San Luis*, "so near that the boats were beaten off with musket-shot." The galleasses came to their assistance, while the *Rata* and other vessels endeavored to support the threatened Spanish vessels in so far as the light airs permitted. Howard in the *Ark* and Lord Thomas Howard in the *Golden Lion* were towed into the fight with their long-boats. "There was many good shots made by the *Ark* and *Lion* at the galleasses," reads the account, "in the sight of both armies, which looked on and could not approach, it being calm."

Meanwhile another heavy engagement was taking place at the northern end of the battle line. Here Sidonia's flagship, the *San Martin*, was attacked by a number of large English ships, probably Frobisher's squadron. "They came nearer than the first day," reports Sidonia, "discharging their large pieces from the lower deck, and cut the capitana's mainstay, slay-ing also some soldiers." Other Spaniards came to their leader's rescue, notably the Portuguese galleon *San Luis*, the Biscayan ships *San Juan* and *Gran Grin*, the Castilian ships *San Cristobal* and *San Juan*, Oquendo's flagship, the *Santa Ana*, and the Levant ship *San Juan de Sicilia*. The *Triumph*, much damaged, "discharged pieces," says Sidonia, "to show her need of succour, and was now towed by eleven of the enemy's long-boats." "The *Bear* and the *Elizabeth Jonas*," writes Howard, "perceiving her distress, bare with her for her rescue and put themselves, through their hardiness, into like perils." Just as the Spaniards had hopes of boarding, a fresh breeze sprang up from the southward and Frobisher sailed clear.

Hawkyns and Drake now closed on the southern wing of the Armada and "there began some fight," in which Howard mentions the *Nonpareil* and *Mary Rose* as being heavily engaged. While this attack was not generally pressed home, its long-range fire harassed the vessels at the tip of the wing, so that they fell into confusion. "The duke, seeing that in the proposed assault the advantage no longer was with us and that we were now near the Isle of Wight, discharged a piece and proceeded on his course, the rest of the Armada following in very good order, the enemy remaining a long way astern."

Sidonia then despatched a messenger to Dunkirk to advise Alexander of recent occurrences, and that "it was fitting that he should come out with as little delay as possible to join with this fleet." The disabled *Santa Ana* during the night made off for Havre, where she was wrecked. This was the only result of the day's hard fighting, in which the Armada tactically had at least held its own. The continuous fighting, however, was undoubtedly wearing down the Armada and slowly breaking its resistance. The British still had powerful reinforcements upon which to rely.

On Friday there was no fighting. "Now," says the English account, "for as much as our powder and shot was well wasted, the Lord Admiral thought it was not good in policy to assail them any more until their coming near unto Dover, where he would find the army which he had left under the conduction of the Lord Henry Seymour and Sir William Wynter, knight, ready to join his flagship, whereby our fleet should be much strengthened, and in the meantime, better store of our munition might be provided from the shore." Howard then, "as well in reward of their good services in the former fights, as also for the encouragement of the rest," called aboard the *Ark* and knighted with full ceremony Lord Thomas Howard, Lord Sheffield, Sir Roger Townshend, Sir Martin Frobisher, and Sir John Hawkyns.

On the same day Sidonia sent a pinnace to Parma "to obtain from him shot of four, six and ten pounds, because much of his munition had been wasted in the several fights." He also asked for forty flyboats to enable him to come to grips with the fast-sailing English ships. He again asked Alexander to join him the day he arrived off Dunkirk.

During Saturday the fleets kept on up the channel, the English constantly receiving reinforcements of ships and men, together with ammunition and provisions. At 4 P.M. the Armada arrived off Calais. "There were divers opinions," says Sidonia, "as to whether we would anchor there or go further"; but the duke, understanding from the pilots who were with him that if he went on further the currents would carry him out of the English Channel and into the North Sea, he resolved to anchor in Calais Roads. At 5 P.M., therefore, the Armada came to anchor in the open sea, some twenty miles from Parma's first base at Dunkirk. Another messenger was sent off to tell him that "he could not tarry there without endangering the whole fleet."

Seymour was lying with thirty-six ships in the Downs, when he received orders from Howard to join the fleet at Calais. Although many vessels had but three days' food, he immediately proceeded and about 8 P.M. joined the flag. The entire fleet was now anchored about one and a half miles west of the Armada, about 136 vessels in all. The Dutch fleets of 150 vessels, mostly small craft, lay along the coast from Dunkirk to Flushing, making it absolutely impossible for Alexander's army to put to sea or for him to send out the flyboats and ammunition requested. Ostend was held by a British garrison, thus providing a convenient base for the Dutch vessels and a position from which cavalry could make raids deep into Spanish territory.

At dawn on Sunday Captain D. Rodrigo Tello, whom Sidonia had sent to Parma on the 15th, returned to Calais with the news that no embarkation of troops had been commenced at Dunkirk. This, however, could hardly have been expected, because it was not until the next day that Alexander received information of the fleet's arrival at Calais, and naturally the troops could not be embarked in their small boats and fishing craft until actually ready to sail.

Sunday morning Lord Howard held a council of war and adopted Wynter's proposal to attack the Armada with fireships. Even if no ships were burned, this could be expected to force its vessels from their anchorage under conditions where loss of anchoring gear and collisions were probable.

At midnight eight fireships were sent down with wind and tide toward the densely-packed Armada. "The duke seeing them approach and that our men did not hinder them, fearing that they should be explosion-machines, gave orders to weigh." This order was the turning point in the campaign. The Antwerp "hell-burners" were reaping their final harvest. A panic ran through the Armada. The galleasse *San Lorenzo* lost her rudder in a collision with the *San Juan de Sicilia.* Sidonia, after clearing the fireships, again anchored and some few ships did likewise, but the rest of the fleet was borne off with the tide and scattered for a distance of twenty miles.

Early on Monday Sidonia, "seeing his Armada was very far off, and that the enemy was coming under a press of sail, weighed anchor to collect his fleet and therewith endeavor to recover the place they had been in." The *San Lorenzo* ran aground in trying to enter Calais Harbor.

The English fleet followed the Armada in five squadrons. Drake was on the right flank nearest the Flemish coast; then came in order Hawkyns, Howard, Frobisher, and Seymour. The right squadrons appear to have been more advanced than the left. It had been arranged at Sunday's council that Howard was to make the first attack, followed in order by Drake and Seymour, but both Howard and Seymour were tempted from their missions by the desire to pillage the grounded *San Lorenzo.* Pinnaces and long-boats attacked at short range and after a sharp fight she was carried and sacked, most of the crew swimming to the shore. Howard had lost his opportunity to win a great victory for the pillage of a disabled ship.

Meanwhile Sidonia was doing his best to assemble his ships. Before the S.S.W. wind the Armada was drifting toward the Dunkirk shoals, and the pilots assured him that his only hope lay in sailing close-hauled on the port tack to the westward. Though far in the rear and accompanied only by the *San Marcos,* Sidonia gallantly showed his intentions to the fleet by tacking toward the English squadrons, "discharging his ordnance and sending off pinnaces to order all the ships to keep a close luff, as otherwise they would drive on to the banks of Dunkirk." He was immediately attacked by Drake, followed by Hawkyns and Frobisher. "The enemy admiral," says Sidonia, "with the greater part of their fleet, assaulted our capitana with great shooting of ordnance, approaching within musket-shot or even harquebus-shot."

The *San Martin* kept on this westerly course until the fleet was clear of the shoals. Then Sidonia set the course N.N.E. and was able about 9 A.M. to concentrate into a crescent some fifty of his best ships. "This day," he says, "the duke wished to turn on the enemy with the whole Armada, so as he would not leave the channel; but the pilots told him that it was impossible, because with the wind and sea from the northwest, setting straight to the coast, they must go by force into the North Sea, or else the whole Armada would drive on the banks." His statement as to the wind does not agree with the English accounts, but the duke gives a second and more probable reason: "Thus in no way could they avoid leaving the channel; nearly all the best ships being spoiled and unable to resist longer, as well from the damage they had received as for not having shot for their ordnance."

From 10 A.M. to 5 P.M. a furious rearguard action was fought. "I deliver it unto your honor," writes Wynter, "upon the word of a poor gentleman, that out of my ship there was shot 500 shot of demi-cannon, culverin and demi-culverin; and when I was furthest off in discharging any of my pieces, I was not out of shot of their harquebus, and most times within speech of one another." Ubaldino, who wrote Drake's history of the campaign, says: "That day Sir Francis' ship was riddled with every kind of shot, and was letting fly every way from both her broadsides, so that she seemed to repeat her fire as rapidly as any harquebusier."

One by one the damaged ships began to fall behind. Don Francisco de Toledo in the *San Felipe* tried to grapple with the English ships, "whereupon they assailed him, and by shooting of ordnance brought him to great extremity." The *San Felipe* apparently was the "great galleon assailed by the Earl of Cumberland and Mr. George Raymond in the *Bonaventure* most worthily." Don Francisco continued to defend himself with the utmost heroism. "He fought," writes Padre Geronimo, "neither more nor less than most valiantly, placing himself in the hottest of the fight and fighting with twelve or fifteen galleons without help except from God, and moreover close enough to use his muskets."

Don Diego Pimentel in the *San Mateo* gallantly came to his assistance, only to be attacked by Seymour in the *Rainbow* and Wynter in the *Vanguard.* The *San Mateo,* according to the same friar, fought with about thirteen ships until "she was a thing of pity to see, riddled with shot like a sieve. All her sails and rigging were torn and sorely destroyed; of her sailors many perished; and of her soldiers few were left in the galleon." Nevertheless, all demands to surrender were received with taunts to try to board.

Recalde and Mexia then entered the action, and they in turn were supported by the *Valencera, Begoña,* and *San Juan de Sicilia.* The Spaniards tried to grapple with their enemies, the latter "fighting with their great ordnance, and our men defending themselves with harquebus-fire and musketry, the distance being very small."

Sidonia, seeing his rearguard in distress, gave the order for the Armada to come about and actually rescued the damaged vessels. He found, however, that the *San Felipe* and *San Mateo* "had suffered much damage and were unable for the service, all their people being slain or wounded." The *San Juan de Sicilia* "was able to follow us, though much spoiled."

Now about 5 P.M. the action ceased. "And when every man was weary with labor," writes Wynter, "and our cartridges spent, and munitions wasted—I think in some altogether—we ceased and followed the enemy."

Although the duke ordered the *San Felipe* and *San Mateo* abandoned, Don Diego Pimentel refused to leave his ship. Most of the crew of the *San Felipe* were taken off by the storeship *Doncella,* but hearing a cry that the latter also was going down, Don Francisco de Toledo "said that if he was to be lost, he would be lost in his own ship, and therewith returned to her and went towards Zeeland." The *San Martin* was just kept afloat. The Biscayan galleon *Maria Juan,* which had been in collision with the *San Juan de Sicilia,* and later engaged by the *Hope,* went down in a squall which sprang up as the action closed, and only eighty of her crew were saved. The Spanish loss was about 400; the English about sixty.

It was not until this day that Alexander heard that the Armada had arrived at Calais. Proceeding immediately to Nieuport, he embarked 16,000 troops that night and at dawn on Tuesday arrived at Dunkirk, where the embarkation was quickly completed. For two days the troops lay packed in their boats until finally the news of the Armada's defeat was received. The Dutch fleets prevented Parma from even attempting to put to sea. "Our fleet," reported the States of Zeeland to the queen, "under the charge of Justinus of

Nassau, being happily arrived and riding off Dunkirk at the very time of the discovery of the Armada of Spain, the forces of the Prince of Parma, then ready to put to sea, were by the same closely locked in and stayed within the same Dunkirk."

The *San Mateo*, in a sinking condition, was assaulted by Admiral van der Does of the Holland fleet and after a brave resistance for two hours, Don Diego Pimentel hauled down his flag, which for many years hung in the great church at Leyden. The *San Felipe*, dismasted and foundering, drifted toward Nieuport, to which city Don Francisco de Toledo and his officers escaped. This ship also was captured and, with the *San Mateo*, taken to Flushing, where both sank. The Dutch took 400 prisoners. Another ship is reported to have been driven ashore near Ostend.

Tuesday morning found the Armada in a perilous position off the Dutch coast, the pilots saying that with the existing N.W. wind the entire fleet would go on the shoals. "Being in this peril," writes Sidonia, "without any sort of remedy, and in six and a half fathoms of water, God was pleased to change the wind to W.S.W., whereby the fleet stood toward the north without hurt to any ship."

Howard held a council of war and, much to Seymour's disgust, ordered the latter's squadron back to the Narrow Seas to watch Parma, while he followed the Armada. "Notwithstanding that our powder and shot was well-nigh spent," he wrote, "we set on a brag countenance and gave them chase, as though we had wanted nothing." The same evening Sidonia called a council. Having lost eight ships, while all the best of his remaining ships were badly damaged, the Armada had been much reduced in fighting strength; the English, on the other hand, had not lost a single vessel. Added to this, all the Spanish ships which had been heavily engaged were out of ammunition, while there was a general lack of provisions and water. On one of the best-provided vessels five men a day were dying. "The council," reported Sidonia, "was wholly of opinion that they should go back to the channel, if the weather would permit it." But the wind increased from the S.S.W. and continued from the same general direction for some days, and finally Sidonia resolved to round the British Isles and return to Spain.

Howard was perfectly willing to let them go, "partly because we saw their course and meaning was only to get away that way to the northward to save themselves, and partly also for that many of our fleet were unprovided of victuals." On Friday, August 2, Howard turned back toward Dover.

Of the total of 130 Spanish vessels, scarcely half returned to Spain. Leyva was lost off the Irish coast; Recalde and Oquendo died from exposure. The broken spirit of the men is well typified by the statement of a Portuguese prisoner in Ireland. "He saith also," says the examination by his captors, "that it is a common bruit among the soldiers, if they may once get home again they will not meddle with the English."

When the news was broken to Philip his expression did not change. "Great thanks," he said, "do I render to Almighty God, by whose generous hand I am gifted with such power that I could easily, if I chose, place another fleet upon the seas. Nor is it of very great importance that a running stream should be sometimes intercepted, so long as the fountain from which it flows remains inexhaustible."

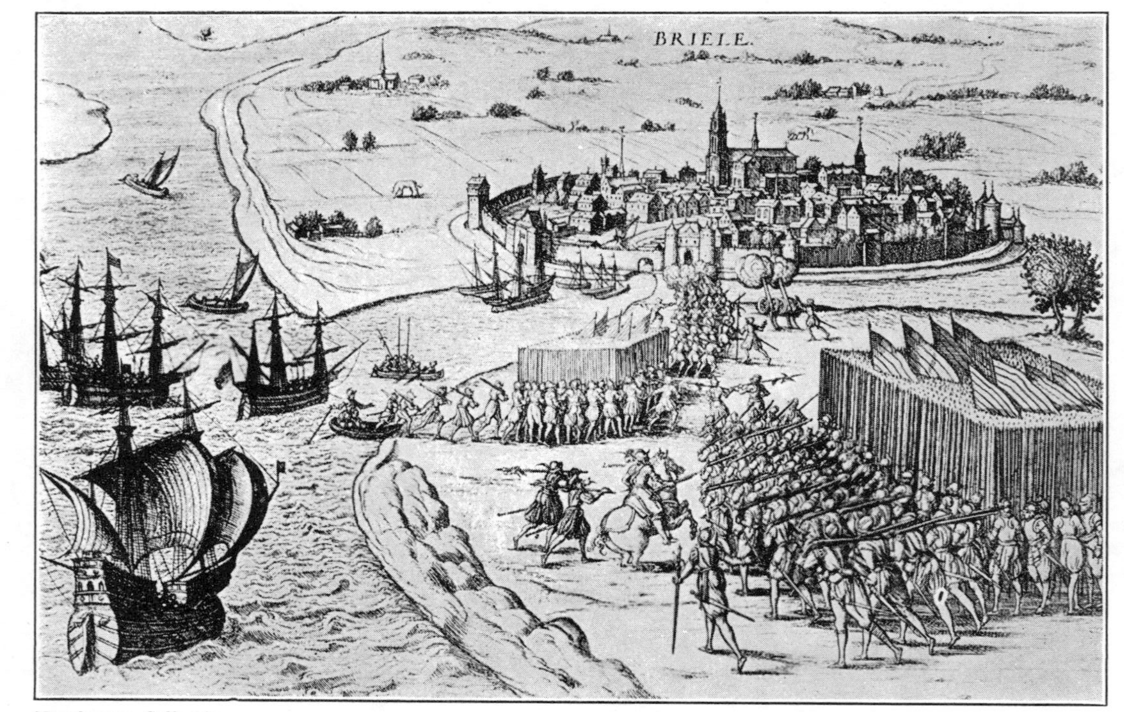

Macpherson Collection

THE CAPTURE OF BRILL, 1572

CHAPTER IV

Gibraltar

LOUIS of Nassau commenced the Dutch wars of independence in 1568 by invading Friesland and defeating a Spanish army near the monastery of Heiliger Lee in the very country where Hermann more than fifteen centuries before had annihilated the legions of Varus.

For some years William of Orange and his brother Louis of Nassau attempted to meet the veteran troops of Spain with hastily assembled armies of German mercenaries. But after repeated defeats in the open field it was found that their two greatest assets were the remarkable capacity of the Dutch burghers for defending their cities and the ferocity with which their seamen swept the Spaniards from the seas and rivers.

Some years before the actual revolution had broken out, a number of the highest Dutch and Flemish nobles had presented a remonstrance to Margaret, Duchess of Parma. On this occasion Berlaymont, a supporter of the Spanish régime, had said to the duchess: "What, madame! Is it possible that your Highness can entertain fears of these beggars?" That night a wild drinking bout was held by the nobles who had presented the remonstrance, during which the fiery Brederode, describing Berlaymont's jest, shouted out: "They call

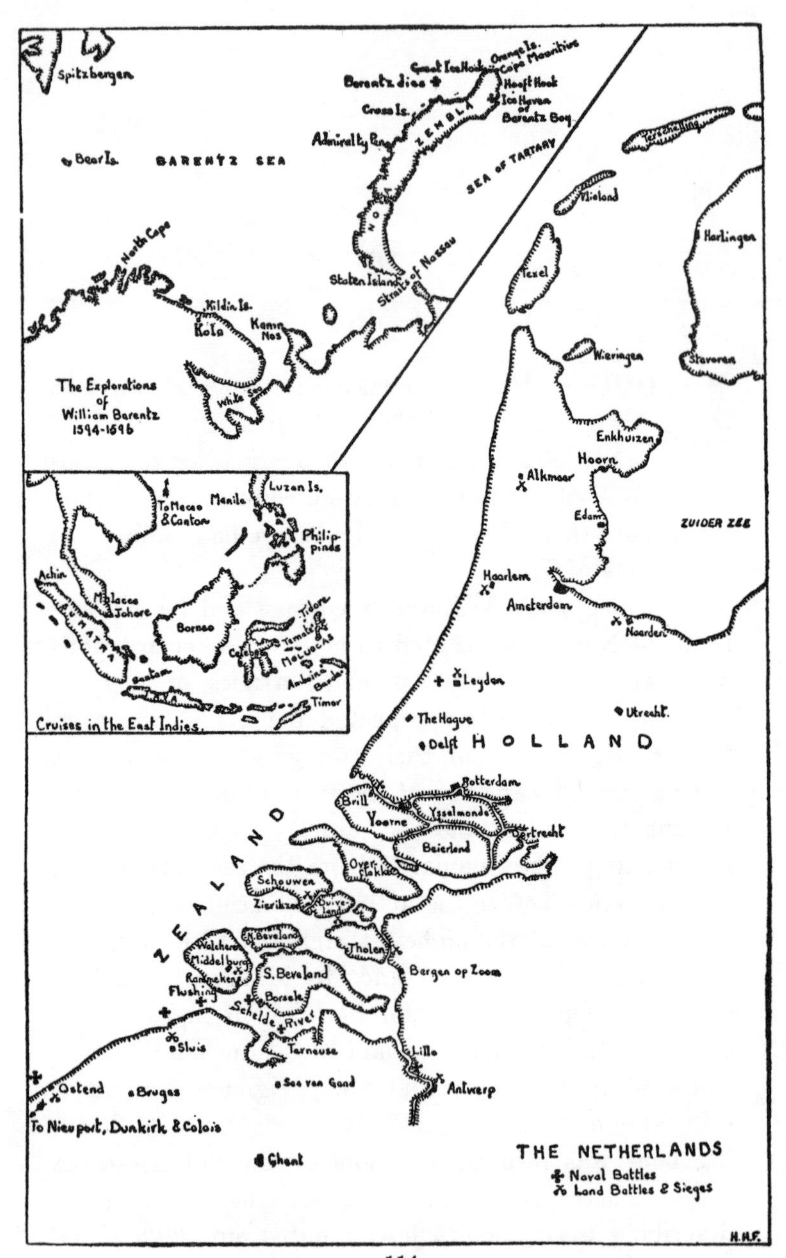

Spitzbergen
Barentz dies
Orange Is.
Cape Mauritius
Hooft Hook
Cross Is.
Ice Haven of Barentz Bay
Admiralty Pen.
Bear Is.
BARENTZ SEA
ZEMBLA
SEA OF TARTARY
North Cape
Staten Island
Straits of Nassau
Kildin Is.
Kola
Kanin Nos
White Sea
The Explorations of William Barentz 1594-1596
Luzon Is.
To Macao & Canton
Manila
Philippines
Achin
Malacca
Johore
SUMATRA
Borneo
Tidore
Ternate
Celebes
MOLUCCAS
Amboina
Banda
Bantam
Timor
Cruises in the East Indies.
Terschelling
Vlieland
Harlingen
Texel
Wieringen
Stavoren
Enkhuizen
Hoorn
Alkmaar
Edam
ZUIDER ZEE
Haarlem
Amsterdam
Naarden
Leyden
Utrecht
The Hague
Delft
HOLLAND
Rotterdam
Brill
Voorne
Ysselmonde
Dortrecht
Beierland
Overflakke
ZEALAND
Schouwen
Zierikzee
Duiveland
N. Beveland
Walcheren
Middelburg
Rammekens
Flushing
S. Beveland
Tholen
Bergen op Zoom
Borsele
Schelde River
Terneuse
Sluis
Lillo
Antwerp
Ostend
Bruges
Sas van Gand
To Nieuport, Dunkirk & Calais
Ghent
THE NETHERLANDS
Naval Battles
Land Battles & Sieges
H.H.F.

us beggars! Let us accept the name! Long live the beggars—Vive les gueux!" "Then," says Motley, "for the first time, from the lips of those reckless nobles, rose the famous cry which was so often to ring over land and sea, amid blazing cities, on bloodstained decks, through the smoke and carnage of many a stricken field."

When open fighting commenced, the uniform successes of the Spaniards ashore drove many Zeelanders and Hollanders to the sea. These men were given letters of marque and fitted out fleets of privateers in English waters as early as 1569. They swept the Spanish flag from the coasts and rivers of the Netherlands and became known as the "sea-beggars." Though they were little better than pirates, William of Orange had to use every instrument which might help him in the fight he was waging against the mighty Spanish empire. He therefore appointed William de la Marck as the admiral of the sea-beggars.

By 1572 the fleet of the sea-beggars had been built up to twenty-four small vessels, manned by some 300 of the wildest and most ferocious seamen who have ever lived. One of the captains, Treslong, suggested that they attack the little town of Brill in Zeeland. By pure bluff and plenty of good luck the town was captured and this for the first time gave the patriots a foothold on the seacoast.

The name Brill was spelled almost the same as the Dutch word for spectacles, and the Dutch circulated with great effect a cartoon of de la Marck stealing the spectacles from the Duke of Alva's nose; a verse,

On April Fool's day
Duke Alva's spectacles were stolen away,

was passed by word of mouth through the country. Such was sixteenth century propaganda.

The capture of Brill proved the spark to the magazine. No less than sixteen coastal cities revolted to William of Orange in addition to many inland towns. In all Zeeland the Spaniards retained only the capital city of Middelburg; here the famous Mondragon easily held head to the besiegers. While the Zeelanders endeavored to maintain the blockade from their base at Flushing, the Spaniards endeavored to provision it by sea. There was frequent fighting of the most desperate character. Even in those early days Sebastian de Lange showed the heights to which Dutch seamen could rise in adversity. When his ship had grounded and boarders from four Spanish vessels were pouring over the side, this heroic captain fired his own magazine, carrying with him to death many of his triumphant enemies.

A small squadron of twelve Zeeland ships under Ewout Worst and Joost and John de Moor attacked a Spanish merchant fleet at the entrance of the Scheldt, dispersed it with heavy losses and took booty to the amount of half a million florins, which proved most useful in financing the revolution.

Alva ordered Sancho d'Avila, a noted Spanish general, to raise the siege of Middelburg. He equipped a fleet of over fifty vessels and sailed from Antwerp down the Scheldt. At Terneuse, d'Avila met the Dutch fleet under Admiral Ewout Worst. After several days of skirmishing, the wind came up strong from the west and the Dutch drove in before it upon the Spanish fleet at anchor, and at the same time sank hulks in the channel to hinder its retirement toward Antwerp. Several heavy caracks touched on this obstacle and were badly shot up before they could get clear; a number of smaller craft were overtaken and captured.

Several days later d'Avila returned to the attack, and a furious action was fought near Borsele. Two Zeeland captains, Groeneven and Everkitte, grappled with the largest Spanish galleon, named the *Elephant*, commanded by the Seignior de Blicqui, a noted Walloon officer. In the desperate fighting all three captains were killed, but finally the *Elephant* was taken by the Zeelanders. Another Spanish vessel, the *Promised Land*, grounded under the guns of one of their own batteries; but this did not prevent gallant Joost de Moor from storming the ship and driving the enemy out of the battery. Another vessel was burned and four more captured. The enemy then anchored under the guns of the château of Rammekens.

Despite these repulses the determined Spanish leader made a third attempt to carry out his orders and this time he did succeed in provisioning Middelburg; but before he could regain Antwerp the Zeelanders captured two more of his ships and damaged many others with gunfire, so that d'Avila was glad to turn his attention to military operations, where he and his soldiers were more at home. These early battles were of immense importance, not only materially but morally, for they established a Dutch ascendancy at sea which was as pronounced as that of the Spaniards ashore.

While d'Avila was operating in the Scheldt to provision Middelburg, Alva himself was endeavoring to reduce the cities of Holland which had hoisted the flag of revolution. His success at the little town of Haarlem cost him seven months in time and 12,000 lives. "Never," he wrote to his king, "was a place defended with such skill and bravery as Haarlem, either by rebels or men fighting for their lawful prince." Among the defenders was a company of 300 women who fought gallantly through the entire siege under a lady of distinguished family. The Spaniards next laid siege to Alkmaar.

While these operations were proceeding in Holland, Alva endeavored to assist them by gaining the command of the Zuider Zee. Admiral Comte de Bossu, who had recently beaten the Hollanders on the lakes of Haarlem, had been campaigning there against Admiral Cornelius Dirkzoon, in command of the Frisian naval forces. Flying his flag in the great galleon *Inquisition*, of thirty-two guns, and accompanied by a fleet of twenty-nine other well-equipped vessels, Bossu left Amsterdam on October 3, 1573. In addition to their crews, his vessels carried more than 1300 soldiers. On the afternoon of the 5th, Dirkzoon attacked him with twenty-four vessels and a two days' battle commenced. The Spanish ships were the best sailers and their guns had the longer range. On the other hand, the Frisians were short of powder and endeavored to grapple with their enemies. After much long-range fighting, Captain Jacob Til grappled with a Spanish vessel which had become separated from its fleet, killed or captured its crew and removed its guns before the approach of Bossu made it necessary to abandon the prize. Captain Taams Frederikzoon also grappled with a Spanish vessel, whereupon the *Inquisition* and three other vessels bore down upon him. Even then Frederikzoon held on to his prey until one of its crew cut the grapnel line. The fighting now became very fierce and the losses were heavy on both sides; at the end of the second day the fleets parted without either having gained a decision.

Bossu, hearing that Alva had been compelled to raise the siege of Alkmaar after a most decisive repulse, was determined to renew the fighting at the first opportunity, but Dirkzoon's instructions were most conflicting. While the States of Friesland ordered him not to waste his powder, but to board, Sonoy, lieutenant-governor of North Holland, ordered him to avoid battle. The admiral decided the issue by throwing Sonoy's letter into the fire without telling a soul of its existence. At noon of the 11th the two fleets came into close action, John Floriszoon steering the Dutch flagship full into the *Inquisition.* Three other captains also grappled with Bossu's flagship: Peter Bak, Jacob Tryntjes, and Boer. While the Dutch threw up burning pitch hoops to the *Inquisition's* deck, the Spaniards threw down pots of fire and forced Captain Boer, who had taken station under the high poop, to shove off. Another Spanish vessel of nine guns was sunk by gunfire, five smaller vessels were taken and a wild panic swept over their fleet. Vice-Admiral Rol wished to come to his leader's assistance, but his soldiers forced him to withdraw toward Amsterdam, which he could do only by throwing over all his guns so the shoals could be passed.

Meanwhile a most desperate conflict raged between Bossu and the three Dutch vessels. All night long the fight continued, the Dutch receiving reinforcements from the shore to take the place of their wounded. In the early morning John Haring of Hoorn—called the Dutch Horatius for his famous exploit of holding the Diemer dyke single-handed against 1000 Spaniards—sprang up the *Inquisition's* sides, fought his way across the bridge, climbed into the rigging, and hauled down the ensign, only to be killed by a musket-shot from below. Finally, in the afternoon, after twenty-eight hours' fighting, only fifteen Spaniards remained on their feet and Bossu surrendered. Despite his former cruelties, his life was spared in consideration of his remarkable resistance. This battle left the Dutch in complete command of the Zuider Zee, and, coming just three days after the siege of Alkmaar was raised, it showed that at last victory was inclined toward the Orange standard.

After these defeats the Duke of Alva retired in disgrace from the Netherlands and was relieved by Don Louis de Requesens. The new commander resolved to take the offensive in Holland on land by besieging Leyden and in Zeeland by relieving Middelburg by sea. Sancho d'Avila again assembled thirty large vessels at Antwerp, while de Glimes and Julian Romero equipped a fleet of sixty vessels at Bergen-op-Zoom. William of Orange assembled a Zeeland fleet of forty-four large and thirty small vessels at Flushing, under Admiral

Louis Boisot, the first great Dutch sea captain. On January 29, 1574, de Glimes and Romero were attacked by Boisot in the Scheldt River off Roemerswaal. As the vessels of the rival admirals were about to ram each other, de Glimes discharged two guns, loaded with grapeshot, into Boisot's bridge with deadly effect. Brave Captain Schot, who had risen from a sickbed to fight his last battle, was killed and also his first officer; Admiral Boisot lost an eye from a splinter. Captain Adrian Corneliszoon came to his leader's relief and grappled with de Glimes' ship, while other ships came to grips with no less than eight of the largest Spanish vessels. Gaspard Leunszoon performed a famous feat by springing to the bridge of the Spanish flagship, climbing the mast, striking the Spanish ensign and bringing it back to his own ship.

Julien Romero, seeing the admiral's flag come down, hoisted another on his own ship and grappled with Boisot's vessel. Sixty Spaniards poured over upon her bridge, only to be blown into the air by a powder-charge which had been hidden there. The Spaniards now gave way. De Glimes was killed and his ship burnt; eight other vessels were captured; Romero escaped only by swimming; more than eight hundred of his men were killed. After this defeat Mondragon, who had held Middelburg for over two years, surrendered the town. To complete his success, Boisot sailed past the forts of Antwerp, attacked d'Avila's squadron and took or destroyed some fifteen ships, including that of the vice-admiral. All Zeeland and the Scheldt as far as Antwerp were now in the hands of the patriots.

In March, 1574, the siege of Leyden was temporarily raised, but in May, after the defeat of Louis of Nassau at Mook, it was resumed. The city was defended with desperate courage, but after four months lack of food had reduced the defenders to the last extremity. As no Dutch army could beat the Spaniards in the open field, it would be necessary to bring the sea to Leyden. "As well," shouted the besiegers, "can the Prince of Orange pluck the stars from the sky as bring the ocean to the walls of Leyden for your relief." The city was full fifteen miles from the outer dyke; relief from the sea might well seem impossible, had not such men as William of Orange and Admiral Boisot been at the helm. After the outer dykes were pierced, there were no less than three additional lines of dykes held in force by the Spaniards, who had erected sixty-two redoubts and forts about the city. The besiegers under Valdez numbered some 10,000 veteran troops, while the relieving force under Boisot consisted of some 200 light-draft vessels, manned by 2500 seamen. But these were veterans of many a sea fight and among them 800 Zeeland sea-beggars.

"A wild and ferocious crew," writes Motley, "were those 800 Zeelanders. Scarred, hacked, and even maimed, in the unceasing conflicts in which their lives had passed; wearing crescents in their caps, with the inscription, 'Rather Turkish than Popish'; renowned far and wide as much for their ferocity as for their nautical skill, the appearance of these wildest of the sea-beggars was both eccentric and terrific. They were known never to give nor to take quarter, for they went to mortal combat only, and had sworn to spare neither noble nor simple, neither king, kaiser, nor pope, who should fall into their power."

On September 10 the fleet arrived within five miles of the city almost without encountering resistance, but it required twenty-three days for the three remaining dykes to be carried by storm and for the ocean to be brought to Leyden. On October 3 the city was relieved and the Spaniards withdrew with heavy losses.

The province of Zeeland, being composed of large islands separated from the mainland by wide estuaries, could easily be defended by the Zeeland squadrons and seemed secure against any attack. The Spaniards, however, became proficient in a novel method of warfare. On several occasions they made long night marches along carefully charted shallows between the islands, where at low tide they could wade. A famous march on this order by Mondragon had given them possession of Tholen Island, and now from there Don Osorio de Ulloa led 1500 picked troops over six miles through the shallows to Duiveland; most of this distance the water was breast high and frequently up to the necks of his men. The passage commenced at midnight and required six hours, during which the soldiers in the water were almost constantly under gun and musketry fire from the Zeeland vessels, which advanced as far as the depth of water would permit; small boats came so close to the line of march that frequently there was hand-to-hand fighting; by such tactics the Zeelanders delayed the march so much that a number of men at the rear of the column were drowned by the rising tide.

After having reached Duiveland it was a simple matter for Don Osorio to make a further march to Schouwen and besiege Zierikzee, its capital.

Admiral Boisot determined to attempt the relief of this important city by sea. Mondragon, who had gone over to command the besiegers, had built a line of piles across the harbor entrance. The admiral believed that he could break through this obstacle and drove his flagship at it under full sail. This gallant attempt, however, was unsuccessful; and as the tide ebbed, his ship was fast aground under the enemy batteries. After dark the crew tried to save their lives by swimming, but most of them, including the brave Boisot, were drowned in the cold water.

For many years no naval actions took place, so complete was the Dutch command of the sea. The fleet did what it could to relieve Antwerp, but the great bridge across the Scheldt built by Alexander of Parma prevented it from coming up the river, and a landing attack on the Kowenstyn dyke failed after desperate fighting. During the Armada campaign the Dutch cooperated with the British navy by keeping in port Parma's flotillas.

This defeat marked the beginning of the downfall of Spain, which was hastened four years later by the death of the greatest general of the age, Alexander of Parma. Prince Maurice of Nassau now built up the Netherlands army so that it could contend with the Spanish troops in the open field; eventually it became the finest in Europe. The chief handicap to the United

Provinces was the tremendous financial burden of the war.

However, the overseas trade from Dutch ports grew to such proportions that not only could these heavy burdens be met, but capital remained for continued economic expansion. The Dutch merchant fleet became three times that of any other nation. This trade expansion encouraged remarkable voyages of discovery to locate shorter routes to the markets of Asia. These voyages were stimulated by the return to Holland of John Huygen van Linschoten after a stay of thirteen years in India, during which time he had carefully compiled a detailed account of conditions in the Far East. He conceived the idea that this rich region could be reached by cruising through the Arctic Ocean north of Russia far easier than by way of the Cape of Good Hope.

To prove the correctness of this theory he sailed from Holland in four vessels in the spring of 1594. With two vessels he passed through the Straits of Nassau, between Nova Zembla and Russia, into the Sea of Tartary. After penetrating its waters for a distance of 150 miles, however, he ran into field ice and had to sail back before a fierce northeasterly storm. William Barentz, with the other two vessels, sailed up the western coast of Nova Zembla to its northeastern point in Lat. 77°, by far the most northern point yet reached by land. In a great storm his vessels, drifting in a dense fog among masses of icebergs, were almost lost, and he also was forced to beat a retreat. During this cruise his small boats were often attacked by great companies of walruses, now seen for the first time by Europeans, and whenever his men landed on ice or the shore they had to resist the attacks of ferocious polar bears.

Linschoten seems to have drawn too rosy conclusions from his first voyage, for the next year he set out with a fleet of seven vessels prepared to trade with China. Again he completely failed in the accomplishment of his mission, and his voyage is noted only because of its famous leaders: Linschoten, Barentz, and Jacob van Heemskerk, that great sea captain who here first appears on the world's stage. The principal event of this cruise was a fight on Staten Island, at the southern end of Nova Zembla, between a polar bear and a party of twenty men, two of whom were killed before the bear could be killed. The sale of his skin was the only financial asset of the voyage that Linschoten could claim.

Despite these two failures, the intrepid Barentz still was confident of success and on May 18, 1596, he sailed with two little ships on what proved to be the first polar expedition. He with Jacob van Heemskerk sailed on one ship, while John Cornelius van der Ryp was captain of the other.

Barentz decided to sail more to the northward than before. Already on June 5 he ran into icefields; four days later a small island was sighted; because of a fight with a bear, it was named Bear Island, and so it appears on some maps to this date. On the 19th mountainous land was sighted in Lat. 80°, which they called Spitzbergen, the base from which in 1926 Byrd flew to the North Pole. Here the explorers went ashore and saw flocks of the same kind of wild geese which visited Holland in the summer. Never before had the eggs of these birds been seen by a European. "Therefore," wrote Gerrit de Veer in his diary, "some voyagers have not scrupled to state that the eggs grew on trees in Scotland, and that such of the fruits of those trees as fall into the water become goslings, while those which drop on the ground burst in pieces and come to nothing. We now see that quite the contrary is the case." On the maps showing the greatest latitudes reached by Arctic explorers there still often is seen a cross at the northern end of Spitzbergen with the notation, "Barentz, 1596."

On June 23 the explorers sailed to the south to avoid the icefields which were closing in around them and a week later they again came to Bear Island. From here the two vessels proceeded separately, Ryp going back to the northward and Barentz to the eastward toward Nova Zembla, reaching its western coast on July 17. A few days later an unarmed party exploring Cross Island was suddenly confronted by two great bears. Heemskerk stopped a momentary panic, saying quietly: "The first man that runs shall have this boat-hook of mine in his side. Let us remain together and face them off." While Heemskerk looked the bears squarely in the eye the party retired deliberately and regained their boats without being attacked.

Now for day after day the little ship was tossed about among icebergs, while snow and fog added to their dangers. Once they made fast their anchor to a towering berg, only to have it burst into pieces with a terrific crash. On August 15 the Orange Islands at the northeastern point of Nova Zembla were reached; to Barentz' delight he saw the sea to the eastward free of ice. They set sail in this direction with high hopes, but these were doomed to bitter disappointment when dense icefields were encountered. Barentz decided to try to work his way down the eastern coast of Nova Zembla and return through the Straits of Nassau. But even this proved impracticable; at Ice Haven the ship was caught in the ice and buffeted about by great cakes. A dense snowstorm and the ceaseless crashing and groaning of the ice added to the terrors of the crew. "It was enough," records de Veer, "to make the hair stand on end to witness the hideous spectacle."

By September 1 the ship was frozen solidly in the ice and it became evident that there was no possibility of escape until the spring. Fortunately the ship was close to the land and a providential current had borne great masses of driftwood to the shore. Instead of bemoaning their ill-luck, these brave seamen offered up thanks to God for having provided them with wood which they could use for fuel and for the construction of a house. Their building operations were delayed for days at a time by tremendous snowstorms, and bears constantly had to be beaten off. At the end of September, when the house was only half finished, the carpenter died, but the remaining sixteen men continued their work. On one occasion Heemskerk and two comrades were set upon by several bears. The firearms of those days were not very accurate and the bears

Macpherson Collection

BARENTZ IN THE ARCTIC, 1596

were close upon the men, when as a final resort a volley of sticks and stones were thrown. This amused the bears, who began to chase these missiles like dogs. While one of the men kept throwing sticks the others kept up a fire with their muskets, until finally a shot took effect and the bears withdrew.

Early in October a formal housewarming was celebrated, and instead of the usual maypole a long icicle was set up. The two whaleboats and all the supplies were brought ashore and great quantities of fuel were collected.

On November 4 the sun disappeared and with it went the bears. The moon shone constantly and white foxes became plentiful. Many of these were killed for food and complete suits were made from their furs. Snow fell almost constantly and for days at a time the house was covered with drifts. On January 25 Twelfth Night was celebrated according to the Dutch custom. The dinner consisted of pancakes, one hard biscuit apiece and a small portion of wine. Gerrit de Veer thus set forth their feelings: "We were as happy as if we were having a splendid banquet at home. We imagined ourselves in the fatherland with our friends, so much did we enjoy our repast." Finally, when lots were drawn and the gunner had received the winning chance, he was formally proclaimed King of Nova Zembla.

The day before the feast both Heemskerk and de Veer had claimed having seen the sun on the edge of the horizon. Barentz maintained that they must have been mistaken. They were in Lat. 76°; therefore it was necessary for the sun to reach a declination of 14° S. before it would show above the horizon, and by all calculations this date was February 10. On January 27 the whole party distinctly saw the whole disc of the sun; this mystery excited the wonder of Europe until Tycho Brahe published his refraction tables.

With the return of the sun the polar bears again appeared on the scene and almost daily battles were waged with them. One of the men died and the others were greatly weakened by their inactive life and poor food. When on April 17 the ice began to break up they were anxious to commence their homeward voyage, but Barentz and Heemskerk decided that they should wait until the end of May. This decision was cheerfully accepted, "for they were all ready to submit to his better judgment." Work on the two whaleboats was commenced, but by the end of May so little progress had been made that Heemskerk had to urge them to hurry their work, saying that "if the boats were not soon under way, we must be content to make our graves here as burghers of Nova Zembla."

The noble William Barentz was now fast dying, but continued his work to the end. He wrote up three detailed accounts of the voyage, one of which he left in a powder-horn in the house, where it was found intact two and a half centuries later. On June 14 he was carried down into one of the boats and they shoved off on their perilous cruise, "trusting themselves to God." Up the eastern coast they worked their way past Hooft Hook and Cape Mauritius, until on the 16th they were off Great Ice Hook. Here the hero was lifted up so that he could look on the great ice cape for the last time. The same afternoon a storm drove the frail boats in among a mass of icebergs. Brave de Veer sprang out on a block of ice and jumping from one piece to another made a line fast to a large iceberg, so that the boats could ride in its lee. On the 20th, as the open sea was reached, Barentz breathed his last. "And thus the hero," writes Motley, "who for vivid intelligence, courage, and perseverance amid every obstacle is fit to be classed among the noblest of maritime adventurers, had ended his career. Nor was it unmeet that the man who had led those three great though unsuccessful expeditions toward the north pole should be laid to rest, like the soldier dying in a lost battle, upon the field of his glorious labors." The wide sea in which he was buried still bears his name.

For six weeks longer the two boats struggled down the coast of Nova Zembla; on July 28 they were delighted to meet Russian fishermen, who gave them food and wine and sailed with them as far as the Straits of Nassau. On August 18 Kanin Nos was reached and on the 25th Kildin Island; here, after having been seventy-six days in their boats, they found to their astonishment Captain Ryp, who had come north to Kola on a trading voyage. On November 1 they arrived at Amsterdam, and here, still clad in their fox-skins, they were brought before the authorities to tell the thrilling story of their arctic adventures.

While William Barentz was attempting to find a northeast passage to Cathay, Cornelius de Houtman was making a venture toward the same objective along the Portuguese routes past the Cape of Good Hope. In April, 1595, he had set out with four vessels, the *Hollandia*, the *Mauritius*, the *Amsterdam* and the *Pigeon*. After touching at the Cape Verde Islands and Port Elizabeth, near Cape Town, the squadron arrived at Madagascar. After suffering terrible privations there, they started for Java in December, but scurvy forced them to return to Madagascar. Now internal dissensions came near ruining the cruise. In the middle of February a second attempt was made and this time the expedition reached Sumatra in June. Houtman remained nine months in the Indies, but found the Portuguese so firmly intrenched that he could accomplish little. The *Amsterdam* had to be destroyed and only a small amount of nutmegs and spices could be bought. In February, 1597, the ships started for home, arriving in August of the same year with only eighty-nine men of the 284 who had comprised the original crews. While the expedition was far from a commercial success, it had gathered information which was essential to the success of later cruises.

During these years of exploration in the arctic and tropics the war with Spain was continued with its usual bitterness. In 1596 Elizabeth decided to repeat Drake's attack on the Spanish coast, and this time not only to singe but burn the king's beard. Despite the fact that this year there was a large Spanish army in the field in the Netherlands, the Dutch agreed to assist in this attack on the condition that Elizabeth desist for a time her demands for the repayment of her loans. Twenty-four naval vessels, averaging 300 tons, were provided. They were manned by 3000 Hollanders and Zeelanders, commanded by Admiral Warmond. On board was a contingent of 2200 troops of the Dutch regular army, under the famous Sir Francis Vere. The British furnished thirty-three naval vessels under Lord Howard and 3800 troops under the brilliant young Earl of Essex. Among the noted volunteers were Sir Walter Raleigh and Count Louis Gunther of Nassau.

On June 30 the combined expedition arrived off Cadiz. There was found a great fleet. The galleon *St. Philip* was of 2000 tons, mounted eighty-two guns, and carried 1200 men as a crew. The galleons *St. Matthew, St. Thomas* and *St. Andrew* each mounted fifty guns. There were some twenty-five other war vessels, mounting from fifty-two to eighteen guns, and a convoy of fifty-seven armed merchantmen about to sail for the Indies. The allies, far from being deterred by this formidable fleet, drove their ships immediately upon it. Soon the four great galleons were either captured or burned and a landing party of 1300 soldiers attacked the city. Louis Gunther led the assaulting party and soon the colors of William of Orange waved from the walls. Next day the citadel surrendered and the Spaniards burned thirty-two war vessels to prevent their capture. The cautious attitude of Lord Howard prevented the permanent retention of Cadiz or an attack upon Lisbon. Elizabeth highly complimented Admiral Warmond in a personal letter for the most efficient services of the Dutch forces in this campaign.

In 1598 the Dutch commenced another series of enterprises to reach the Far East. While Houtman again succeeded in doing so by way of the Cape of Good Hope, two expeditions attempted to reach this rich region through the Straits of Magellan. The first expedition of five vessels, under Admiral Mahu, sailed in July. After long delays on the African coast, where the crews were much reduced by disease, the expedition reached the Straits of Magellan in April, 1599. For no less than five months did they struggle through the terrible straits. When the fleet reached the Pacific it was beset by a succession of storms and scattered over the face of the ocean. The *Geloof*, captained by Sebald de Weert, turned back through the straits and reached home with but thirty-six men. Dirk Gerrits, in the *Blyde Boodschap*, sailed so far to the southward as to discover the southern continent, which was rediscovered some two centuries later in the position reported by him. With only nine men fit for duty, Gerrits surrendered his ship to the Spaniards at Valparaiso. A third vessel, the *Liefde*, appeared in Japan with only twenty-four of her crew of 110 still alive. An Englishman, Will Adams, who was serving as pilot, became a great favorite with Ieyasu, the Japanese dictator, and greatly assisted the lucrative trade of England and Holland with that people. The *Trouwe*, with Admiral de Cordes, after remarkable adventures, reached the East Indies, but was treacherously captured by the Sultan of Tidore. The *Hoop* was lost with all hands in the Pacific.

A month after Admiral Mahu left Holland, Olivier van Noord followed in his tracks with a second expedition of four vessels toward "the kingdom of Chili, the west coast of America, and, if need be, the islands of the Moluccas." His flagship was the *Mauritius;* the vice-admiral, Jacob Claesz, was in the *Hendrik Frederik.* The yacht *Eendracht* and a merchant vessel named the *Hope* were the other vessels. After watering at a little island in the Gulf of Guinea, van Noord arrived off Rio de Janeiro, but was prevented by the Portuguese from getting any supplies. At an island off the coast he obtained water, fruit, wild fowl, and fish, but lost six men from an attack by the natives. For some time he was so harassed by Portuguese detachments that his food and water were nearly exhausted and his men were dying daily. Fortunately he found a small uninhabited island, called Santa Clara, and here after three weeks ashore his sick men recovered. On June 28, 1599, the squadron sailed for the south, after the *Eendracht* had been burned and her crew distributed among the other vessels.

When the three remaining vessels reached the straits they were in such bad condition that van Noord decided that they must be overhauled. For this purpose he lay for three months at Porto Deseado, which had been located only a few years before by Cavendish, the third man around the world. Here the captain of the *Hope* died and the former captain of the *Eendracht* was appointed to relieve him. The name of the *Hope* was changed to the *Eendracht.*

On November 5 van Noord entered the straits, but it was not until February 29 that he emerged into the Pacific; it is said that the last mile took him four weeks. During this passage he was in company for a few days with Admiral de Cordes in the *Trouwe*. After gaining the Pacific the *Hendrik Frederik* separated in a storm. The other two ships sailed up the Chilian coast and at the island of Santa Maria captured the *Buen Jesus*, a large Spanish ship. Learning that a Spanish fleet was waiting for him at Lima, van Noord decided to surprise Valparaiso; he burned or captured every ship in port. He then set sail across the Pacific. After a very successful cruise, broken by two days in the Mariana Islands, he arrived on October 14 at Luzon in the Philippines. By pretending that his ship was French, van Noord obtained water, provisions, and two native pilots.

For some weeks now van Noord cruised through the Philippines, capturing vessels and burning villages. He then boldly cruised into Manila Bay and pillaged a number of small vessels. While thus engaged two great galleons attacked him. With only some fifty men in the *Mauritius* and twenty-five in the *Eendracht* the little expedition now seemed to have met its fate. One galleon captured the *Eendracht*, while the other grappled with the *Mauritius*. Boarders poured over the side, but brave van Noord swore that he would blow up his ship sooner than surrender, and his crew fought with such fury that the Spaniards were driven clear. Then a fortunate gunshot below the waterline sank the galleon and practically her entire crew was drowned. Van Noord lost no less than thirty-one men killed and wounded.

Now the *Mauritius* cruised along the coasts of Borneo and Java; van Noord did not dare to put into

Macpherson Collection

THE ATTACK ON CADIZ, 1596

Bantam for a load of spice in his crippled condition, and set sail for the Cape of Good Hope. While cruising to the northward off St. Helena in June, 1601, he met a fleet under Heemskerk en route to the East Indies. In August he arrived home after a three years' cruise with only forty-four of the 248 men who had sailed with him in such high hopes. The *Mauritius* was the fourth vessel to circumnavigate the globe.

The *Hendrik Frederik* sailed alone across the Pacific and arrived at Ternate. As too few men remained to work the ship, it was sold to the sultan, and, building a new sloop, the crew sailed to Bantam, where they took passage for home in van Heemskerk's squadron.

While the expeditions of Mahu and van Noord had been struggling through the Straits of Magellan, other cruises were being made along Houtman's track past the Cape of Good Hope. In May, 1598, Jacob van Neck and Heemskerk left Holland in eight vessels. Trade relations were entered into with the native chiefs of Bantam, Ternate, and Tidore and a rich cargo of spices was brought back to Holland, thus giving the expedition a profit of 100 per cent.

In 1601 thirteen merchant vessels sailed for the Far East; of these five were under the command of Wolfert Herman, while four others were under Jacob van Heemskerk. As Wolfert Herman arrived in the East Indies he heard that a powerful Portuguese fleet was blockading Bantam. Arriving there, he found himself opposed by no less than eight galleons and about twenty smaller vessels, all under the command of Admiral Mendoza. Although the Portuguese flagship alone was more powerful than his five little vessels, Herman fought them at long range for two full days, taking advantage of his better speed and gunnery. After seven of his ships had been lost the Portuguese admiral withdrew from the fight, leaving the Dutch to establish their first trading stations in the Far East at Bantam, Banda, and Achin, the chief city of Sumatra. The king of the latter city sent an embassy in Wolfert's ship to Holland. Off St. Helena on the return voyage a great Portuguese carack from Goa was taken by two of his ships; the rich cargo, valued at a million and a half florins, contributed much to the success of the venture.

Jacob van Heemskerk with his detachment skirted the coasts of India and established relations with the king of Johore. In the Straits of Malacca with two small ships he took the great Portuguese carack *St. Catherine,* manned by 700 men, and carrying a cargo worth more than a million florins. Next he proceeded to Macao and made commercial treaties with the Chinese.

While these expeditions were being made to all parts of the world the war at home proceeded with its customary bitterness. Prince Maurice now had built up a professional army which developed military science to the highest level of the age. In 1600 he defeated the Spaniards in the famous battle of Nieuport. In the next year commenced the remarkable siege of Ostend by Ambrose Spinola. This adventurer, a member of a rich Genoese family and absolutely without military experience, was placed in command of the Spanish army and astonished Europe by his feats of warfare. His brother, Frederick Spinola, operated privateers from Sluis against Dutch shipping. As a financial venture he manned and equipped eight great galleys, similar to the galleasses of the Spanish Armada which had done such good service. In September, 1602, Spinola set out from Spain with this reinforcement for his Sluis squadrons.

Off the Portuguese coast an English squadron attacked the galleys and sank two of them. On October 3 Spinola brought the six remaining vessels along the English coast into the Straits of Dover. Each galley carried a large number of soldiers in addition to 250 galley-slaves. At sundown two Dutch galiots, the *Tiger*, Captain Peter Mol, and the *Pelican*, Captain Lubbertzoon, having been informed by Sir Robert Mansel in the British ship *Hope*, sighted the galleys and tracked them. Their gunfire signals passed the alarm to Vice-Admiral John Kant, who, with the *Mackerel*, *Half-moon*, and two other war galiots, lay at anchor off the Flanders coast.

The .Dutch squadron concentrated on the galleys for attack. Off Gravelines, where only fourteen years before the great Armada had been put to rout, the moon came over the horizon and about ten o'clock a breeze ruffled the waters. The *Mackerel* led off by pouring a broadside into the *San Felipe*. John Kant now showed that sailing ships as well as galleys could use their rams. With full sail set on the *Half-moon*, he crashed full into the *San Felipe*, and then, swinging around, discharged a broadside with guns and a volley with his muskets into the rowing benches. A third galiot rammed the doomed galley with such force that she sank with all hands. Captain Gerbrand Sael rammed the *Lucero* with such effect that the water came up to the waists of the rowers. Then he and Captain Hartman cannonaded her at close range until she sank. The other vessels meanwhile had also been closely engaged with the remaining four galleys. The *San Luis*, Spinola's flagship, was able to make Dunkirk; two more got into Nieuport, but the fourth was detained by the French at Calais.

In March, 1603, the Dutch lost the assistance of England when the great Elizabeth died. With all her caution and miserliness, she had been a staunch friend of the United Provinces. James I immediately declared the neutrality of England and even leaned toward the side of his country's traditional enemy.

Frederick Spinola still thought that the galley, if used in calm weather, could beat the Dutch galiot. This time he built his vessels in Sluis so that they would not have the perilous passage from Spain to make. Early one morning in the following summer Admiral Joost de Moor, whom we have seen taking part in the earliest campaigns of the Zeeland sea-beggars, and who was now commanding the Sluis blockade, saw eight great galleys rowing out to attack him, followed by four smaller vessels. On each of the larger galleys there were 200 soldiers in addition to the rowers.

De Moor's squadron consisted of four galiots and the *Black Galley* of Zeeland, which was commanded by Captain Jacob Michelzoon. It was dead calm, and of the Dutch forces only the *Black Galley* could move. Conditions were perfect for Spinola and victory seemed certain, when two of his galleys hit the *Black Galley* so squarely that their rams stuck fast in her stout sides. But even with their greatly superior numbers every attempt of the Spaniards to board was beaten back by the Zeelanders and broadsides carried death into their rowing benches. Captain Michelzoon was killed; but Lieutenant Hart, although himself wounded, promised to blow up the ship rather than surrender. Sebastian de Lange had already proved that Dutch captains were capable of this supreme act of heroism. Finally the Spaniards withdrew, leaving their rams in the sides of the *Black Galley.*

Meanwhile four other galleys had attacked the galiot of Captain Logier and had rammed it in succession. But here again attempts to board were beaten back and the galleys backed off under Logier's broadsides. Three more Spaniards went for de Moor's flagship, but his gunfire and musketry were so lively that they did not attempt to ram. Spinola, whose bravery and energy were worthy of a better cause and result, signaled for a final attack on the *Black Galley.* By this time, however, Logier had drifted down close enough to assist Hart in his defense, and between them they repulsed this last attack. When brave Spinola fell riddled with the discharge of a gun on the *Black Galley,* and a freshening breeze was bringing other Dutch vessels into range, the Spaniards withdrew to port, having lost very heavily, and having proved to their own satisfaction that even under the most favorable conditions they were no match for their blockaders. Admiral de Moor celebrated his victory by calling his crew to quarters and reciting with them the 34th Psalm. With Spinola's death the privateering operations from Sluis ceased.

Meanwhile the Dutch East India Company had been formed and in December, 1603, a fleet of twelve ships, under Stephen van der Hagen, sailed for the East Indies. In 1605 Matelieff de Jonge followed him with eleven large ships and other smaller vessels.

Van der Hagen first entered into agreement with one of the chiefs of Malabar on the coast of India, permitting the Dutch to build forts as a counterpoise to the Portuguese capital of Goa. Next he sailed for Amboina in the Moluccas and captured the Spanish castle. After touching at Banda, the expedition sailed for the famous clove islands. In the summer of 1605 van der Hagen arrived at the little island of Ternate and entered into alliance with the native sultan. Assisted by native levies, he moved against the neighboring island of Tidore, where the Spaniards had built a formidable castle. First he sent Captain John Mol to seize two carracks moored under the guns of the castle. This was easily accomplished, and after twelve large guns and a supply of powder had been removed from them they were fired. Mol established a battery ashore, breached the walls, and led the first assault. This attack was repulsed and the brave captain was carried off the field badly wounded. But a fortunate shot ignited the castle's magazine and created such havoc that the second assault was successful. This gave the Dutch entire possession of the Moluccas, except for a Portuguese foothold in Timor.

In 1606 Matelieff arrived in the Far East with eleven ships, manned by 1400 men. Despite the fact that his was a distinctly commercial venture, he saw that almost constant fighting would be necessary to maintain the prestige of his nation. He first besieged for four months the Spanish castle at Malacca, but was forced to raise the siege by the arrival of an armada from India, consisting of fourteen galleons and twenty smaller vessels. Although greatly outnumbered, Matelieff ordered battle. The result could well be called a draw, for two vessels were lost on each side. Matelieff drew off to Johore to repair his damages. Hearing that the Spanish forces at Malacca had been reduced to seven galleons and three galleys by the partial dispersal of the armada, Matelieff with nine ships returned to the attack. The enemy unwisely awaited the attack at anchor. Three galiots ran alongside the *St. Nicholas* and captured her after a desperate struggle; three other galleons were taken or burnt. The Spaniards then withdrew into the harbor and during the night destroyed their remaining vessels and retired into the castle. The Dutch admiral now exchanged prisoners at the rate of twenty Spaniards for one Dutchman.

The squadron next proceeded to Banda, and from here three richly-laden vessels were sent home. With the other six Matelieff went on to try to recover Ternate and Tidore, which had been taken by a great fleet from the Philippines. Being unable to reduce the Spanish strongholds on these islands, he established a fort on Ternate and left there a garrison of forty-five Hollanders with four yachts. Next Matelieff went with three ships to China; here he could accomplish little and narrowly escaped from six Portuguese galleons off Macao. Again he visited Ternate and heard that the little garrison had successfully withstood a siege. With five vessels laden with spices the expedition now sailed for home. As he left the East Indies, Paul van Kaarden arrived with eight warships at Bantam, to be followed by others which consolidated the Dutch holdings in these valuable territories and eventually made their retention permanent.

During the last years military operations in the Netherlands had been decreasing in intensity. In August, 1604, Prince Maurice captured the important city of Sluis and a month later Ambrose Spinola finally took Ostend; this little town had resisted for three years and two months, and it was estimated that no less than 100,000 lives had been lost in the opposing armies. From this time to the end of the war there were no military operations of importance. Maurice and Spinola manœuvered against each other, neither daring to risk a pitched battle; they contented themselves with taking and retaking small towns and with skirmishes here and there. Under these conditions the States-General reduced the army and increased the naval forces for operations off the Spanish coasts and attacks on Spanish colonies.

In line with this strategy Admiral Haultain was sent to the Spanish coast in the summer of 1606 to intercept the convoys returning from the Indies. Minor successes only were won, and in a storm six of his best ships were separated from the fleet. On the sixteenth

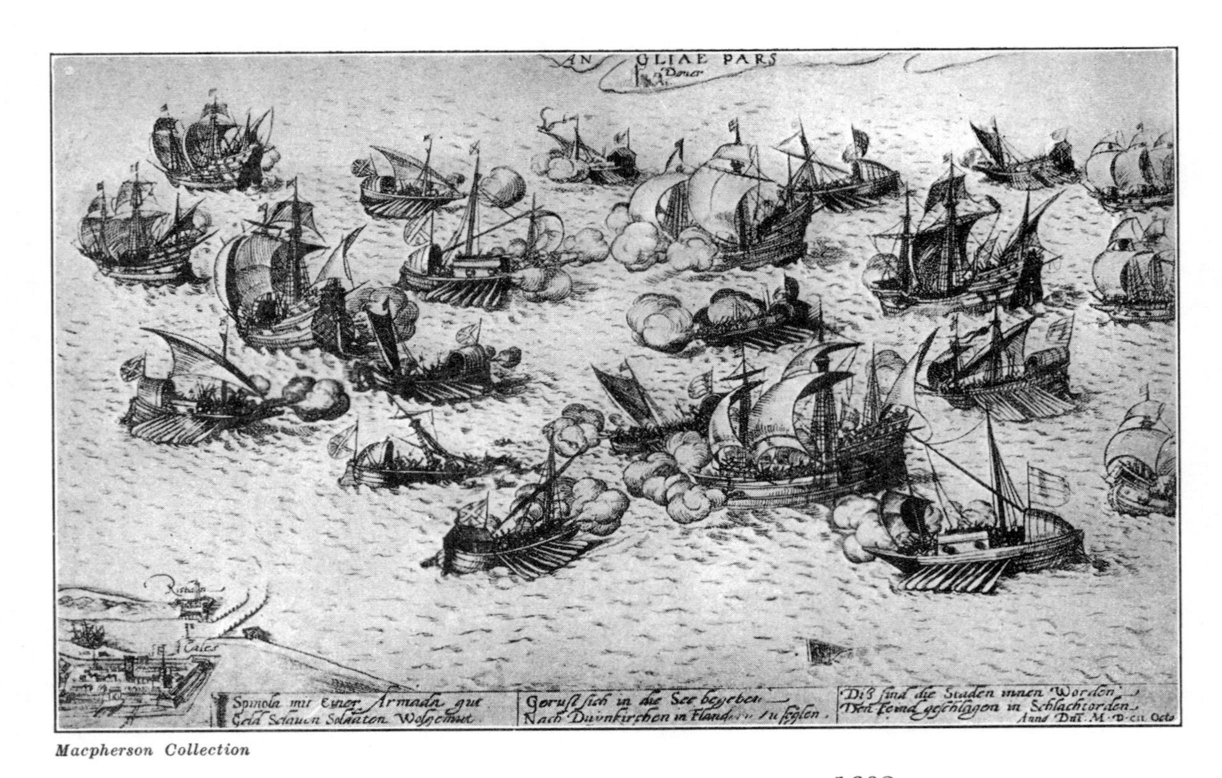

Macpherson Collection

THE BATTLE IN THE STRAITS OF DOVER, 1602

of October, while cruising off Cape St. Vincent with the remainder of his squadron, Haultain ran into an armada of eighteen galleons, eight galleys, and other smaller craft. The Spaniards had the weather-gage and their galleons came down before a fresh wind upon the Dutch force; the heavy sea compelled the galleys to seek shelter near the coast. Haultain manœuvered to gain the weather-gage, but his ships became scattered and all save one made the best of their way out of the enemy's clutches. It was fortunate for the honor of the Dutch navy that Regnier Claassens was serving as vice-admiral of the fleet. He alone disdained to fly and single-handed engaged the Spanish fleet. His mainmast was carried away and Haultain momentarily disengaged him with five ships. But as night came on, Don Luis de Fazardo, the Spanish commander, stood down again and the galiots made off, leaving their vice-admiral in the midst of the enemy.

Now occurred a fight without parallel in naval history, one which far surpassed that of Sir Richard Grenville in the *Revenge,* immortalized by Tennyson's poem. For two entire days and nights Regnier Claassens lay helpless among the galleons. The Spaniards did not dare to board, for fear that their foe would blow up their own ship, but kept up an almost constant cannonade, which Claassens answered as well as he might. Repeated demands to surrender, with offers of quarter, were made and refused. Finally there remained only sixty men, many of them badly wounded. The crew agreed to a man with their admiral's determination never to surrender, and while they knelt in prayer on deck he lighted off the magazine. The Spaniards picked up two wounded men who died soon after telling their marvelous story.

Next spring the States-General determined to avenge Haultain's defeat and to re-establish their prestige over the Spanish navy. They fitted out twenty-six war galiots and at their head placed the greatest sea captain of the age, Jacob van Heemskerk, whose stirring exploits in arctic and tropic seas we have followed.

On April 10 the Dutch fleet arrived off the Tagus and here spies informed the admiral that no rich convoys were to be expected for some time, but that a great war fleet was cruising in the Straits of Gibraltar to attack shipping coming out of the Mediterranean. Heemskerk immediately decided to attack this fleet, although it was reported to be greatly superior to his own. Head winds held him back, and it was not until the 23d, when off Cape St. Vincent, that he heard from a Flushing ship that the enemy was sailing toward Cadiz. Heading toward the coast, Heemskerk passed that port during the 24th and that evening learned from a French vessel that his enemy was lying under the guns of Gibraltar. During the forenoon of the 25th the Spanish fleet was sighted.

The Spanish armada consisted of ten galleons, supported by eleven galleys. The general, for so the Spaniards termed their leader, was Don Juan Alvarez de Aviles; his flag flew from the *St. Augustine;* with him on that vessel was the governor of the infantry, Diego de Aguilar y Castro, and the sergeant major, Pedro Alvarez de Herrara. Vice-Admiral Tomas Guerrero de la Fuente was in the *Señora de la Vega*, while the rear-admiral sailed in the *Madre de Dios*. According to Dutch accounts the crews of the galleons averaged 400 men; the *St. Augustine* alone is said to have had 700 men and twenty-one bronze cannon. The galleys were rowed by about seventy slaves and had a fighting force of soldiers in addition. Many nobles and volunteers augmented the Spanish crews, among whom were veterans of Lepanto. The Spanish accounts state that the galleons averaged only eighty sailors and one hundred soldiers, but this appears to be an understatement.

The Spanish squadron already had captured fourteen Dutch merchant vessels, when information came in of a Dutch squadron off Cape St. Vincent. The three flagships and two large galleons, the *Portuguesa* and *Campechana*, were anchored in an outer semicircle under the guns of Gibraltar; the five remaining galleons were anchored in an inner line, and all preparations were made for resisting the attack.

As Aviles saw the little Dutch galiots coming to the attack he called up Skipper Govert, so the old accounts tell the story, who had been captured from a Dutch merchant vessel, and asked him if he had any idea as to what might be their purpose. "Either I am entirely mistaken in my countrymen," replied the Hollander, "or they are coming for the express purpose of offering you battle." The Spaniard then boasted that he would sink the entire Dutch fleet with his flagship alone.

Meanwhile Heemskerk had assembled his captains on his flagship, the *Æolus*. There they found the admiral in complete armor with orange plumes and sash. Standing before the mast he addressed the captains, as reported by the old Dutch historians, about as follows: "Remember that you have no choice between triumph and destruction. I have led you into a position whence escape is impossible—and I ask of none of you more than I am prepared to do myself—whither I am sure that you will follow. The enemy's ships are far superior to ours in bulk; but remember that their excessive size makes them difficult to handle and easier to hit, while our vessels are entirely under control. Their decks are swarming with men, and thus there will be more certainty that our shot will take effect. Remember, too, that we are all sailors, accustomed from our cradles to the ocean, while yonder Spaniards are mainly soldiers and landsmen, qualmish at the smell of bilge-water, and sickening at the roll of the waves. This day begins a long list of naval victories which will make our fatherland forever illustrious; or lay the foundation of an honorable peace by placing, through our triumph, in the hands of the States-General, the power of dictating its terms."

In those early days there was little science in naval tactics. The best plan that Heemskerk was able to offer was for two galiots to attack each of the galleons, while the smaller vessels were to take station on the flanks to prevent the escape of the enemy. He in the *Æolus* and Lambert Hendrikzoon in the *Tiger* were to attack the great *St. Augustine*, which with her four decks towered high above them. On every ship the men knelt in solemn prayer and the loving cup was passed from hand to hand. The blood-red flag, the signal for a general attack, broke out from the yardarm of the *Æolus*.

At 3:30 P.M. the two fleets came into action. Heemskerk headed before the freshening breeze directly for the *St. Augustine*, ordering his men to withhold their fire "until you hear it crack." Aviles, seeing that the spearhead of the attack was directed at his flagship, cut his cable so as to drift back a bit from his exposed position. The *Æolus* and *Tiger* passed several galleons and kept straight for their objective. The Spanish flagship opened the battle by firing a broadside at the *Æolus*, but then the latter crashed into her, firing her bow guns and a volley of musketry. As the vessels ranged alongside, the Spaniards fired their second broadside directly across the decks of the *Æolus*. Admiral Heemskerk fell, like Nelson, mortally wounded. "He fell on deck," writes Motley, "and, knowing himself to be mortally wounded, implored the next in command on board, Captain Verhoef, to fight his ship to the last and to conceal his death from the rest of the fleet. Then prophesying a glorious victory for the republic and piously commending his soul to his Maker, he soon breathed his last. A cloak was thrown over him and the battle raged. The few who were aware that the noble Heemskerk was gone burned to avenge his death and to obey the dying commands of their beloved chief. The rest of the Hollanders believed themselves under his directing influence, and fought as if his eyes were upon them. Thus the spirit of the departed hero still watched over and guided the battle."

The *Æolus* now fired a broadside with terrible effect

through the high sides of her opponent, killing the Spanish admiral. The *Tiger* then secured on the other side of the *St. Augustine*, and fierce hand-to-hand fighting commenced. Vice-Admiral Alteras in the *Red Lion* engaged two galleons and, probably with the assistance of other vessels, sank one and drove the other ashore. Captains Bras, Adrian Roest, and Marin Hollaert engaged the *Vega* and set her on fire; so close aboard were they that their own sails caught fire. The *Vega* was burned to the water's edge, her guns going off and powder exploding; only eleven men saved themselves by swimming.

Captain Harry Janszoon fired another galleon, but was himself killed by a musket-ball. Still another galleon was sunk by gunfire, and Captain Kleinzorg in the *Griffin* burned another vessel. Captain Tromp commanded one of the Dutch vessels, and his son Martin, who afterward sailed the channel with a broom at his masthead, although only nine years old, accompanied him through the battle.

After several hours' desperate fighting a terrible catastrophe overtook the Spaniards. A large galleon, engaged with two galiots, was hit in the magazine by a hot shot and was blown to pieces. Two other galleons caught fire and were destroyed. Only on the *St. Augustine* did resistance continue; here the *Æolus* and *Tiger* were reinforced by the *Griffin*. It was not until sunset that she was boarded and her flag hauled down by the trumpeter of the *Griffin*.

Incensed at recent Spanish cruelties, orders for which, signed by the king, were found in the cabin, the Dutch gave no quarter. Every galleon and most of the smaller vessels were destroyed or captured. Never was a victory more complete. The Spaniards admit the loss of ten galleons, but claim to have set fire to the five in the inner line themselves; this is entirely probable. They say nothing of the galleys, which evidently were considered of little importance. Had the admiral lived, more strategical results would have been gained from the tactical success.

Heemskerk's body was sent home and buried with great pomp in Amsterdam, being accorded the first public funeral in the history of the Dutch Republic. There on his tomb in the Nieuwe Kerk his epitaph reads:

Heemskerk, who dared through polar ice and iron hau to steer,
Left to his country fame; at strong Gibraltar life; his honored body here.

A few days before the great battle the armistice between the United Provinces and Spain had been agreed to and published. The Dutch naval victories, particularly that off Gibraltar, had a decided effect on the peace negotiations which in 1609 were concluded with the actual, if not the formal, acknowledgment by Spain of the independence of the United Provinces, with practically the same frontier which exists to this day.

The brave and self-reliant Dutch seamen, led by Cornelius Dirkzoon, Louis Boisot, Wolfert Herman, Joost de Moor, John Kant, Admiral Warmond, William Barentz, Cornelius Houtman, Olivier van Noord, Matelieff de Jonge, Regnier Claassens, and Jacob van

Heemskerk, had raised their little country for a time to the pinnacle of world power. Their favorite name, Staten Island, appeared on the world maps off the coast of Nova Zembla in the Arctic Ocean, off Cape Horn at the southern tip of South America, in the Kurile Islands north of Japan, and at the approaches to New Amsterdam on the Atlantic coast of North America.

CHAPTER V

The Nile

THE wars of the French Revolution were waged without decisive result until 1796, when Bonaparte, only twenty-seven years old, received the command of the Army of Italy and announced to his starving soldiers: "I will lead you into the most fertile plains of the world. Rich provinces, great cities will be in your power; there you will find honor, fame and riches."

Now, as this fiery young general led his troops through an amazing series of victories, the tide of war turned in favor of France. Parma and Modena treated for peace. Naples signed an armistice and closed her ports to the British fleet. The Pope was glad to come to terms, while French troops seized the British naval and commercial base at Leghorn. French influence grew in Genoa, and uprisings against the English commenced in Corsica. On August 19 Spain entered the war as an ally of France; in October a Spanish fleet entered Toulon and brought the allied force there to no less than thirty-eight ships of the line. Sir John Jervis, with but twenty-two of the line, was reduced to a most perilous situation, which was further aggravated by the fact that one of his subordinates sailed for home with seven ships without even informing his commander-in-chief. An uprising on a large scale further endangered the only remaining naval base in Corsica. That island, therefore, was evacuated, the troops deposited in Elba, and in November Jervis himself was forced by shortage of food to withdraw from the Mediterranean.

While Bonaparte continued his victories in Italy, the Spanish fleet of twenty-seven of the line sailed from Toulon, passed the Straits of Gibraltar and on February 14, 1797, while off Cape St. Vincent, was beaten by Jervis with only fifteen of the line and driven back into Cadiz. But this victory was more than offset by French successes on land; Austria asked for an armistice; Russian promises of support vanished with the death of Catherine II; Holland entered into alliance with France and mobilized her fleet. In France internal tranquillity was re-established by the *coup d'état* of the 18th Fructidor, which confirmed the supremacy of the Directory. The king of Sardinia ceded that important island to France; Venice was occupied by French troops, its fleet seized, and Corfu, its important naval base, garrisoned. The British channel fleet was in open mutiny; Nelson's expedition against Teneriffe was completely repulsed and its leader very severely wounded; to cap the climax, Austria was browbeaten by Bonaparte into signing the Treaty of Campo Formio, in which Belgium was ceded to France. "The present moment," wrote Bonaparte, "offers us a fine game. Let us concentrate all our activity upon the navy and destroy England. That done, Europe is at our feet."

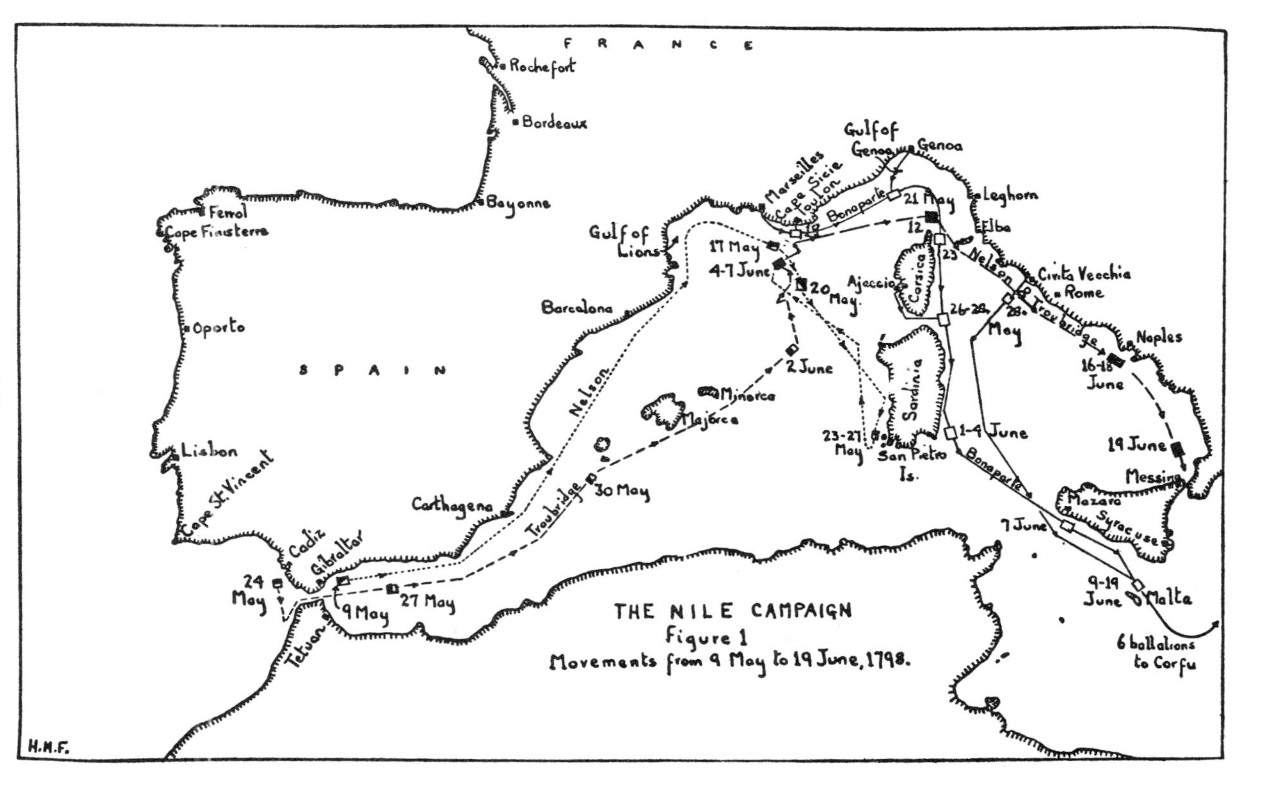
THE NILE CAMPAIGN
Figure 1
Movements from 9 May to 19 June, 1798.
FRANCE
SPAIN
Rochefort
Bordeaux
Bayonne
Ferrol
Cape Finisterre
Oporto
Lisbon
Cape St. Vincent
Cadiz
Gibraltar
Tetuan
Carthagena
Barcelona
Gulf of Lions
Marseilles
Cape Sicie
Toulon
Gulf of Genoa
Genoa
Leghorn
Elba
Civita Vecchia
Rome
Naples
Messina
Syracuse
Mazara
Malta
6 battalions to Corfu
Corsica
Ajaccio
Sardinia
San Pietro Is.
Minorca
Majorca
Nelson
Troubridge
Bonaparte
24 May
9 May
27 May
30 May
17 May
4-7 June
20 May
2 June
23-27 May
19
21 May
12
23
26-28
28 May
1-4 June
7 June
16-18 June
19 June
9-19 June
H.N.F.

On land, French aggression continued. General Brune, by an able campaign, occupied Switzerland and seized the Swiss treasury. Berthier took Rome, to the great advantage of his country's exchequer. But here the French tide reached its highwater mark. Duncan's victory over the Dutch fleet off Camperdown eased the situation greatly for the English, and on February 23 Bonaparte announced to the Directory that an invasion of England was impracticable. "Make whatever efforts we will," he wrote, "we shall not for many years acquire the control of the seas. To make a descent upon England without being master of the sea is the boldest and most difficult operation ever attempted."

Seeing that nothing could be accomplished by a direct attack upon England, Bonaparte urged upon the Directory the expedition against Egypt which he had been considering for some time. "In Paris they can remember nothing," he said. "If I remain without doing something, I am lost." Seeing that the time was not ripe for him to overturn the Directory, which soon would fall of its own accord, and not wishing to be identified with any political party, he saw in the attempt against Egypt an opportunity to play Caesar's part in Gaul, and believed also that it was the most effective blow which France could strike against England.

On March 5 secret preparations were commenced for the expedition. Admiral Brueys was appointed to command the escorting squadron of thirteen of the line, fitting out at Toulon. In addition there were eight French frigates, two Venetian 64s and six frigates, and small craft to bring the men-of-war to a total of seventy-two. Four hundred merchant vessels were assembled at Toulon, Marseilles, Genoa, Civita Vecchia, and Ajaccio; troops were concentrated in the ports of embarkation to a total of fifty-six battalions and twenty squadrons, 30,500 men in all. Only 300 horses were carried, but harness was brought for 6000 to be obtained in Egypt. On April 12 "Citizen Bonaparte" was named "General-in-Chief of the Army of the Orient" and given complete authority over Admiral Brueys. The destination of the force was kept so secret that even after it had sailed the senior officer at Toulon wrote: "I know no more of the movements of this squadron than if it did not belong to the republic." To deceive the British the Spanish fleet in Cadiz was ordered to simulate preparations to sail, and Bonaparte himself did not leave Paris until May 3.

Meanwhile the victory off Camperdown and the inactivity of the French fleet at Brest, coupled with information of French preparations on a large scale in the Mediterranean, induced the British to again enter that sea. On April 29 the Admiralty wrote to Jervis that he was to send a detachment of at least nine or ten of the line into the Mediterranean and that these would be replaced by eight from England. It was intimated that Rear-Admiral Sir Horatio Nelson should be given the command of the Mediterranean detachment.

This gallant officer had been convalescing for ten months in England following the loss of his right arm in the attempt on Teneriffe. On April 30 he had rejoined Jervis before Cadiz in the *Vanguard* (74). On May 9 he sailed into the Mediterranean, in company with the *Orion* (74), *Alexander* (74), *Emerald* (36), *Terpsichore* (32), and *Bonne Citoyenne* (20), to determine the intentions of the French armada. On the 10th the Admiralty's orders arrived at Cadiz; they were accompanied by a personal letter to Jervis, a paragraph of which beautifully summarizes the traditional British strategy of the old days: "I am as strongly impressed, as I have no doubt your Lordship will be, with the hazardous nature of the measure which we have in contemplation; but I cannot at the same time help feeling how much depends upon its success, and how absolutely necessary it is at this time to run some risk, in order, if possible, to bring about a new system of affairs in Europe which shall save us from being overrun by the exorbitant power of France." On the 19th Jervis sent the *Alcmene* frigate, Captain Hope, to notify Nelson that ten of the line would be sent to him shortly and that he was to come to Gibraltar to join this reinforcement, leaving the cruisers *Emerald* and *Bonne Citoyenne* to track the French fleet should it proceed to sea, sending the *Transfer* to Naples with instructions to the British minister there.

Five days later Captain Troubridge was detached with *Culloden*, *Bellerophon*, *Minotaur*, *Defense*, *Zealous*, *Goliath*, *Majestic*, *Swiftsure*, and *Theseus*, all 74s, and sailed for Gibraltar to join Nelson—all ships being provisioned for six months. On the 30th the *Audacious* (74), the *Leander* (50), and the *Mutine*

(18) joined Troubridge and he entered the Mediterranean.

Meanwhile Nelson had arrived in the Gulf of Lions; on the 17th he captured, off Cape Sicie near Toulon, a French corvette, from which he learned that the French armament was expecting to sail daily. He sent the prize under escort of the *Caroline* to Gibraltar with this intelligence for Jervis. Two days later, before a strong northwesterly wind, Bonaparte sailed from Toulon with the forces assembled there and the Marseilles detachment, saying to his soldiers and sailors in one of his famous proclamations: "Hold together. Remember that on the day of battle you will each need the other." Heading into the Gulf of Genoa, a heavy northerly gale broke upon his fleet, but, being under the lee of the land, he received little damage. On the 21st the convoy from Genoa joined the fleet; on the 23d it reached the northern point of Corsica and then ran down the east coast. On the 26th the southern point of the island was reached and the convoy from Ajaccio joined the flag. Knowing that the Civita Vecchia convoy of seventy ships had sailed from that port on the 28th, Bonaparte remained at this rendezvous until the 30th. Then he proceeded slowly down the eastern coast of Sardinia, and here it was that on June 3 he first heard that Nelson was in the Mediterranean with three of the line and was expecting to be joined by ten more.

Bonaparte then sailed for Sicily. "The squadron," he writes in his *mémoires*, "navigated in the finest order, in three columns, two of four vessels, that of the center of five vessels. Captain Decies scouted ahead with a light squadron. * * * The convoy, duly escorted, scouted also on every side." On the 7th the armada passed within sight of Mazara and kept on along the southern Sicilian coast; on the 8th the course was set for Malta. There he arrived the next day and found the Civita Vecchia convoy. On the 12th Malta with its dependent islands surrendered and received a garrison of three battalions. Six battalions proceeded for Corfu under frigate escort.

While Bonaparte was commencing his great enterprise with so much precision and success, Nelson was being subjected to an unusual series of mishaps. On the 17th he could not have missed the enemy by more than fifty miles. On the 20th, when only seventy-five miles south of Hyères Islands, he experienced the same storm which Bonaparte had passed through in the Gulf of Genoa, but had the misfortune to lose his foremast and the main and mizzentopmasts. The *Emerald*, *Terpsichore*, and *Bonne Citoyenne* parted with the *Vanguard* after this accident and proceeded to Minorca, where they met the *Alcmene*, and informed Captain Hope that they believed that the *Vanguard*, *Orion*, and *Alexander* had gone to Gibraltar to refit. Captain Hope had already met the *Caroline* off Barcelona, and upon receiving this news from the frigates, he sent the *Emerald* and *Bonne Citoyenne* to search for the enemy and bring all the information they could obtain to Gibraltar. Intending also to withdraw soon in that direction, Hope remained off Minorca for the present with the *Alcmene* and *Terpsichore*.

The day after the *Vanguard's* mishap the *Alexander*

Macpherson Collection

THE BATTLE OF GIBRALTAR, 1607

took her in tow, but on the 22d both vessels were nearly carried by the westerly swell on the Sardinian coast. At one time Nelson even ordered the *Alexander* to let go the line, but Captain Ball finally brought the crippled flagship under the lee of San Pietro Islands, at the southern end of Sardinia, on the 23d. By great exertions new spars were fitted to the *Vanguard* by the 27th and Nelson sailed for Cape Sicie, the rendezvous appointed for the frigates. In so doing he sailed up the western coast of Sardinia, while Bonaparte sailed down the eastern.

As Troubridge was entering the Mediterranean on the 30th he ran into the *Caroline* and opened the despatches for Jervis. He also heard that the *Caroline* had spoken the *Alcmene* off Barcelona. In order to intercept Nelson, should he be coming to Gibraltar in accordance with the orders carried for him by the *Alcmene*, Troubridge sent the *Mutine* north of Majorca, while he proceeded south of it with his ships of the line spread on a scouting line. In case the *Mutine* met Nelson the latter was to be informed that Troubridge was heading for the Cape Sicie rendezvous. The *Mutine* fell in with the *Alcmene* and *Terpsichore* off Minorca and exchanged news with them. Captain Hope, on hearing that Troubridge was to the southward of Minorca, decided to search for him and try to persuade him not to go to Cape Sicie, but to proceed around the southern end of Sardinia to intercept the French fleet off Naples, where it was thought they would go. He tried to persuade Hardy to go with him in the *Mutine*, but this he very wisely refused to do, saying that he must go to the rendezvous as ordered. Fortunately the *Alcmene* did not find Troubridge. The movements of this and the other frigates are now obscure; they did not make contact with Nelson during the remainder of the campaign, although two of them discovered the French fleet in Aboukir Bay some time before the battle of the Nile.

On June 4 Nelson reached the rendezvous, but none of his frigates were at hand. The next day the *Mutine* arrived and brought two interesting items of information: First, Troubridge with ten of the line was on his way to the rendezvous. Second, the frigates were either en route to Gibraltar or had no intention of coming to the rendezvous. The *Orion* and *Alexander* were spread on either side of the *Vanguard* to facilitate the concentration of Troubridge with the flag.

On the 7th Troubridge joined. He brought word of having met a vessel which had sailed from Toulon on May 28 and reported that Bonaparte had sailed on the 19th. As nineteen days had already elapsed since this time, Nelson sailed at once for the northern point of Corsica, leaving the *Leander* to inform the *Orion* and *Alexander* as to the route along which they were to follow him. Now began the long search which was to last for almost two months. Nelson's underlying thought during this heartbreaking period is expressed in a letter to the First Lord of the Admiralty: "Be they bound for the Antipodes, your Lordship may rely that I will not lose a moment in bringing them to action and endeavour to destroy their transports." Passing Corsica on the 12th and thence sailing slowly down

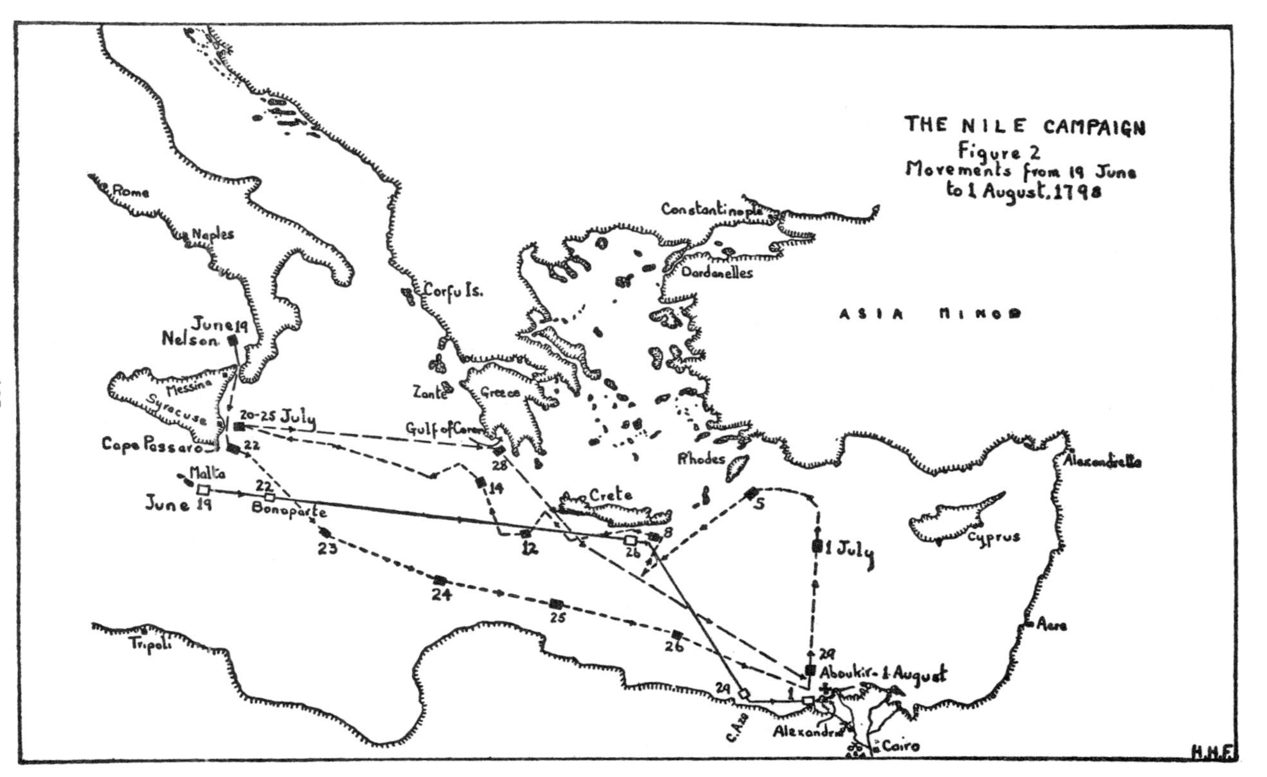
THE NILE CAMPAIGN
Figure 2
Movements from 19 June
to 1 August, 1798
Rome
Naples
Corfu Is.
Constantinople
Dardanelles
ASIA MINOR
June 19
Nelson
Messina
Syracuse
20-25 July
Cape Passaro
22
Malta
June 19
22
Bonoparte
Zante
Greece
Gulf of Coron
28
14
Crete
Rhodes
5
8
26
12
23
24
25
26
1 July
Alexandretta
Cyprus
Acre
Tripoli
29
Aboukir - 1 August
29
C. Aza
Alexandria
Cairo
H.H.F.

the Italian coast, Nelson received information from a Tunisian cruiser on the 14th that the French had been seen off the western point of Sicily on the 4th, sailing to the eastward. On the 17th Naples was reached and word was received that the French had been off Malta on the 9th. The *Orion*, *Alexander*, and *Leander* had meanwhile rejoined the flag.

The British squadron on the 20th passed through the Straits of Messina and skirted the Sicilian coast until Cape Passaro was reached. Here on the 22d three French frigates were sighted in the distance, but Nelson feared that to chase them would disperse his squadron. The same afternoon a ship from Malta brought word that it had surrendered to the French and that the armada had sailed again on the 16th. This information was only partly correct, for it was not until the 19th that Bonaparte had set sail for Crete. Believing that the French had six days' start instead of the three they actually had, Nelson called on board the *Vanguard* the four captains in whom he had the greatest confidence—Saumarez, Troubridge, Ball, and Darby. Their opinions as to the course of action to be taken were stated in writing. With the prevailing westerly winds it was considered that such a great force as the enemy's could not go to the westward of Malta. It was also evident that nothing was to be attempted against Sicily. The three most likely objectives were Corfu, Constantinople, and Alexandria. Nelson believed that an attempt against the latter would involve the greatest danger to his country's interests and boldly decided to proceed under full sail for that port. "I am just returned from on board the Admiral," records Saumarez, "and we are crowding sail for Alexandria. * * * Some days must now elapse before we can be relieved from our cruel suspense; and if, at the end of our journey, we find we are on a wrong scent, our embarrassment will be great indeed."

As the British squadron sped on before the favoring wind it crossed in rear of the French armada from left to right and speedily outdistanced it. On the 28th, after a quick voyage of only six days, Nelson arrived off Alexandria and discovered nothing in port. On the next day he started on his return voyage to Syracuse. On the same day Bonaparte was making out the Egyptian coast in the distance.

His cruise had been directed with remarkable skill. On the 26th he had sailed along the southern coast of Crete and the next day learned from a frigate coming from Naples that Nelson had been off that port ten days before. As a final precaution, Bonaparte wisely sailed for a point on the African coast seventy miles west of Alexandria, sending a frigate to reconnoiter that port. On the 29th he made his landfall at Cape Aze and commenced to work his way slowly along the coast to the eastward. On July 1 he arrived off the town of Marabout, a few miles west of Alexandria. Leaving nothing to chance, he worked all night getting troops ashore and by the next morning 4500 men were available for a forward movement. Although no artillery had been landed, Bonaparte, with this small vanguard, stormed the walls of the city, and the transports and a few frigates then entered the port.

With his usual activity Bonaparte commenced only three days later the advance toward Cairo, the army being assisted by a flotilla manned by the navy. On the 13th, at Shubra-Khet, the advance guard of the Mamelukes was beaten back with loss. On the 21st the army came in sight of the pyramids and there found ranged against them 10,000 Mamelukes, the finest horsemen of the world. "From these pyramids," said their enthusiastic young leader, "forty centuries look down upon you"; and the French squares completely routed their picturesque enemies. On the next day Cairo was occupied.

While these operations were in progress Bonaparte had issued the instructions necessary for the security of the fleet. On July 4 he ordered Brueys to sound the old port of Alexandria and, if the depth of water permitted, to secure the fleet there. If it were not possible to get the squadron into the old port it was to be moored in Aboukir Bay, provided that a good defensive position could be found; if neither of these alternatives proved possible, Brueys was to go to Corfu. On July 8, while the old port was being surveyed, Brueys went to Aboukir Bay. On the 18th the soundings were completed and showed that the ships could be brought into the old port during good weather, but Brueys still remained inactive at Aboukir, trusting that the British would not return. On August 1, when their topsails appeared over the horizon, he was taken completely by surprise.

We left Nelson on the twenty-ninth of June sailing north from Alexandria. On July 4 he touched the southern coast of Asia Minor, then passed along the shores of Crete, and on July 20 came to Syracuse, without having the slightest positive knowledge of the French expedition. He did know, however, that it had not gone to Tunis or Corfu and also that it had not been reported west of Sicily. Alexandria seemed to be the only objective remaining, and on the 25th, after filling with water and taking on twenty bullocks per ship, he again started for the east, heading for the southwestern point of Greece. On the 28th Troubridge was sent into the Gulf of Coron and captured a French brig laden with wine. Information from two independent sources showed that the French had steered southeast from Crete four weeks before, and the Turkish governor assured Troubridge that they were in Alexandria. Nelson headed in that direction, "constantly keeping," as says Captain Miller of the *Theseus*, "the worst sailing ship under all sail."

On July 31, as the fleet was nearing the port, Nelson sent on the *Alexander* and *Swiftsure* to reconnoiter. The next morning they were some nine miles ahead of the other vessels. At 10:30 A.M. the *Alexander* signaled that she had sighted the land. At noon the squadron was some twenty miles northwest of the city and just able to make out its towers in the distance. "We had a fine breeze of north wind," writes Captain Miller of the *Theseus*, "smooth water, and fine weather, the body extending about three miles easterly and westerly without being in any order of sailing, and going about five miles an hour under topsails, generally. The *Culloden* under all sail about seven miles astern, with the wine brig in tow (an article of which the fleet was running short), the *Alexander* and *Swiftsure* being far ahead on the lookout."

At about 12:50 the *Alexander* sighted two French ships of the line—in reality the Venetian 64s—and six frigates in the port and reported them by signal. At 1:30 Captain Ball hailed the *Swiftsure* and ordered her to attack a French ship off the harbor entrance, but at 2:15 Nelson signaled to both of them to "leave off chase," and they tacked to the northeast to join the flag. The reason for this signal is described by Captain Hood of the *Zealous:* After the *Alexander* had reported the French vessels in Alexandria, "I immediately kept," he writes, "well to the eastward of the admiral to try if I could make out anything at Aboukir, as also did the *Goliath*. At about half-past one o'clock the man at the masthead said he saw a sail and instantly a fleet at anchor. I sent a glass up and they told me there were sixteen or eighteen large ships, they thought sixteen of the line. I instantly made the signal to the admiral." Apparently no less than four separate signals were made by the *Zealous*, the first about 2:00 and the last about 2:45. By this time the French fleet could be made out by the entire squadron, bearing slightly to the southward of east. At 2:55 the admiral hoisted the general signal to sail close-hauled on the port tack; this would make the course about E.N.E., or just northerly enough to clear the shoals to the north of the French anchorage. Five minutes later the *Culloden* was ordered to cast off her tow.

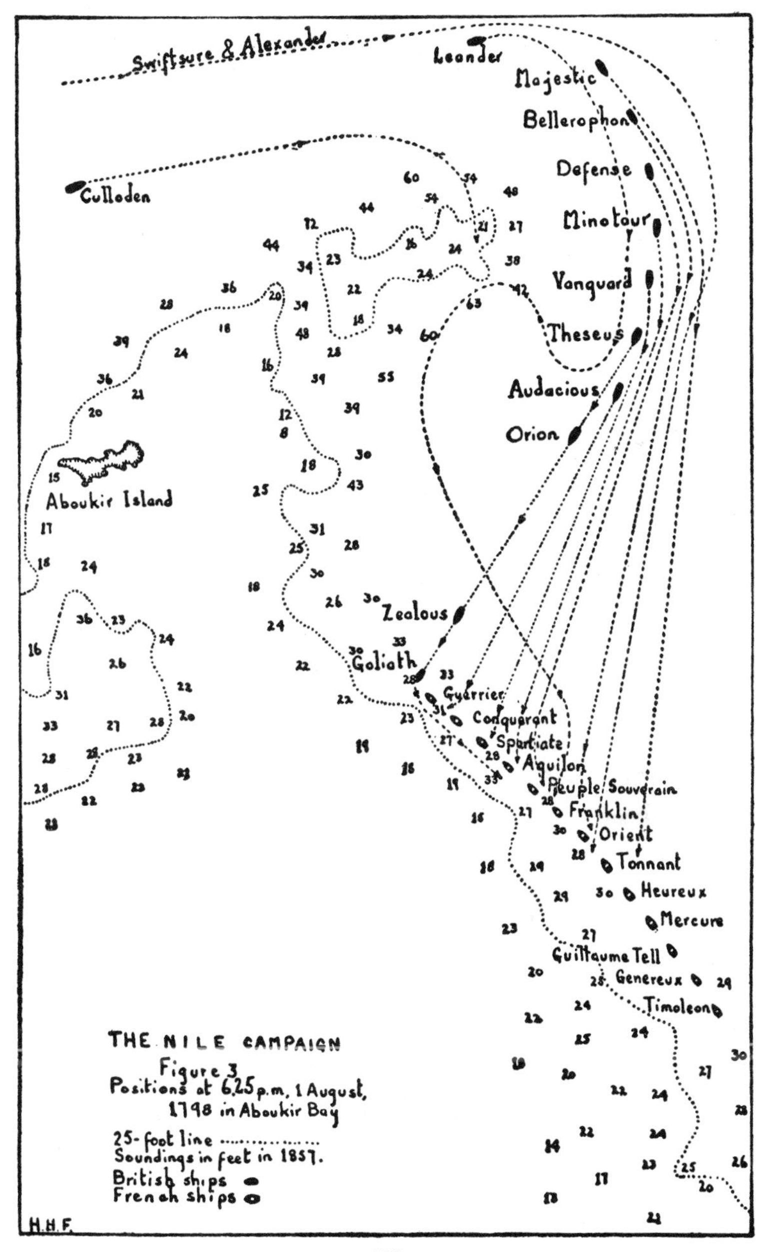
Swiftsure & Alexander
Leander
Majestic
Bellerophon
Defense
Minotaur
Vanguard
Theseus
Audacious
Orion
Culloden
Aboukir Island
Zealous
Goliath
Guerrier
Conquerant
Spartiate
Aquilon
Peuple Souverain
Franklin
Orient
Tonnant
Heureux
Mercure
Guillaume Tell
Genereux
Timoleon
THE NILE CAMPAIGN
Figure 3
Positions at 6.25 p.m. 1 August, 1798 in Aboukir Bay
25-foot line
Soundings in feet in 1857.
British ships
French ships
H.H.F.

Now let us examine the dispositions made by Admiral Brueys to receive the enemy. His thirteen ships of the line were moored in a single line. The van or northernmost vessel was about 2600 yards southeast from Aboukir Island. From that ship, the *Guerrier*, to the seventh ship, the flagship *Orient*, the line ran southeast; from the *Orient* it ran southeast by south to the *Timoleon*, the thirteenth and rear ship. According to Chevalier, a leading French authority, there were 160 yards of open water between the ships. Allowing seventy yards as the length of the ships, we see that the thirteen ships presented a slightly curved line about 2830 yards long. The wind was about N.N.W., and as each ship had out but a single anchor, the lines of their keels were from ten to twenty degrees to the right of the line through their foremasts. It had been arranged in advance that upon the sighting of an enemy each ship was to lay out an additional bower-anchor ahead, a small anchor astern, to run a hawser to the ship ahead and to put springs on the anchor already down, so that the ship could be swung about to bring her broadside to bear in any direction.

Rear-Admiral Villeneuve, who in the *Guillaume Tell* commanded the rear, states that signals had been arranged for the van ships to weigh and stand down the line should the enemy concentrate upon the rear, but that no arrangements had been made for the rear ships to assist the van should it be concentrated on. While such a manœuver would have been difficult with the prevailing northwesterly winds, Villeneuve in making his escape the day after the battle was to prove that it was not impossible, and its omission from the French plan was a grave error.

A second defect was the excessive distance between ships, which threw away the greatest advantage of fighting at anchor, the massing of a great number of guns in the shortest line of battle. It also permitted the British to break through the line.

Another defect of the French position was that the leading French ship was anchored in thirty feet of water, whereas a 74 drew from twenty-two to twenty-four feet. This left a space ahead and inside of the French line through which attacking ships might pass, although it must be admitted that such a dangerous manœuver would not be probable.

In addition, there were no lookout frigates scouting off the coast to give warning of the approach of a hostile force. The frigate which should have performed this duty on the day of the battle had been forced to return to her anchorage by lack of food and water. Some ships had food remaining for only six days. The ships' boats were ashore with working parties bringing off water, while twenty-five men from each ship formed the permanent garrison of a fort established to protect them as they worked.

But a more underlying defect of the squadron was the inferior quality of its seamen. "It will, doubtless, be easy for you to judge," Flag-Captain Ganteaume reported to the minister of marine, "whether the crews of a fleet, so hastily fitted out as ours, could be reasonably expected to be well composed; and whether we could hope to find among men collected at random, as it were, almost at the very instant of departure, able mariners and skilful and experienced cannoneers." On the other hand, the French had a slight material advantage, for they had one 120-gun ship, three very powerful 80-gun ships, nine 74s and four frigates, against thirteen 74s and one 50-gun ship.

At 2:00 the *Heureux* signaled twelve sail to the W.N.W.; soon sixteen sail were sighted and made out to be fourteen of the line and two brigs, the *Leander* being taken for a two-decker. As the *Mutine* was seen sounding ahead of this advancing force, the brigs *Alerte* and *Railleur* were sent out against her. At 3:00 signals were made to recall all boats, stow all hammocks and make ready for an engagement at anchor. The frigates were ordered to send as many men of their crews as they could spare to the ships of the line to take the places of the men away watering.

Admiral Brueys called a council of war. Admiral Blanquet, commanding the van in the *Franklin*, urged that the fleet fight under way, and possibly his idea was entertained for a time, for Brueys signaled for the topgallant yards to be crossed. Villeneuve and Ganteaume urged that lack of men prevented this and argued that the battle should be fought at anchor. The admiral, who was very seriously ill, decided in their favor. Consequently at about 5:00 the signal was made to fight at anchor in accordance with the prearranged plan. Unfortunately, as many of the boats had not returned, some of the ships were not able to lay out the additional anchors and to run hawsers to the ships ahead; all seem to have been able to put springs on their riding cables. All the French ships were much below their normal complements of men when the action commenced.

But if the French were suffering from certain disadvantages, the British also were confronted with many difficulties. First, there was only one rough sketch of Aboukir Bay in the squadron, which did no more than indicate the presence of many dangers to navigation without definitely fixing their position. Second, the squadron was not formed in regular line of battle, but in an irregular body, with three ships so far astern that they could not engage until after dark. Third, there was no opportunity for explaining the plan of attack to the captains, an almost essential feature of an attack upon a prepared position, nor of even arranging the ships in their normal order. "But," says Flag-Captain Berry, "the admiral viewed the obstacles with the eye of a seaman *determined on attack*." At 4:22 the *Vanguard* signaled, "Prepare for battle anchoring with springs and sheet cable taken in at the stern port." William James describes this method of anchoring as follows: "Each ship, accordingly, made fast a stream-cable to her mizzenmast, and, passing it out of one of her gun-room ports, carried it along her side just below the first-deck ports, to several of which it was slung by a slight rope-yard lashing, and then bent it to an anchor at her bow: so that, when the anchor was let go, the ship ran over her main-cable, or that out of the hawse-hole, and brought up by the cable from her stern. This was to avoid the risk of being raked while swinging head to wind, as well as to enable the ship, by slackening one cable and hauling upon the other, to spring her broadside in any direction she pleased."

At 4:52 Nelson hoisted signals 45 and 46, meaning "Attack enemy's van and center." "By attacking the enemy's van and center," he wrote to Lord Howe, "the wind blowing directly along their line, I was enabled to throw what force I pleased on a few ships. This plan my friends readily conceived by the signals." At 5:30 he signaled, "Form line of battle as convenient." At this time the *Vanguard*, *Zealous*, and *Goliath* were sailing along abreast of each other on a northeasterly course, the *Vanguard* outside, the *Zealous* in the center, and the *Goliath* nearest the shore. Close astern of the *Vanguard* was the *Theseus;* on the latter's port quarter was the *Bellerophon* and on her starboard quarter the *Minotaur*. The *Railleur* brig was now within gunshot of the leading British vessels; her captain endeavored to entice them over the shoals, but they refused to follow him.

"As we got abreast of the end of the shoal at the entrance," writes Captain Hood of the *Zealous*, "being within hail of the admiral and on his lee bow, Sir Horatio asked me if I thought we were far enough to the eastward to bear up round the shoal. I told him I was in eleven fathom, that I had no chart of the place, but if he would allow me I would bear up and try with the lead, which I would be attentive to, and lead him as close as I could with safety, it appearing to shoal regularly. He said he would be obliged to me." As Nelson replied to Hood, he took off his hat and wished him success. "Captain Hood," writes Lieutenant Webley of the *Zealous*, "in endeavoring to do the same, let his hat fall overboard, and immediately said, 'Never mind, Webley! there it goes for luck! Put the helm up and make sail!' This was done directly, and as speedily followed by the *Goliath*, who, when the course was shaped, had the lead of the *Zealous* (in consequence of being inside) about a ship's length." It was at this time, 5:39, that Nelson made the signal, "Alter course to starboard"; each ship wore in succession and gradually eased up into the wind, until it was on the starboard beam.

A few minutes later the French mortar battery on Aboukir Island opened on the leading British ships. "At six," reports Ganteaume, "the admiral threw out the signal for commencing the engagement; and, shortly after, the two headmost ships began firing."

At about 6:10, when about three miles from the enemy, the *Vanguard* hove-to in order to speak the *Mutine* and obtain from her boat some Arab fishermen whom she had picked up for use as pilots. "I took this opportunity," writes Captain Miller of the *Theseus*, "to pass the admiral to leeward and endeavor to obtain the honour of leading the fleet into battle, as the *Culloden*, the only ship ahead of us in the regular line, was still considerably distant; but Captain Berry hailed as we passed, and gave me the admiral's order to become his second ahead, in consequence of which I hove-to close ahead of him, and the *Orion* and *Audacious* passed us." Astern of the *Vanguard* were the

Minotaur, *Defense*, *Bellerophon*, *Majestic*, and *Leander*, completing the line of eleven ships.

At about 6:15, just as the French ships hoisted their colors, the admiral gave the order to "Make sail after lying by." While he had been hove-to, the *Goliath* and *Zealous* had opened out quite an interval between them and the next vessels. "The two ships," writes Lieutenant Webley, "continued to run in this way until they got within shot of the enemy, when Captain Hood said to me, 'I see Foley does not like to give up the lead; let him take it; he is very welcome to it; therefore shorten sail, and let him place himself. I suppose he will take the van ship.'" At this time, about 6:20, the French van opened fire, but though they were placed to rake the British ships as they came on, their fire was singularly ineffective.

Captain Foley now, on his own responsibility, but in accordance with that freedom of action which Nelson always granted his captains, made a daring and brilliant decision: to pass ahead of the enemy and attack them on their inner side. While doubtless Nelson had discussed such a move during the conferences which he held to acquaint his captains with his ideas, its execution by a captain who knew nothing of the ground and had not even a sketch of the bay, was one of the most remarkable feats in naval history, and deserves to be classed with the famous example of daring and originality given by Nelson himself at the battle of Cape St. Vincent. At 6:25 the *Goliath* passed a ship's length ahead of the *Guerrier* and poured a raking

Macpherson Collection (From a color aquatint by and after R. Dodd, published 1799)

THE BATTLE OF THE NILE, AUGUST 1, 1798—THE MORNING AFTER

broadside into her. "All sail was now taken in," writes an officer of the *Goliath,* "except the mizzentopsail, which was thrown aback, and, when thus very slowly passing the bow of the *Guerrier,* within a ship's length, the action was commenced on our side by a most dreadfully destructive raking fire. The anchor was at the same time dropped from the bow, the cable being in at the stern port; but *having no after-bitts,* when the ship swung stern to the wind, and the sails began to fly loose from the running rigging being cut, it became difficult to stopper the cable. It kept surging for some minutes, and at last carried all away, and ran out to the clinch, placing the *Goliath* on the quarter of the second, and bow of the third ship of the French line, so as to engage both." The *Goliath's* log states that she anchored abreast of the second ship, the *Conquerant.* The time of anchoring was about 6:28. It must be stated here that all the times of this account are necessarily only approximate, but it is believed that they give throughout the correct sequence of events.

Captain Hood of the *Zealous* decided to take the place which the *Goliath* had missed, and, running past the *Guerrier,* he cut away his sheet-anchor and brought up on the cable running out of his gun-room port on her port (or inner) bow, at 6:28. "I commenced," he wrote, "[such] a well-directed fire into her bow within pistol shot a little after six that her foremast went by the board in about seven minutes, just as the sun was closing the horizon; on which the whole squadron gave

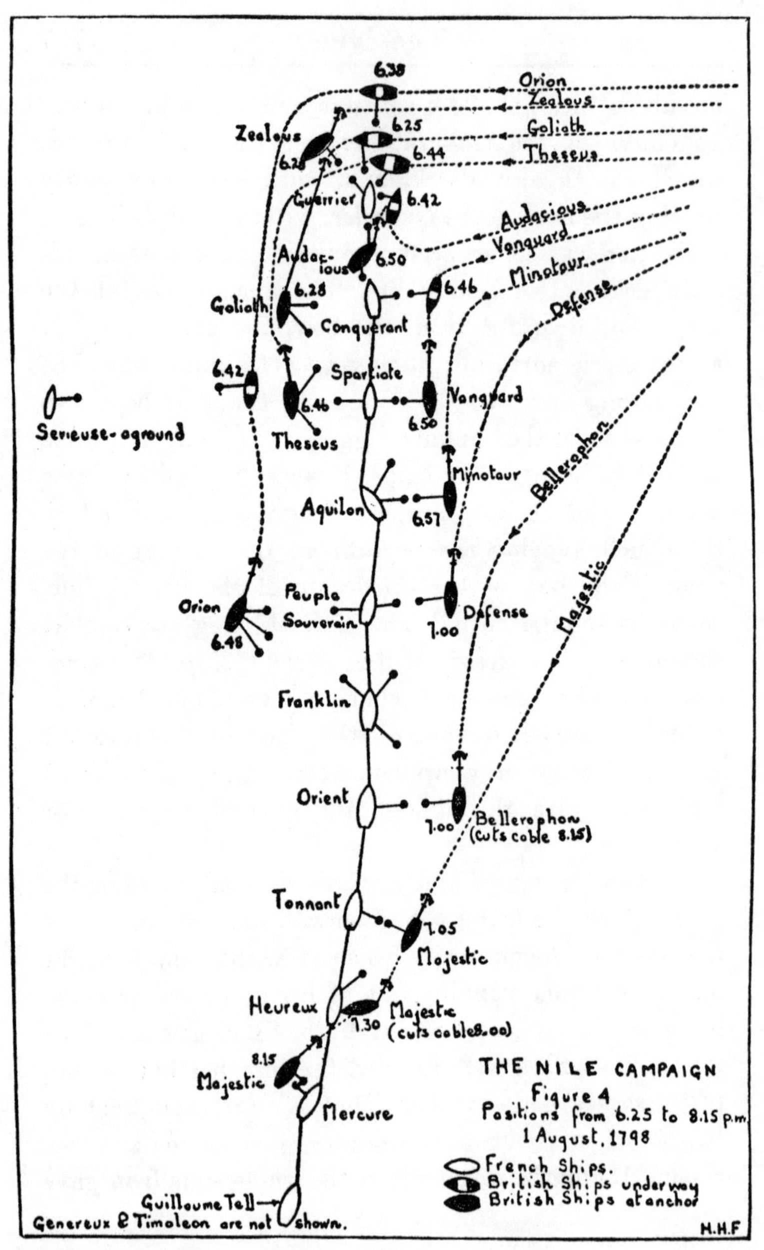
6.38
Orion
Zealous
6.25
Goliath
Zealous
6.28
6.44
Theseus
Guerrier
6.42
Audacious
Vanguard
Audac-
ious
6.50
Minotaur
6.28
6.46
Defense
Goliath
Conquerant
6.42
Spartiate
Vanguard
6.46
6.50
Serieuse-aground
Theseus
Bellerophon
Minotaur
Aquilon
6.57
Majestic
Orion
Peuple
Souverain
Defense
6.48
7.00
Franklin
Orient
7.00
Bellerophon
(cuts cable 8.15)
Tonnant
7.05
Majestic
Heureux
Majestic
7.30
(cuts cables 8.00)
8.15
Majestic
Mercure
THE NILE CAMPAIGN
Figure 4
Positions from 6.25 to 8.15 p.m.
1 August, 1798
French Ships.
British Ships underway
British Ships at anchor
Guillaume Tell
Genereux & Timoleon are not shown.
H.H.F

three cheers, it happening before the next ship astern of me had fired a shot and only the *Goliath* and *Zealous* engaged." This success was due largely to the fact that the French were unprepared to fight on their port side. The *Guerrier's* lower-deck guns were not even run out and the upper-deck ports were full of bags and lumber. The *Zealous* had only seven men wounded.

Captain Saumarez, in the *Orion*, passed the *Guerrier* at 6:38, delivered his broadside into her and then turned outside the *Zealous* and *Goliath*. As he passed the third French ship, the *Sérieuse* frigate commenced firing at him. At 6:42 the *Orion* returned this fire with her starboard guns so effectively that her masts came down and she went aground. The *Orion* let go her best-bower-anchor at 6:45, just as the *Vanguard* broke the general signal to "engage closer." The ship was allowed to swing head to wind and bring up at 6:48 abreast, or a little abaft the inner beam, of the fifth French ship, the *Peuple Souverain*. While most of her fire was directed at that vessel, some of her after-guns played on the *Franklin* and *Orient*, the two next ships.

The *Audacious*, Captain Gould, was brilliantly handled. She was headed for the gap between the *Guerrier* and the *Conquerant*, but when just short of the French line she luffed up into the wind into a position on the *Guerrier's* starboard beam and close aboard; at 6:42 she "fired three broadsides (larboard guns)," according to her log, "and her mainmast fell." The *Zealous* still was firing on the *Guerrier*, and at the same instant the *Theseus* also added her fire to the concentration. "I closed them suddenly," writes Captain

Miller, "and running under the arch of their shot, reserved my fire, every gun being loaded with two and some with three round shot, until I had the *Guerrier's* masts in a line, and her jibboom about six feet clear of our rigging; we then opened with such effect that a second breath could not be drawn before her main- and mizzen-mast were also gone. This was precisely at sunset, or 44 minutes past 6."

The *Audacious*, after her three broadsides at the *Guerrier*, dropped back a bit and let go her small bower-anchor. By veering away on its cable and holding on to a spring leading to her port quarter she was able to hold a position slightly on the port bow of the *Conquerant* so that her full broadside could bear at forty yards' range, while the French ship could reply only with a few guns. At about 7:30 the *Conquerant's* mainmast went by the board, and soon was followed by the mizzen. Her crew consisted of but 400 men; being fifty years old, she carried only 18- and 12-pounders, where a ship of her rate usually carried 24s and 18s.

After the *Theseus* passed the *Guerrier*, Captain Miller turned between her and the *Zealous*. Then he went outside the *Goliath* and anchored by the stern abreast the *Spartiate*, the third ship, and at 6:46 opened a heavy fire on her. "As the *Theseus* passed the *Goliath*," writes an officer of the latter ship, "she gave us three such cheers as have been seldom heard. They were returned by the *Goliath's* crew, and an attempt was made to do the same by the French ships engaged, but it was so truly ridiculous that it caused peals of laughter on board the English ships, loud enough to be heard by both parties. Such enthusiastic cheers were certainly very disheartening to the French, and they readily acknowledged it after the battle."

The *Vanguard* stood down the outer side of the French line and, letting go her best-bower-anchor, came up at 6:50 on the cable leading through her gun-room port abreast the *Spartiate*, distant eighty yards and exactly in line with the *Theseus*. This compelled that vessel to cease fire for fear her shot would go into the *Vanguard*. Captain Miller therefore directed that all his guns forward of the mainmast should fire on the *Aquilon* and those abaft it on the *Conquerant*, "giving up," he says, "my proper bird to the admiral." The *Aquilon*, not yet being engaged, used her springs to haul her stern out to the eastward, and bring her broadside to bear full on the *Vanguard*, from a position directly under her bow. This fire caused severe casualties on the flagship until, at about 6:57, the *Minotaur* anchored by the stern exactly on the *Aquilon's* outer beam and commenced using her heavy upper battery of 32-pounder carronades with smashing effect. The *Defense*, at 7:00, anchored by the stern outside the *Peuple Souverain*. Thus was effected almost to perfection the concentration in thirty-five minutes of eight British ships against the five 74s of the French van.

There remained five 74s and the *Leander* with which to effect the concentration on the French center; this was to prove a much more difficult task. In the first place, only the *Bellerophon* and *Majestic* were immediately available. In the second, among their opponents were the great three-decker *Orient*, twice as powerful as a 74, and the *Franklin* and *Tonnant*, which while rated only as 80-gun ships, actually carried 92 guns and, according to James, were as powerful as British three-deckers of 98 guns.

And now also approaching darkness was rendering more difficult the task of the British captains, which thus far had been performed so exceptionally well. At 7:00 the British ships hoisted their recognition signal of four horizontal lights. The *Bellerophon*, instead of anchoring opposite the *Franklin* or on the *Orient's* bow, came down until, anchoring by the stern, she brought up directly under the *Orient's* broadside at 7:00. Even though the *Orient* could not man over half her upper-deck 12-pounders, her 24s and 36s on the main and lower decks so overwhelmed the *Bellerophon* that at 8:00 her mizzenmast came down, followed shortly by her fore- and main-masts. Her guns were silenced and, cutting her cable, she wore out of action, receiving the fire of the *Tonnant* and *Heureux* as she drifted down the line. Her casualties were heavy, 197 out of a complement of 584. Although the time of this incident is much in dispute, the preponderating weight of evidence seems to place it at 8:15.

At 7:05 the *Majestic* let go her sheet-anchor and brought up by the stern on the *Tonnant's* starboard quarter. This French ship was probably the best trained and disciplined in the fleet, and her heavy battery opened on the *Majestic* with great effect, while the *Heureux* fired into her with her bow guns. At 7:30 Captain Westcott was killed and the command devolved on Lieutenant Cuthbert. To make matters worse, the anchor dragged until her bowsprit ran into the *Heureux's* mizzen-rigging. Captain Etienne of that ship called away boarders, but Cuthbert then, at about 8:00, slipped his stern cable and passed along the *Heureux's* side, exchanging several broadsides. His ship drifted clear and through the French line; very skilfully letting go his bower-anchor with a spring out his gun-room port, Cuthbert at 8:15 brought his ship up in a position even with the *Mercure's* port bow; by this brilliant manœuver he was enabled to fire on the *Mercure* with his starboard battery and still play on the *Heureux* with his port-bow guns. In this desperate close-range fighting the *Majestic* lost 193 men, while the *Mercure* alone had 253 killed or wounded. Captain Etienne of the *Heureux* was so badly wounded that he had to relinquish the command.

The *Culloden* was some two miles astern of the *Majestic*, and Captain Troubridge in his eagerness to get into battle tried a short cut over the reef extending out from Aboukir Island, only to hit hard and fast on a rock at 6:40. The *Leander* put about and sent in a boat to offer assistance. Troubridge directed her captain "to lose no time in joining the fleet." He kept only the *Mutine* with him and signaled for the *Swiftsure* and *Alexander* to give him a wide berth.

The grounding of the *Culloden*, the delay to the *Leander*, and the unavailability of the *Swiftsure* and *Alexander* might well have cost the British dear had Villeneuve used the same energy as did the British captains in entering the battle. The *Guillaume Tell*, *Genereux*, and *Timoleon* did not fire a shot. Captain Trullet of the last-named ship at 8:15 hoisted his topsails as an indication of his desire to enter the action, but Villeneuve made no signal to get under way. He later alleged the difficulty of getting up his anchors and beating up against the wind, but twice during the latter part of the action he did not hesitate to cut his cables, and finally the next morning it proved easy enough for him to sail out of the bay. The intervention of his three fresh ships, one of 80 guns, against the *Swiftsure* and *Alexander* might well have counterbalanced a British victory in the van with a defeat in the center. With the British commander out of the action with a serious wound, no one can say how the action would have terminated. It is certain that the result would have been more favorable to the French than it actually was.

Now let us revert to the fighting in the van. The *Conquerant* was under a terrible concentration of fire from the *Goliath*, *Audacious*, and *Theseus*. Her casualties reached 210, over half her crew, and at 8:30 she hauled down her colors and was occupied by the *Audacious*. In gaining this success the British had suffered little; the *Goliath* lost only sixty-two men, but had both her main- and mizzen-masts badly wounded.

After the *Conquerant's* surrender the *Audacious* continued firing her port-bow guns into the *Guerrier*, and commenced fire on the *Spartiate* with her starboard-quarter guns. The former ship had already been raked by the *Goliath*, *Orion*, and *Theseus* and

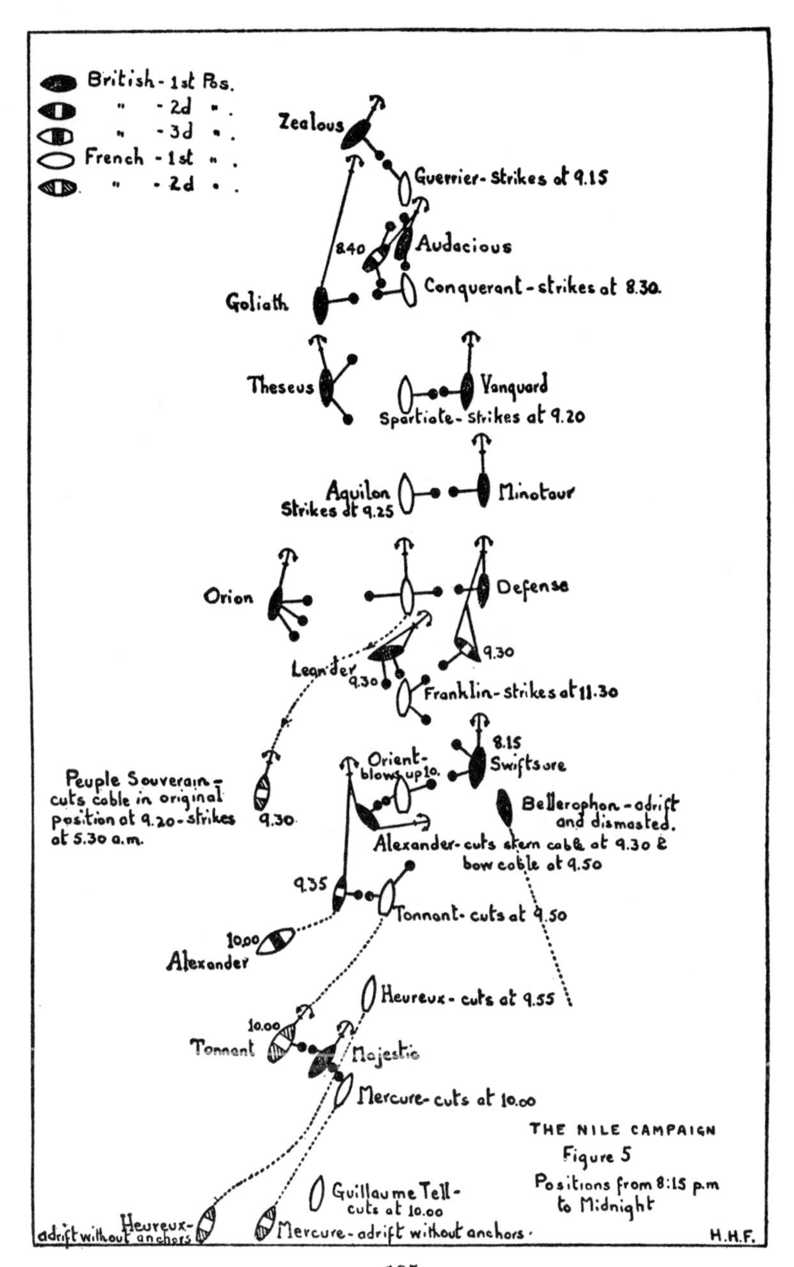

British - 1st Pos.
" - 2d " .
" - 3d " .
French - 1st " .
" - 2d " .
Zealous
Guerrier - strikes at 9.15
8.40
Audacious
Conquerant - strikes at 8.30.
Goliath
Theseus
Vanguard
Spartiate - strikes at 9.20
Aquilon
Strikes at 9.25
Minotaur
Orion
Defense
9.30
Leander
9.30
Franklin - strikes at 11.30
8.15
Swiftsure
Orient - blows up 10.
Peuple Souverain - cuts cable in original position at 9.20 - strikes at 5.30 a.m.
9.30
Bellerophon - adrift and dismasted.
Alexander - cuts stern cable at 9.30 & bow cable at 9.50
9.35
Tonnant - cuts at 9.50
10.00
Alexander
Heureux - cuts at 9.55
10.00
Tonnant
Majestic
Mercure - cuts at 10.00
THE NILE CAMPAIGN
Figure 5
Positions from 8:15 p.m to Midnight
Guillaume Tell - cuts at 10.00
Heureux - adrift without anchors
Mercure - adrift without anchors.
H.H.F.

engaged continuously by the *Zealous* from a favorable position on her port bow. All three of her masts had fallen early in the action. Her crew were driven from the upper decks by the canister and musketry of the *Zealous,* and her port side was stove in for half its length, the deck beams falling over the guns on the main deck. "But," says Captain Hood, "I could not get her commander to strike for three hours, although I hailed him twenty times, and seeing he was totally cut up and only firing a stern gun now and then at the *Goliath* and *Audacious.* At last being tired firing and killing people in that way, I sent my boat on board her and the lieutenant was allowed with the jolly-boat to hoist a light and haul it down to show his submission." The *Guerrier's* resistance until about 9:15 was most creditable, and tied down the British ships in the van for so long that they were unable to attempt the concentration on the French rear which Nelson ultimately hoped to effect.

The *Spartiate,* a ship completed only six months previously, made a splendid resistance. First she had been attacked by the *Theseus* on the inner side; then the *Vanguard* had anchored on her outboard beam. In addition she received some fire from the *Minotaur's* starboard-quarter guns, and after 8:30 the *Audacious* poured in a raking fire from ahead. Finally, at about 9:20, only two guns remained intact, her captain was wounded and her total casualties reached 214 out of 500 men, and she then lowered her colors; she was occupied by the *Vanguard's* marines. In this desperate action the *Vanguard* lost no less than thirty killed and seventy-six wounded. Lord Nelson was badly wounded in the forehead by a piece of iron and had to be carried below. Even though he believed himself mortally wounded, the admiral insisted on calling on board Captain Louis of the *Minotaur* to tell him that his support had prevented the *Vanguard* from being obliged to haul out of the line.

The *Aquilon*, a well-built ship only five years old, made a most determined resistance. On her inner bow the *Theseus* was engaging her with half her battery, while on her outer beam was the *Minotaur*, which had for her upper battery a tier of 32-pounder carronades, a heavier gun than carried by any 74 in either fleet. By 9:25 no less than 300 of her crew were killed or wounded, her brave Captain Thevenard being among the former, and she then surrendered. In addition to causing part of the *Vanguard's* losses, she inflicted eighty-seven casualties on the *Minotaur*.

The *Peuple Souverain* had been attacked by the *Orion* on her inner beam and the *Defense* on her outer beam. Her fore- and main-masts came down, 223 of her crew were out of action, and at 9:20 her cable parted. She reanchored about ten minutes later 400 yards on the *Orient's* inner beam. The *Peuple Souverain* seems to have aimed high, for while she inflicted few casualties, the *Defense's* foretopmast fell by the board, and all three lower masts as well as her bowsprit were injured. The *Orion* had her fore- and mizzen-masts shot through, and also was narrowly missed by a blazing boat set adrift by the *Guerrier*.

During the early part of the action the *Franklin*

had scarcely been engaged. She had received some fire from the *Orion's* port-bow guns and possibly fired on the *Defense* and *Bellerophon*.

Thus, by 9:30 the French van had been decisively beaten and five ships captured or driven from the line. In the center the *Franklin* had scarcely been engaged; the *Orient* by 8:15 had driven off the *Bellerophon;* the *Tonnant* had inflicted heavy losses on the *Majestic*, only to have her make a brilliant manœuver at 8:15 to turn the tables on the *Heureux* and *Mercure*. At this time the *Swiftsure*, *Alexander*, and *Leander* were close at hand, and with unerring judgment their captains selected as their objectives the *Orient* and *Franklin*, leaving the *Tonnant* still practically out of the fight.

A few minutes after 8 o'clock the *Swiftsure* sighted a dismasted ship, which Captain Hallowell hailed. The reply showed that it was the *Bellerophon* going out of action. The *Swiftsure* immediately let go her small bower-anchor and brought up by the stern outside the French line opposite the interval between the *Franklin* and *Orient*, distant about 200 yards from each. At 8:15 she opened fire with her starboard battery, the after guns on the *Franklin* and the forward guns on the *Orient*.

The *Alexander* was handled with beautiful precision. As she plunged through the interval between the *Orient* and *Tonnant* she raked the former and let go her small bower-anchor and allowed the cable to run out the gun-room port. Then luffing into the wind, she dropped her best-bower-anchor on the *Orient's* port beam; veering out on this cable, while holding on to her stern hawser, she hung in a perfect position on the *Orient's* port quarter and poured in at 8:30 a terribly effective fire. For one hour the fight in the center continued thus.

Then the gap in the line left by the *Peuple Souverain* afforded an opportunity to the *Leander* which Captain Thompson was quick to grasp. Anchoring by the stern at 9:30 slightly on the *Franklin's* port bow, he sprang his broadside so that his port guns fired right down the French line. According to French accounts, the balls which missed the *Franklin* smashed into the *Orient* and *Tonnant*. The *Orion* had to cease firing into the *Franklin* when the *Leander* intervened in the line of her fire. When the *Peuple Souverain* left the line, the *Defense* at about 9:30 veered her cable and by means of springs brought her full broadside full upon the *Franklin*.

Let us now see the effects of this constantly increasing concentration on the French flagship. At about 8:00 Admiral Brueys, who had taken his station on the poop, was wounded in the body and head. Coming down to the quarterdeck, his left leg was carried away by a round shot; saying that a French admiral should die on his quarterdeck, he refused to allow his friends to carry him below, and met death with calm heroism. "Obliged to defend ourselves on both sides," reports Ganteaume, "we gave up the 12-pounders; but the 24s and 36s kept up their fire with all possible ardour." Soon after 9:00 an explosion on the after part of the quarterdeck set fire to the wreckage there. "The fire pumps," says Ganteaume, "had been dashed to pieces by the enemy's balls and the tubs and buckets rendered useless. An order was given to cease firing, that all hands might be at liberty to bring water; but such was the ardour of the moment, that in the tumult the guns of the lower deck still continued their fire. Although the officers had called up all the people from below, the flames had in a very short time made a most alarming progress; and we had but few means in our power of checking them."

The British ships, seeing a great success within their grasp, redoubled their fire on the men fighting the flames and shot down the *Orient's* main- and mizzen-masts, which added to the confusion on board. "She was," writes Captain Miller, "soon in a blaze, displaying a most grand and awful spectacle, such as formerly would have drawn tears down the victor's cheeks, but now pity was stifled as it rose by the remembrance of the numerous and horrid atrocities their unprincipled and bloodthirsty nation had and were committing."

It was now apparent that the French flagship was doomed, and on all sides friend and foe began to draw clear and make preparations to prevent their being set on fire by the approaching explosion. At 9:30 the *Alexander* cut her stern cable and veered with her bow cable until she was abreast the *Tonnant,* which she engaged. At 9:50 the bow cable also was cut to prevent the blazing *Orient* falling down upon her. The impending explosion also had a most unfortunate effect upon the whole French line in rear of the *Orient.* The

Tonnant had to cut her cable, and as she drifted down on the *Heureux* that vessel did the same. The *Heureux* crashed into the *Mercure*, which then also cut her cable. The *Tonnant* reanchored on the *Majestic's* port beam, but the *Heureux* and *Mercure*, having no more anchors fit for use, drifted down inside the line. The three vessels of the rear seem to have veered or slipped their cables until they were about 400 yards in rear of their original positions. The *Franklin*, ahead of the *Orient*, was in a dangerous position, particularly as at 9:30 her main- and mizzen-mast fell and all her main-deck battery was out of action.

Shortly after 10:00 the *Orient* blew up and her wreck drifted down the line. Some of her crew were able to swim ashore; others swam to near-by ships. The *Bellerophon* picked up two, the *Orion* fourteen, the *Swiftsure* eleven, while the *Alexander's* log states, "Served to the French prisoners saved from the *l'Orient* when blown up, and came on board naked, shirts twenty-eight, trousers twenty-eight pair." So close was the *Alexander* that her jib- and main-royal-sail caught fire; the ship drove down before the wind and seems to have remained under way for several hours. The *Franklin* was covered with blazing fragments but was able to put out the numerous fires which sprang up.

For some ten minutes friend and foe were so awed by the explosion and so occupied in preventing the fire from spreading to their own ships that not a shot was fired. Then the gallant *Franklin* reopened the action and was concentrated upon heavily by the *Swiftsure*, *Defense*, and *Leander*. "The *Franklin*," writes a staff officer on board, "anxious to preserve the trust confided to her, recommenced the action with a few of the lower-deck guns; all the rest were dismounted: two-thirds of the crew were killed, and those who remained most fatigued. She was surrounded by the enemy's ships, who mowed down the men at every broadside. At half-past eleven, having only three lower-deck guns that could defend the honor of the flag, it became necessary to put an end to so disproportionate a struggle; and Citizen Martinel, capitaine de frégate, ordered the colours to be struck."

Thus before midnight the seven leading French ships had been lost and the remaining six thrown into complete confusion. Only the *Tonnant* continued resistance. We have seen how she reanchored on the *Majestic's* port beam. A prolonged and desperate action now occurred between these two ships, it being the fourth distinct engagement for the British 74. Some of the *Tonnant's* bow guns greatly annoyed the *Swiftsure*, which could not reply because the *Alexander* was in the line of fire, apparently beyond the *Tonnant*. Possibly the *Alexander*, while thus under way, took some part in this action, but this is not indicated by her log. At 12:15, however, she did anchor and joined the fight. The *Tonnant*, whose crew was animated by the fine spirit of her captain, Petit-Thouars, made a splendid resistance against these odds and at 1:30 A.M. shot down the *Majestic's* main- and mizzen-masts. However, her brave captain was killed and her casualties reached 260 men. Only a few of her guns remained in action, and at 2:00 all three of her masts crashed down.

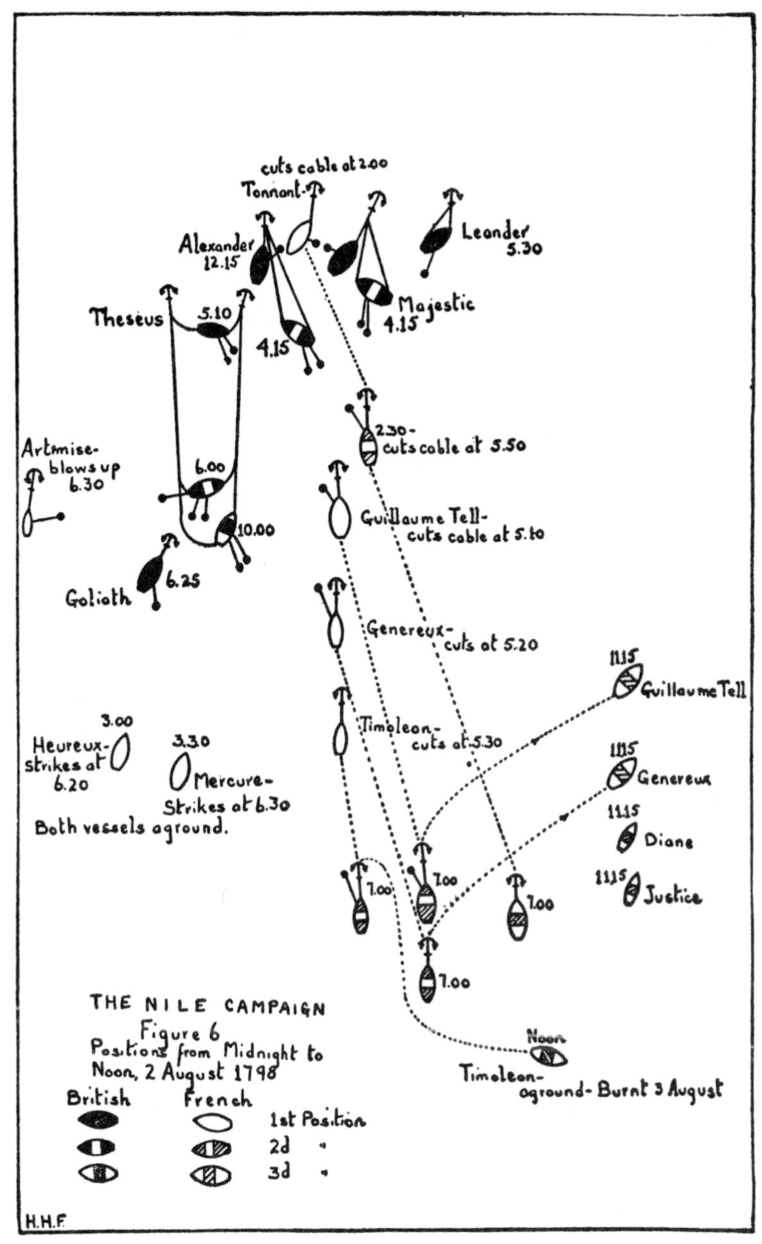
cuts cable at 2.00
Tonnant
Alexander
12.15
Leander
5.30
Theseus
5.10
Majestic
4.15
4.15
2.30-
cuts cable at 5.50
Artemise-
blows up
6.30
6.00
Guillaume Tell-
cuts cable at 5.10
10.00
Goliath
6.25
Genereux-
cuts at 5.20
11.15
Guillaume Tell
3.00
Heureux-
strikes at
6.20
3.30
Mercure-
Strikes at 6.30
Both vessels aground.
Timoleon-
cuts at 5.30
11.15
Genereux
11.15
Diane
11.15
Justice
7.00
7.00
7.00
7.00
THE NILE CAMPAIGN
Figure 6
Positions from Midnight to
Noon, 2 August 1798
Noon
Timoleon-
aground- Burnt 3 August
British
French
1st Position
2d "
3d "
H.H.F.

Her cable was cut and she drifted off with colors still flying, anchoring ahead of the *Guillaume Tell.* Fire now ceased; both sides were completely exhausted; the night battle was at an end.

But now other misfortunes overtook the crippled *Heureux* and *Mercure.* When the former vessel had reached the vicinity of the *Guillaume Tell* and the lieutenant who had succeeded to the command attempted to anchor, he found that the only remaining anchor had been smashed by a cannon-shot. While trying to make sail, his ship, which was low in the water due to leaks, took the ground at 3:00 and could not be moved. The *Mercure* likewise had no anchors remaining and half an hour later grounded near the *Heureux.* It was not even possible to evacuate and destroy the ships, because all the boats had been destroyed.

As dawn broke, about 4:00, the *Alexander* and *Majestic* discovered only four French vessels still in line. First was the dismasted *Tonnant,* then the *Guillaume Tell, Genereux,* and *Timoleon,* none of which had been appreciably under fire. At 4:15 the two British ships reopened fire at long range, but ceased after about half an hour. This cannonade was of use only to invite attention to the fact that all the spoils of battle had not yet been gathered.

Meanwhile the *Theseus* had occupied the *Sérieuse* frigate, and Captain Miller, seeing three more frigates to the southward, sent a boat to sound toward them. The *Orion* occupied the *Peuple Souverain.*

At 4:30 A.M. Captain Hood came aboard the *Theseus* to propose action against the French frigates. The bower-anchor was being lifted for this purpose, when an officer from the *Swiftsure* came on board to say that "the admiral wishes us all to go to the assistance of the *Alexander* and *Majestic.*" When hoisting the stern-anchor an officer of the *Alexander* came on board with an even more urgent message. These two officers apparently passed on to the *Goliath, Zealous,* and *Audacious.* The *Vanguard* signaled the *Leander* to assist the *Majestic.*

The *Theseus* was the only vessel able to move for some time. At 4:55 she was under way and about fifteen minutes later moored with two anchors inside the French line so that her starboard battery bore on the *Tonnant, Guillaume Tell,* and *Genereux* at ranges between 500 and 1000 yards. Astern and inboard of her was the *Artemise* (36), and still farther off, at extreme gunshot, the *Justice* (40), and *Diane* (40). On her starboard quarter were the *Heureux* and *Mercure,* which, Captain Miller says, "did not appear to have been at all in action." The *Theseus* did not immediately commence firing, in hopes that other British vessels would arrive before the action recommenced. "My people were also so extremely jaded," the captain writes, "that as soon as they had hove up our sheet-anchor they dropped under the capstan-bars, and were asleep in a moment in every sort of posture, having been working at their fullest exertion, or fighting, for near twelve hours."

At sunrise, or about 5:15, the *Guillaume Tell* drifted down in line with the *Genereux,* and then the *Theseus* opened up, followed by the *Alexander* and *Majestic,* and somewhat later by the *Leander* at very long range. A shot from the *Alexander* cut the *Tonnant's* cable and she drifted off to the southeast. The remaining three French ships slipped their cables and drifted down to the southeast so fast that by 6:00 the *Theseus*, although she had veered-to 400 yards of cable on each anchor, had to cease fire. In a few minutes she reopened fire on the *Heureux* and *Mercure* on her starboard quarter, and the other British vessels also contributed a few rounds. At 6:20 the *Heureux* struck and was occupied by Lieutenant Brodie of the *Theseus*. At 6:25 the *Goliath* anchored on the starboard quarter of the *Theseus* and commenced firing on the *Mercure*, but ceased when Captain Miller hailed to say that he had already sent a boat to demand her surrender. Five minutes later the *Mercure* hauled down her colors and was occupied by the *Theseus*, which later resigned this prize to the *Alexander*. At about 6:30 the *Artemise* fired a broadside at the *Theseus* and hauled down her colors, "but such," reads an old English account, "was the unwarrantable and infamous conduct of the French captain, that after having surrendered, he set fire to his ship, and with part of his crew made his escape to the shore."

The *Zealous* was under way and standing toward the French rear at 7:00, when the *Vanguard* signaled her to chase to the eastward after the *Justice*, which seemed to be trying to escape. When she turned back, the *Zealous* was ordered to go to the assistance of the *Bellerophon*, which was anchored some three miles to the eastward.

At about 7:00 the *Guillaume Tell, Genereux,* and *Timoleon* had again anchored at extreme range from the *Theseus,* and many large boats from the shore were seen passing from ship to ship. The *Diane* and *Justice* anchored close by. Now for three whole hours neither side made a move to commence the action, although it would seem that overwhelming numbers could have been brought against the small French force remaining. Had Nelson been unwounded it is certain that Villeneuve's fate would now have been sealed. Captain Miller of the *Theseus* was the only captain with the energy and initiative necessary to reopen the fight. At about 10:00 he opened fire. "I caused," he writes, "a cool and steady fire to be opened on them from our lower deckers only, all of which being admirably pointed by Lieutenant England, who commanded that deck, they soon drove the boats entirely away from their ships, and doubtless hulled them frequently, particularly the *Timoleon.*"

At 11:00 the French vessels got under way and stood to the eastward. The *Timoleon* was farthest to leeward and had received injuries to her rigging from the fire of the *Theseus.* Twice she attempted to wear after the other ships, but, failing in this, the captain headed her straight for the shore, her foremast falling as she struck. The *Vanguard* hoisted signals for the *Zealous, Goliath, Audacious,* and *Leander* to chase, but only the *Zealous* was able to execute the signal. "Though I did them a great deal of damage," reports Captain Hood, "they were so well prepared as to cut every bowline, boom, topmast and standing rigging, sails, &c., away."

No less than forty round shot passed through the mainsail of the *Zealous* in this brief engagement. "Found we had one pipe of wine," says the log of the *Zealous*, "No. 3320, containing 144 gallons, being on deck to serve the ship's company at dinner, and not having time to strike it down, received a shot by which it was stove and the contents lost." Perhaps this is the way Captain Hood diplomatically accounted for having served out an extra allowance.

Nelson's first act after firing had ceased was to issue the following memorandum:

Vanguard, off the Mouth of the Nile,
2d Day of August, 1798.

Almighty God having blessed his Majesty's arms with victory; the admiral intends returning public thanksgiving for the same, at 2 o'clock this day, and he recommends every ship doing the same, as soon as convenient.

To the respective Captains of the Squadron.

His next step was to issue an order congratulating the "captains, officers, seamen, and marines," and to thank personally the captains who came on board the flagship during the day. He expressed great anxiety to secure the *Tonnant* and *Timoleon*, whose flags were still flying.

Early on the 3d it was discovered that the *Timoleon* had been set on fire and that her crew had abandoned the ship during the night. The *Tonnant* struck to the *Theseus* and *Leander*. "There being no longer an enemy to contend with," writes Captain Miller, "we beat the retreat and solemnly returned thanks to

Almighty God through whose mercy we had been instrumental in obtaining so great and glorious a victory to his Majesty's arms, and I believe from a body of men more fervent gratitude never mingled in prayer."

The battle of the Nile was one of the most decisive in history, from both tactical and strategical viewpoints. The French lost eleven ships of the line, two frigates and, according to Chevalier, some 3000 men killed or wounded; the British vessels all were considerably damaged and lost 896 killed or wounded. The *Tonnant* and *Spartiate* flew the British ensign at Trafalgar, while the *Franklin*, under the name of *Canopus*, remained in active service for many years.

While the French admirals made certain errors, their captains made a brave and skilful defense, and it was to the brilliancy of the British admiral and his captains that the victory was due. Lord Howe correctly said that the action "stood unparalleled and singular in this instance, that every captain distinguished himself." Such a condition reflects great credit upon their immediate commander, Lord Nelson, and their commander-in-chief, Admiral Jervis, who had so painstakingly trained this greatest of all British squadrons.

CHAPTER VI

Mobile Bay

NAVAL warfare in the Civil War was unusual in that the Confederate States were under such industrial disadvantages that they were never able to construct a fleet with which they could dispute the command of the sea. Thus the navy received by default that command of the sea which usually is the prize of a great naval victory. In fact, Northern control of the sea was disputed even less than that of the British navy after the crushing victory of Trafalgar. It permitted Northern fleets to be split up into small detachments to gather all the fruits of this command. Sea forces were used to protect commerce against Confederate raiders, to blockade the coasts of the Southern States, to attack and capture, with the assistance of the army, important Confederate seaports, to assist military campaigns by penetrating into and controlling rivers which extended far into enemy territory, and even to participate in battles between military forces. The Confederate States navy confined its energies to raiding Northern commerce on the high seas and to defending its own coasts and rivers. As these were measures favorable to inferior forces, it was able to do considerable injury to commerce and to oppose a strong resistance to Union attacks on the coast.

The coastal and river warfare of the Civil War, while not marked by great fleet actions, contained far more fighting than usually results in a naval campaign in which two great fleets manœuver against each other for years before engaging. This almost continual fighting brought to the fore that daring and resourcefulness which are our national characteristics and developed captains who were accustomed almost daily to risk their ships and who frequently performed feats of unusual boldness. Mobile Bay was the last and possibly the most brilliant of a series of actions fought by the Gulf and Mississippi squadrons and is a fitting exploit to represent our naval traditions, showing our greatest naval commander at the peak of his career.

Naval warfare in the Gulf of Mexico commenced in 1861 with a most unusual incident. On the recommendation of Mr. Seward, secretary of state, the President directed the organization of a secret expedition to secure to the Union forces Fort Pickens, which commanded the entrance to Pensacola Bay and was then held by but twenty-five men. General Scott was informed of the plan and authorized the chartering of the steamer *Atlantic* to transport 600 troops to Fort Pickens. The President secretly sent Lieutenant David D. Porter, U.S.N., to the New York Navy Yard with orders to relieve the commanding officer of the steamer *Powhatan*, to himself assume the command, and to escort the *Atlantic* to its destination, with the strictest injunctions against letting the Navy Department get wind of the plan, as it was known that Southern sympathizers in the department would divulge it immediately. However, as the expedition left the navy yard the commandant felt it his duty to report the fact to the department. This caused a violent scene between the secretary of the navy and the secretary of state in the presence of the President. The latter yielded and directed Seward to order Porter to cancel the expedition. Porter received the telegram, which did not mention the President, just as he was leaving the harbor. He replied: "I received my orders from the President and shall proceed to execute them." The arrival of the two ships at Pensacola definitely saved Fort Pickens, and with this foothold the Gulf Squadron commenced the blockade.

Meanwhile energetic action was being taken to build up a naval force on the upper reaches of the Mississippi and its tributaries. Three wooden gunboats were quickly commissioned and earned Grant's commendation for their excellent support of his army at the battle of Belmont. Mr. Eads constructed seven fine armored gunboats in one hundred days and in September, 1861, Flag Officer Foote assumed command of the naval forces, Western waters. By the beginning of 1862 all was in readiness for an offensive campaign with the army down the Mississippi, Tennessee, and Cumberland rivers.

Preparations were also being made for an advance of the Gulf Squadron up the Mississippi, and in January Flag Officer Farragut took command, with orders to capture New Orleans and then push on up the river to coöperate with Foote.

In February Grant commenced his offensive down

the Tennessee and Cumberland rivers, accompanied by Foote's gunboats. Fort Henry on the Tennessee first fell before the bombardment of the naval forces and a week later they assisted Grant in the capture of Fort Donelson. Two wooden gunboats played a decisive part in the desperately fought battle of Shiloh, each firing nearly 200 shells at the Confederate troops at point-blank range.

The main body of the naval forces, now under Flag Officer Davis, was transferred to the Mississippi and, in conjunction with a military force, reduced Island Number Ten, Fort Pillow, and Memphis and reached the vicinity of Vicksburg.

Meanwhile in April Farragut had performed an epoch-making exploit in running the Mississippi forts, destroying a Confederate flotilla and capturing New Orleans. He then steamed upriver, ran the batteries of Vicksburg, and joined Davis, but the combined fleets, being without the support of a powerful military force, were unable to reduce this fortress, whose elevated batteries could not be damaged by the ships' fire.

The next year on the river was marked by great activity, many encounters occurring between the Federal gunboats and steamers and the Confederate rams and batteries. Finally, in July, 1863, Vicksburg fell to Grant and Porter, who now commanded the upriver forces, while Banks and Farragut reduced Port Hudson in the same month. These victories placed the river entirely in the possession of the Federal forces. Porter became responsible for its security, while Farragut returned to his station in the Gulf. Soon thereafter he

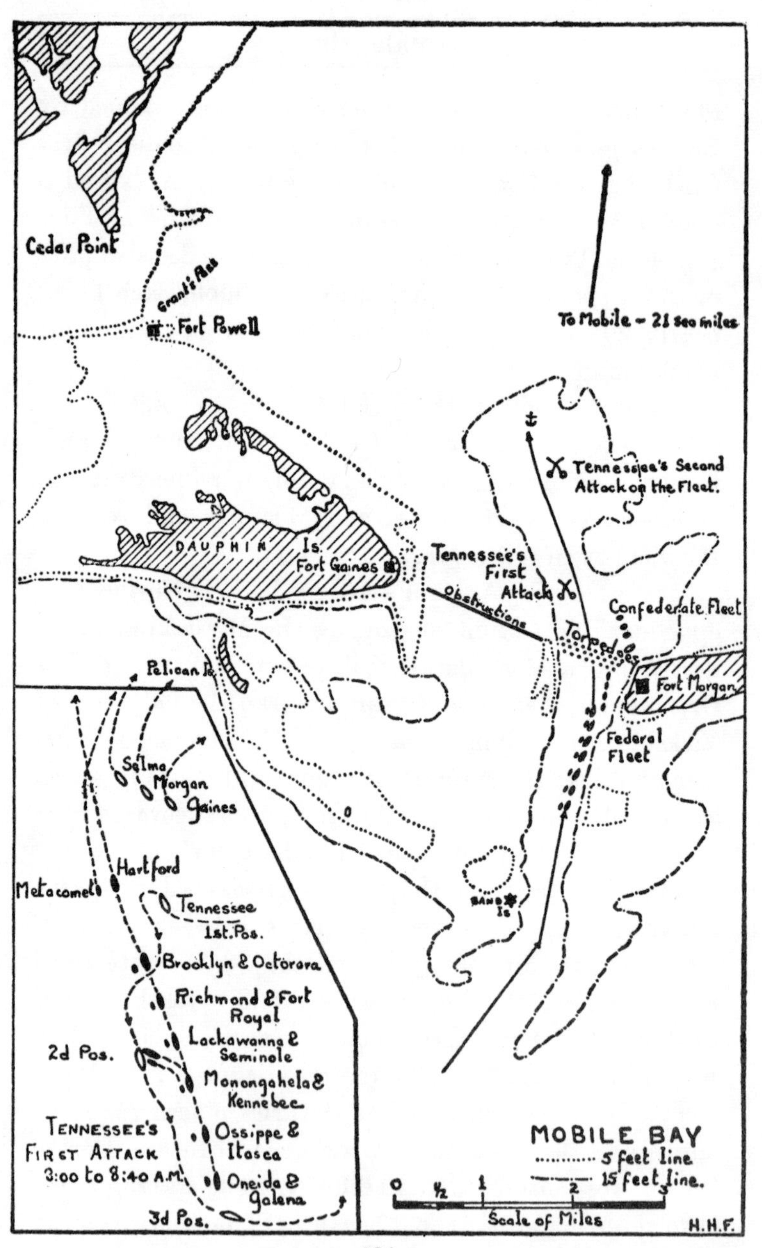

Cedar Point
Grant's Pass
Fort Powell
To Mobile - 21 sea miles
DAUPHIN Is.
Fort Gaines
Tennessee's First Attack
Tennessee's Second Attack on the Fleet.
Obstructions
Torpedoes
Confederate Fleet
Fort Morgan
Federal Fleet
Pelican Pt.
Selma
Morgan
Gaines
Hartford
Metacomet
Tennessee
1st. Pos.
Brooklyn & Octorora
Richmond & Fort Royal
Lackawanna & Seminole
2d Pos.
Monongahela & Kennebec
Tennessee's First Attack 3:00 to 8:40 A.M.
Ossippe & Itasca
Oneida & Galena
3d Pos.
SAND Is.
MOBILE BAY
5 feet line
15 feet line.
0 ½ 1 2 3
Scale of Miles
H.H.F.

sailed north in the *Hartford,* Commodore Bell assuming temporary command of the squadron.

On January 4, 1864, Captain Thornton A. Jenkins, in the *Richmond,* assumed command of the Mobile blockade. He had in addition the *Port Royal, Octorara, Genesee, Kennebec, Pinola, Gertrude, Albatross,* and *Penguin.* The *Lackawanna* and *Oneida* were being repaired at New Orleans and the *Itasca* was about to leave there for the blockade. On the 5th Farragut left New York Navy Yard in the *Hartford* to rejoin his command.

Blockade duty in the Gulf was no sinecure. Its unpopularity is revealed in a report of Captain Jenkins. "When a vessel," he says, "as was the case lately of the *Port Royal,* leaves the station to have repairs requiring, as reported, only about six days, is absent seven weeks; another, in fine weather, the first night after her arrival, her smokestack is carried away by her gaff; the *Itasca,* which broke the anchor stock of her only reliable anchor the first twenty-four hours she was on the station; the *Genesee,* which after a long stay at New Orleans is constantly complained of as being unseaworthy; the *Penguin,* which went to Pensacola to have work done which ought to have required at most two days, is delayed a week, etc., it is beyond the power of war to carry out any systematic plan."

Admiral Franklin Buchanan, C. S. N., one time commander of the *Merrimack,* was then reported to be fitting out the formidable ram *Tennessee* at Mobile, together with a powerful squadron of three smaller rams and three gunboats, and the Confederates were spreading reports that Buchanan would soon break the blockade and even attack Pensacola and New Orleans.

On the 17th the *Hartford* arrived at Pensacola, and Farragut announced that he would proceed to Mobile because of "the report that it is Buchanan's intention to come out with the rams and attack the blockaders. * * * The department is a little uneasy about the *Tennessee*, which Buchanan says is superior to the *Merrimack*." The admiral wrote on the same day to Admiral Porter, asking for two of his monitors, saying: "If I had them, I should not hesitate to become the assailant instead of awaiting the attack."

Three days later Farragut arrived off Mobile and reconnoitered the approaches to the bay in the *Octorara*, being able to count every gun in the forts. On the right or eastern side of the entrance was Fort Morgan, a strongly constructed brick fort of the latest design, mounting forty-eight guns and located at the end of a long peninsula. At the water's edge was an additional battery of seven guns. On the left hand was Fort Gaines, located at the eastern end of Dauphin Island and mounting twenty-six guns. The distance between these forts was about four miles, but the main ship channel was only 1500 yards wide and directly under the guns of Fort Morgan. The shoals extending from Dauphin Island to the main ship channel were obstructed by a line of piles which was plainly visible. It was reported that there were thirty torpedoes, which we would now call mines, planted in the main ship channel, each charged with seventy-five pounds of explosive. To the northwest of Dauphin Island was a gap of some four miles to Cedar Point. Except for Grant's Pass, a very narrow passage, this area was impassable, due to shoals and obstructions. The pass was commanded by Fort Powell, which mounted six guns, later increased to eight. After passing Fort Morgan the main ship channel opened out to a width of about two miles and extended some six miles up the bay, providing an excellent anchorage. The channel to Mobile led across Dog River Bar, which had over it but nine feet of water.

The "Old Salamander," as the admiral was called, was not disturbed by Confederate rumors. "It is depressing to see how easily false reports circulate out here," he reported to the department, "and in what a state of alarm the community is kept by the most absurd rumors. If the department could get one or two of the ironclads down here it would put an end to this state of things and restore confidence to the people of the ports now in our possession. I feel no apprehension of Buchanan's raising the blockade; but with such a force as he has in the bay it would be unwise to take in our wooden vessels without the means of fighting the enemy on an equal footing."

On January 28 reliable information was received from two refugees as to conditions in Mobile. "Provisions and supplies very scarce," they reported. "Ammunition plenty, as two government steamers ran in three weeks ago loaded with ammunition. Prices of everything very high. Flour $160 per barrel; coffee $12 per pound; boots from $120 to $200 per pair;

common overcoat $200; and common suit of clothes from $200 to $300. The spirit of the people is broken, but the officers determined to defend the city to the last."

On February 22 Captain Marchand, who had assumed command of the Mobile blockade in the *Lackawanna*, issued his orders for receiving the attack of the *Tennessee*. "No commanding officer," his instructions read, "will err in risking his vessel by running down the enemy, but the destruction of the ironclad *Tennessee* should be the aim of all." This sounds like Nelson before Trafalgar.

At the end of February an attempt was made to reduce Fort Powell, thus permitting small vessels to enter the bay through Grant's Pass and keep the *Tennessee* from passing Dog River Bar. The fire of the mortar vessels was entirely without effect until March 1, when to his astonishment Farragut believed that he saw the *Tennessee*, another ironclad and three gunboats near Fort Powell. He then abandoned the attack, reduced the blockading forces off the pass to two vessels and hurriedly rejoined his squadron off the main ship channel. It was not until the 9th that he discovered that neither the *Tennessee* nor any other vessels had entered the bay.

The maintenance of the Gulf blockade was a task that required all of Farragut's energies. We find him complaining about provisions in a way that reminds us of Drake and Howard. "The medical officers of the blockading vessels state," he reports to Washington, "that the want of fresh provisions is beginning to tell

From a painting by W. H. Overend—By courtesy of William Pate & Company, New York

THE "HARTFORD" AND "TENNESSEE" AT CLOSE QUARTERS

Farragut overseeing the fight in Mobile Bay, August 5, 1864

upon their crews; that they do not receive one-quarter of the vegetables necessary for health, and have only had fresh beef sixteen days in six months."

The system of signals was in its usual chaotic state. Flag-Captain Drayton first mentions this in a letter to Jenkins: "You will perceive that there is another change of signals, caused, it is understood, by the robbery of a book on the Mississippi. This is the worst yet, as there are two books and two sets of signals." Farragut wrote to the bureau of navigation with much feeling: "You will have to do something to simplify the signals. It has now become a matter of the greatest anxiety to the officers of the fleet. There are nothing but mistakes with two sets of signals. * * * The signals have been changed so frequently that we scarcely learn the flags before they are altered." It was a sad commentary on the Navy's methods of signaling that it had to use army signal officers during the battle of Mobile Bay.

The admiral received a stiff letter from the department on the occasion of the running of the Galveston blockade by the Confederate steamer *Harriet Lane.* "It cannot but be looked upon as a miserable business," writes the secretary, "when six good steamers, professing to blockade a harbor, suffer four vessels to run out in one night."

Another constant bone of contention was the way in which the vessels in Florida ports took from the storeship *Bermuda* provisions and drafts of men claimed by Farragut to be meant for the Mobile Squadron. Thus the admiral on one occasion sent the *Pen-*

guin to Key West to bring off 144 recruits seized by the Federal vessels there. The shortage of personnel was so great that 500 men had to be transferred from the army to make up the complements. Yellow fever was also a cause for great concern. A little later we see the admiral protesting strongly to the department that beef and vegetables meant for him had been appropriated by the vessels at Tampa. The coal supply at times got so low at Pensacola that there was enough to last the squadron only two weeks.

On the other hand, the admiral was able to report many captures of blockade runners, and day by day the Southern States felt with increasing effect the pressure being exerted by his tireless squadron as it rode out gale after gale in the open sea.

Meanwhile Buchanan was working against even greater difficulties in preparing his squadron for sea. Finally on April 1 the *Tennessee* was commissioned with Commander J. D. Johnston in command. Her hull was 209 feet long and forty-eight feet in extreme width. It was decked over eighteen inches above the waterline. To protect her battery a heavy shield or casemate seventy-eight feet in length and eight feet high was constructed over the deck amidships. The sides of this superstructure sloped back at an angle of 33° to the deck and were composed of iron armor from five to six inches thick, backed by twenty-three inches of yellow pine and white oak. At each end of the shield was a 7-inch rifle, while two 6.4-inch rifled guns projected from ports on each broadside. The ram's weak points were her low speed—about six knots—exposed steering gear, and a smokestack which could easily be knocked over.

As the draft of the *Tennessee* was thirteen feet, it was evident that she would have to be lightened four feet to get over the Dog River Bar. Floats were constructed to provide this lift and her coal and ammunition were loaded on two steamers. The first floats were destroyed by fire, but a second set lifted her over the bar on May 20 and she came to anchor inside Fort Morgan.

On the 25th Farragut ran in for a reconnaissance. Referring to Buchanan's reported plans to break the blockade, the admiral wrote: "Let him come; I have a fine squadron to meet him, all ready and willing. I can see his boats very industriously laying down torpedoes, so I judge that he is quite as much afraid of our going in as we are of his coming out. But I have come to the conclusion to fight the devil with fire, and therefore shall attach a torpedo to the bow of each ship and see how it will work on the rebels—if they can stand blowing up any better than we can." Farragut was one of the few commanders who constantly thought of what he could do to the enemy rather than what the enemy could do to him, and this letter is characteristic of his optimistic temperament.

The admiral's superb leadership was greatly raising the morale of the squadron. In June he reports that the number of vessels in the navy yards at New Orleans and Pensacola had been reduced from thirty to four; in consequence, the blockade was constantly becoming more effective, and it was rare that a week passed without the capture of at least one ship trying to run it.

The news as to reinforcements of armored vessels also was good. On July 1 Admiral Porter reported that he was sending the monitors *Winnebago* and *Chickasaw*. On the 8th the *Manhattan* arrived at Pensacola, and four days later Farragut issued his general order to prepare for the attack.

On the 17th General Canby reported that he would send 4000 troops to coöperate with the fleet. The arrival of several drafts of men and a well-loaded collier also eased the situation. On the 30th the fourth monitor, the *Tecumseh*, arrived at Pensacola. By the 2d the troops had arrived and were preparing to land on Dauphin Island. All vessels were ready but the *Richmond*, *Tecumseh*, and *Metacomet* at Pensacola. "We are anxiously looking for you all," writes Drayton to Jenkins, commanding the *Richmond* and senior officer at Pensacola, "and especially the *Tecumseh*. I don't believe the admiral will wait much longer, but go in with the force he has, which will get in if any can."

On the 3d General Granger landed his troops on the western end of Dauphin Island and commenced the siege of Fort Gaines. The admiral was much mortified that the army had commenced action before he was ready. He wrote again to Jenkins: "Send out the *Metacomet* and come out yourself tomorrow morning. I can lose no more days. I must go in day after tomorrow at daylight or a little later. It is a bad time; but when you do not take fortune at her offer you must take her as you can find her."

On the next afternoon Farragut reconnoitered the forts. "The scene on the *Cowslip*," writes Lieutenant Kinney, army signal officer, "that afternoon of the fourth of August was a notable one as she steamed within range of the forts. The central figure was the grand old admiral, his plans all completed, affable with all, evidently not thinking of failure as among the possibilities of the morrow, and filling every one with his enthusiasm. He was sixty-three years old, of medium height, stoutly built, with a finely proportioned head and smoothly shaven face, with an expression combining overflowing kindliness with iron will and invincible determination, and with eyes that in repose were full of sweetness and light, but, in emergency, could flash fire and fury. Next in prominence to the admiral was the tall, commanding form of Fleet-Captain Percival Drayton, the man of all men to be Farragut's chief-of-staff, gentlemanly and courteous to all, but thoughtful and reserved, a man of marked intellect and power."

In the evening the *Tecumseh, Richmond,* and *Metacomet* arrived and at last all was in readiness for the enterprise of the morrow.

The Confederate squadron and forts mounted 103 guns:

Ram		*Gunboats*		*Forts*	
Tennessee	6 guns	Selma	4 guns	Morgan	55 guns
		Morgan	6 guns	Gaines	26 guns
		Gaines	6 guns		

The Federal squadron consisted of eighteen vessels, mounting 188 guns and howitzers:

Monitors		*Sloops*		*Gunboats*	
Tecumseh	2 guns	Hartford	24 guns	Galena	11 guns
Manhattan	2 guns	Brooklyn	25 guns	Octorara	10 guns
Winnebago	4 guns	Richmond	22 guns	Metacomet	10 guns
Chickasaw	4 guns	Lackawanna	14 guns	Port Royal	8 guns
		Monongahela	11 guns	Kennebec	5 guns
		Ossipee	12 guns	Itasca	6 guns
		Oneida	10 guns		
		Seminole	8 guns		

A number of torpedoes were planted in the channel. It seems that sixty-seven originally were laid across the entire channel and that those which were within 500 yards of Fort Morgan were taken up to give a passage for blockade runners. The remaining 1000 yards of deep water were then covered with thirty-six new torpedoes, which would give one to every eighty-six feet. It is probable that the original torpedoes were ineffective at the time of the battle. The minefield was marked by buoys known to the attacking forces.

The fourteen wooden vessels of the attacking squadron were lashed together in pairs, the largest vessels being on the right or eastern side. This had the advantage that the smaller vessels were protected from the fire of Fort Morgan, and that if the larger vessels were injured the smaller ships could carry them through. The time for the attack was specially selected so that there would be a four-knot current setting into the bay, thus expediting the passage of the forts and causing disabled ships to be carried past them. For weeks the ships had been making their preparations: upper masts and spars had been sent down; splinter nets rigged on the starboard side; ramparts of hammocks and canvas built about the pilot houses; anchor chains and sandbags laid over and outside the machinery spaces; and the boats towed along the port side. The ships were to pass to the eastward of the buoys marking the minefields, and upon reaching this position were to stop their engines and drift through, to avoid having their propellers injured by obstructions or fouled by lines. Exact column was not to be used, but each pair was to keep slightly to the right of the wake of the preceding pair, so that all ships could fire ahead.

The monitors were to precede the wooden vessels and engage the forts as the latter advanced. "The service that I look for from the ironclads," reads the order, "is, first, to neutralize as much as possible the fire of the guns which rake our approach; next to look out for the ironclads when we are abreast of the forts, and lastly, to occupy the attention of those batteries which would rake us while running up the bay." It unfortunately was not stated whether the monitors were to precede the wooden vessels past the forts or to form a second column on their right. The order "to look out for the ironclads" would seem to indicate that the monitors were to go ahead, because this is where the enemy ironclads would be. But the diagram issued before the battle shows the monitors on the right and abreast of the wooden ships, and Farragut's report, written after the battle, says that the monitors "had been ordered to take up their positions on the starboard side of the wooden ships, or between them and Fort Morgan." The orders referred to apparently were the instructions to the monitors quoted above and unfortunately were not so clear as the report believed they were.

Buchanan's plan was for his squadron to take station directly ahead of the advancing force, so as to use his full broadside fire against the few guns which they could fire ahead. When the torpedoes were passed, the *Tennessee* was to attack with the ram and guns at close quarters, while the gunboats were to maintain their positions ahead and continue to fire at moderate range.

During the evening of the 4th the Confederates could see that an attack for the morrow was impending, and both sides commenced their final preparations. According to Admiral Porter, several of the coolest officers of the attacking squadron estimated that their losses could not be less than six ships. "At sunset," writes Lieutenant Kinney, "the last orders had been issued, every commander knew his duty, and unusual quiet prevailed in the fleet. The sea was smooth, a gentle breeze relieved the midsummer heat, and the night came on serenely and peacefully, and far more quietly than to a yachting fleet at Newport. For the first hour after the candles were lighted the stillness was almost oppressive. The officers of the *Hartford* gathered around the wardroom table, writing letters to loved ones far away, or giving instructions in case of death. As brave and thoughtful men, they recognized the dangers that they did not fear, and made provision for the possibilities of the morrow. But this occupied little time, and then, business over, there followed an hour of unrestrained jollity. Old officers forgot, for the moment, their customary dignity, and it was evident that all were exhilarated and stimulated by the knowledge of the coming struggle."

In the squadron there was little fear that Fort Morgan could stop their advance; these ships had run the batteries so many times that they knew that it was merely a question as to how many casualties would be inflicted by the guns ashore. The *Tennessee*, however, undoubtedly was a formidable opponent, and her capabilities had been greatly exaggerated. No one could know that her officers, except for her captain, were so inexperienced as Buchanan later reported, or that her primers would fail, a fact, according to her captain, that lost many favorable opportunities to sink Federal vessels. But even beyond this, the torpedoes were recognized as a dangerous, almost inhuman weapon, to which it was not considered chivalrous to resort. The admiral describes this feeling in his report when he says: "Regular discipline will bring men to any amount of endurance; but there is a natural fear of hidden dangers, particularly when so awfully destructive of human life as the torpedo, which requires more than discipline to overcome." Perhaps it was with this thought that he delayed so long for the *Tecumseh*, desiring to have her intrepid captain, T. A. M. Craven, to lead the advance.

In the description which follows, every effort has been made to study and compare all the accounts of the battle, particularly the official reports of the admiral and commanding officers. Unfortunately, while voluminous, they are very conflicting and entirely fail to cover some of the most important points. We have endeavored to build up an account which is reasonable and at least consistent with itself.

A dense fog came up about midnight, but by 5:40 A.M. the ships were lashed in pairs and under way in the prescribed order. There was a light breeze from the southwest and the sky was overcast, with very little sun. The four monitors preceded the wooden ships and kept to their right. At 6:47 the *Tecumseh*, leading the monitors, opened the action with a shell which burst over the fort. Twenty minutes later Fort Morgan opened on the *Brooklyn*, and the action became general at a range of about 1000 yards. In accordance with Farragut's maxim that the best defense was a well-directed fire from his own guns, the fleet covered the fort with a deluge of fire, the monitors using shells and the wooden vessels grape-shot. Due to this fire the fort's return at first was quite ineffective. The three Confederate gunboats, however, took position directly ahead of the line and raked the leading vessels with effect. The *Tennessee* slowly came out.

The *Brooklyn* apparently understood that she was not to pass the monitors and reduced speed to keep in rear of them. When the ship was almost abreast of the fort and approaching the torpedoes, she was close upon the last monitor and distant about 700 yards from the fort. The four monitors apparently had stopped to cover the passage of the wooden ships and were distant about 500 yards from the fort.

At this instant, about 7:25 A.M., the *Brooklyn* was seen to be backing, and the admiral received the following signal from her: "The monitors are right ahead. We cannot go on without passing them. What shall we do?" As the whole line was being thrown into confusion by the *Brooklyn's* action, the admiral replied: "Go ahead."

While this reply was being sent, the *Tecumseh* sighted the *Tennessee* coming out to take position behind the torpedoes. She was firing with effect on the wooden vessels. The two leading monitors had been designated to pay special attention to the ram. There was hardly enough room for the monitors to pass to the eastward of the torpedoes, as the buoy marking their eastward limit was not over 500 yards from the fort, and possibly much less. Although the buoy was seen, Craven decided to take the *Tecumseh* to the westward of it, directly over the torpedoes and at the *Tennessee.* At about 7:30 the *Tecumseh* was seen to list violently to one side and in thirty seconds disappeared beneath the waters, carrying down ninety-three of her crew of 114 officers and men. "Craven and Mr. John Collins, the pilot of the *Tecumseh,*" writes Commodore Parker, "met, as the vessel was sinking beneath them, at the foot of the ladder leading to the top of the turret. It may be, then, that Craven, in the nobility of his soul—for all know he was one of nature's noblemen—it may be, I say, that in the nobility of his soul the thought flashed across him that it was through no fault of his pilot that the *Tecumseh* was in this peril; he drew back. 'After you, pilot,' said he, grandly. 'There was nothing after me,' relates Mr. Collins. 'When I reached the utmost round of the ladder, the vessel seemed to drop from under me.' "

This disaster, seen by both sides, had a great effect—one which might well have been decisive. It caused further confusion in the Federal fleet and elated the Confederate gunners so that they increased their fire. Thinking that the *Brooklyn* was the flagship, their fire was concentrated principally upon her, with deadly effect. The motionless ships, only 700 yards from the fort, offered perfect targets. "Owing to the *Hartford's* position," writes Lieutenant Kinney, "only her few bow guns could be used, while a deadly rain of shot and shell was falling on her, and her men were being cut down by scores, unable to make reply. The sight on deck was sickening beyond the power of words to portray." Now was Buchanan's chance to advance and ram, but he missed it, while Farragut made the momentous decision which changed defeat into victory.

At about 7:35 the *Brooklyn* again signaled: "Our best monitor has been sunk." Farragut's reply was somewhat indefinitely worded. "Tell the monitors," he said, "to go ahead and then take your place." This signal had no effect in getting the fleet again under way. From his position in the main rigging just below the top, the admiral called out to the pilot above him in the top and asked if there were enough room to pass to the left of the *Brooklyn.* When the pilot replied that there was, Farragut decided to take the lead and ordered Captain Drayton, on the deck beneath him, to go full speed ahead. The latter, with cool judgment, had the *Metacomet* back her engines as the *Hartford* went ahead, in order to swing clear of the *Brooklyn.* As the flagship passed, some one shouted over, so tradition has it, that there were torpedoes ahead. To this the admiral replied, or, more probably, said to some one near him, "Damn the torpedoes." While this tradition, as most others, does not appear to be based on any certain authority, the admiral, at any rate, expressed this idea in action, if not in words, with a certainty which no one has denied.

The *Hartford* passed over the torpedoes, and officers believed that they could hear their primers snapping against the hull. The *Brooklyn* followed the flagship at a considerable distance and the rest of the fleet closed up on her. The ships had been stopped under the guns of the forts for about twenty-five minutes.

As soon as the *Tecumseh* was seen to go down, Farragut had directed Captain Jouett of the *Metacomet* to send a boat to pick up survivors. Ensign Nields was in charge of the boat and, according to the official report, "he took her in under one of the most galling fires I ever saw, and succeeded in rescuing from death ten of her crew within 600 yards from the fort." The Confederates were not to be outdone in chivalry. "Here I must note a little incident which challenged my admiration," writes General Page, commanding Fort Morgan and a one-time officer of the United States Navy. "As the *Tecumseh* was going down, a boat was observed to shoot out from under the bow of the leading ship, with oars up and boathook in hand. Seeing her, I gave directions, 'Pass the order not to fire on that boat; she is saving drowning men.' "

As the fleet was passing the fort the three Confederate gunboats had taken position on the starboard bow of the *Hartford*, keeping on a parallel course and using their stern guns with excellent effect. Now the *Tennessee* appeared on the starboard beam endeavoring to ram. Her slow speed, however, prevented this, and, swinging to a parallel course, she followed along on the flagship's quarter and engaged her in a gun duel. Soon, seeing that her fire was not effective and that the *Hartford* was gaining on her, she turned back to attack the rest of the fleet.

Meanwhile these vessels, after a stop of some twenty-five minutes under the guns of the fort, were again proceeding, the *Brooklyn* following the *Hartford* at a distance of one mile, while the remaining vessels were closely bunched behind her. The three monitors were still between the wooden ships and the fort. As the vessels reached a position where their broadsides would bear, the fire of the fort decreased in volume. Due to the fact that its targets were under way, this fire also became less accurate, and few hits were made at this time. However, when about half the wooden ships had passed, the monitors drew past the fort, and as only the stern guns of the wooden vessels then could bear, the Confederate fire again increased in volume and accuracy, and was principally concentrated on the *Oneida*, the rear ship in the column. Her steering gear was shot away and repaired under fire; a raking shot from aft exploded one of her two boilers, scalding the fireroom force of one officer and six men. At about 8:35, however, assisted by her consort, the *Galena*, she was nearly out of range, when the *Tennessee* was seen approaching. But now we must return to a description of that vessel's first attack on the fleet.

After leaving the *Hartford* the ram had stood down toward the *Brooklyn*. For a time it appeared certain that she would strike that ship, and the *Richmond*, next astern, prepared to take advantage of the collision to ram the *Tennessee* in turn. The Confederate vessel did not succeed in hitting the *Brooklyn*, but passed a few yards astern, inflicting severe damage with her gunfire, while the *Brooklyn's* shot bounded off her sloping armor.

Being now on the port hand of the fleet, the *Tennessee* passed the *Richmond* on opposite courses at about seventy-five yards, receiving three 11-gun salvos of 9-inch solid shot, all of which struck and bounced off. The musketry fire directed at the ram's gunports was so effective that she could fire only two or three shells at the *Richmond*, and these passed harmlessly overhead. Passing the *Lackawanna* without anything of moment happening, the ram approached the *Monongahela*. "After passing the forts," says Captain Strong of the latter vessel, "I saw the rebel ram *Tennessee* head on for our line. I then sheered out of line to run into her, at the same time ordering full speed as fast as possible. I struck her fair, and swinging round, poured in a broadside of solid 11-inch shot, which apparently had little if any effect upon her." Both the *Monongahela* and the *Kennebec*, secured alongside, were injured, while the *Tennessee* was undamaged.

The ram next approached the *Oneida*, whose boiler had just been damaged. Now was Buchanan's chance for at least a small success. He appears to have made no attempt to ram, although perhaps his ship steered so poorly and had such slow speed as to make this very difficult. Passing the *Oneida* about 200 yards distant on an opposite course, his primers failed three times and he could get off but one shot, which struck the *Oneida's* after pivot gun. Due to previous injuries to her battery, that ship was able to fire but one shot in return. The ram now turned under the *Oneida's* stern and fired two raking broadsides, wounding the captain severely. "The officers and crew of the *Oneida*," reports her senior unwounded officer to the admiral, "are proud to have served in your fleet, and they are proud of their gallant commander, J. R. M. Mullany, who gave us all so noble an example of unflinching courage and heroism. His coolness in action could not possibly have been surpassed. Having scarcely become acquainted with Commander Mullany, he having only been aboard two days, the highest compliment that can be paid him is the confidence and spirit with which the crew went into action." At about 8:40 Fort Morgan ceased fire, having expended 491 rounds.

From "Battles and Leaders of the Civil War," Vol. IV

SURRENDER OF THE "TENNESSEE," BATTLE OF MOBILE BAY

Let us now return to the head of the line where we left the admiral at about 8:00. "The rebel gunboats *Morgan*, *Gaines*, and *Selma* were ahead," he reports, "and the latter particularly annoyed us with a raking fire, which our guns could not return." A single shell caused fifteen casualties on the *Hartford*, while another killed one man and wounded two on the *Metacomet*. At 8:02 Farragut called down to Jouett to cast off and attack the gunboats. The *Gaines* was heavily hit by the flagship and made for Fort Morgan in a sinking condition; the ship was run aground and the crew saved. The *Metacomet* pursued the *Morgan* and *Selma;* other gunboats cast off and joined in the pursuit. The *Morgan*, not wishing to be cut off from the fort, sheered off in that direction and left the *Selma*, after having had but one man wounded. The *Metacomet* gained rapidly on the latter and soon overpowered her with her heavy battery of ten guns. At 9:10, after a brave resistance, in which eight were killed and seven wounded, among the latter being her captain, Lieutenant Murphey, the *Selma* struck her colors, about ninety prisoners being taken. The *Morgan* escaped to the fort and during the night succeeded in getting to Mobile, as did the crew of the *Gaines* in their boats.

After leaving the *Oneida* at about 8:40, the *Tennessee* headed up the bay toward the *Hartford*, which had just come to anchor. "The thunder of heavy artillery now ceased," writes Lieutenant Kinney. "The crews of the various vessels had begun to efface the marks of the terrible contest by washing the decks and clearing up the splinters. The cooks were preparing breakfast. * * * As if by mutual understanding, officers who were relieved from immediate duty gathered in the wardroom to ascertain who of their mates were missing, and the reaction from such a season of tense nerves and excitement was just setting in, when the hurried call to quarters came and the word passed around, 'The ram is coming.' "

It was about 8:45 when the ram was sighted. Farragut quickly made his preparations for meeting his gallant antagonist. "I was not long in comprehending his intention to be the destruction of the flagship," he reports. "The monitors and such of the wooden vessels as I thought best adapted for the purpose were immediately ordered to attack the ram, not only with their guns, but bows at full speed, and then began one of the fiercest naval combats on record."

While the general signal to ram the *Tennessee* was being prepared, the admiral used the army signal officer to send special signals to the *Monongahela* and *Lackawanna* to "run down the ram." Captain Strong's report is a model of brevity. "Signal was made to my ship to again run into her. I did so." Even though the *Monongahela* struck the ram at full speed, and carried away her own iron prow and cutwater, a careful examination of the *Tennessee* after the battle failed to show where she had been hit. The *Lackawanna* next rushed down under full steam and hit the ram squarely at right angles, but it did no more than list her deeply to one side, while the sloop's bow was smashed in. As the two ships swung alongside, bow to stern, the ram fired two shells into the *Lackawanna's* bow, while all the latter's guns, save one, unfortunately were pivoted on the other broadside. One shot from this gun fired at a distance of twelve feet damaged one of the ram's gunport shutters so that the gun could not be pointed. As the two ships lay alongside, an amusing incident is reported by Captain Marchand. "A few of the enemy," he says, "were seen through their ports, who, using most opprobrious language, our marines opened upon them with muskets; even a spittoon and a holystone were thrown at them from our deck, which drove them away."

The ram now came directly for the *Hartford* and the two vessels approached bows on at full speed. At the last moment the ram sheered off a bit and the two ships crashed into each other, port bow to port bow, and grated alongside. Due to defective primers the *Tennessee* could get off but one shot, but this killed or wounded thirteen men. The *Hartford* fired her full broadside at a distance of ten feet, but the shell bounded off the armor. In order to see better, the admiral sprang upon the rail, holding on to the mizzen rigging. Fearing that he would be knocked overboard from this dangerous position, Flag-Lieutenant Watson passed a line about him.

The shell fired at the *Hartford* was the last shot from the heroic Buchanan. When there was an opportunity to fire, the primers failed in every case, but soon one after another the *Tennessee's* gunports were wrecked by the terrific fire concentrated upon her from all sides and the guns could not be pointed. Her smokestack had been weakened by the ramming, and now a shell from the *Chickasaw* knocked it over, reducing her speed to about three knots. A crowning disaster occurred when the *Manhattan* with a 15-inch shot ripped up the deck plating and wrecked the steering gear. The same vessel broke through the port casemate armor and splintered the wooden backing, while a third shot from her hit the after gunport, killing one man and badly wounding Admiral Buchanan. These two monitors maintained a position astern of the ram, Perkins firing the four 11-inch guns of the *Chickasaw* with great rapidity, while Nicholson in the *Manhattan* fired his 15-inch deliberately. Wood splinters and bolts, washers and nuts holding the armor in place began to fly about the inside of the casemate, wounding several men.

The *Hartford* and *Lackawanna*, in their eagerness to ram the *Tennessee*, collided with each other with serious damage to the former, but the admiral quickly ordered full speed and again approached the ram. By a queer coincidence he narrowly escaped being rammed a second time by the same ship. It was at this time that the admiral said to his signal officer, "Can you say 'For God's sake' by signal?" Upon receiving an affirmative reply, he said: "Then say to the *Lackawanna*, 'For God's sake get out of our way and anchor.' " The admiral later doubtless was glad that his hasty but most natural message failed in transmission.

After standing the concentrated fire of the fleet for over half an hour without being able to fire a shot in return, the *Tennessee* hoisted the white flag, just as the *Ossipee* was about to ram her. So close was that ship when the signal appeared, that even by backing full speed a slight collision could not be avoided. "Suddenly," says Lieutenant Kinney, "the terrific cannonading ceased, and from every ship rang out cheer after cheer as the weary men realized that at last the ram was captured and the day won."

Part of the *Oneida's* list of injuries reads as though the battle was being blamed for all the equipment broken or lost during the past six months: "Mobile Bay chart damaged, 1 spyglass badly damaged, 1 binnacle lamp lost overboard, 2 wardroom chairs broken by shells, 1 lead and line lost overboard, 2 sets of signal halliards cut by shell," etc.

Now that Farragut had forced the entrance, the issue still was far from being decided. In fact, were the three Confederate forts to hold out for a month, his food and coal would be exhausted and it would either have to be sent past Fort Morgan or the fleet would have to leave the bay. His position was thus the same as that in which it was feared the British fleet would find itself after running the Dardanelles. In accordance with this idea, General Gilmer, chief of engineers of the Confederate army, telegraphed to the general commanding at Mobile: "By direction of the President I offer my views. Every effort should be made to hold Forts Morgan, Gaines, and Powell, with the hope of forcing the enemy to withdraw for supplies, or at least gain time to strengthen inner defenses."

Considering the small number of men engaged, the losses were heavy:

Federal Squadron				
Ship	*Hits on hull or spars*	*Killed*	*Wounded*	*Prisoners*
Hartford	20	25	28	0
Brooklyn	30	11	43	0
Lackawanna	5	4	35	0
Oneida	15	8	30	0
Monongahela	5	0	6	0
Metacomet	10	1	2	0
Ossipee	4	1	7	0
Richmond	5 [1]	0	2	0
Galena	9	0	1	0
Octorara	11	1	10	0
Kennebec	2	1	6	0
Tecumseh	..	95	0	4
Manhattan	9	0	0	0
Winnebago	19	0	0	0
Chickasaw	5	0	0	0
	149	147	170	4
Confederate Squadron				
Tennessee	53	2	9	190 [1]
Selma	10 [1]	8	7	90 [1]
Gaines	17	2	3	0
Morgan	6	0	1	0
	86	12	20	280

[1] Estimated.

Fort Powell mounted eight guns, had a garrison of 140 men and additional negro laborers, and was supplied with water for one month and food for two months. The rear bastions, however, had just been commenced and the two guns mounted in this direction were exposed. On the afternoon of the battle the *Chickasaw* bombarded Fort Powell with twenty-five rounds, which had no material but much moral effect. The commanding officer did not consider that he could send his men out in the open to fire the guns which would bear, and during the evening he abandoned the fort, after spiking the guns and blowing up the magazine. This opened Grant's Pass and allowed Farragut to obtain supplies through it.

Fort Gaines was a powerful work, mounting twenty-six guns, and having a garrison of 818 and provisions for six months. Here a long siege was expected, and in fact Granger reported: "Captains McAlester and Palfrey coincide with me that it is neither practicable nor profitable to besiege Gaines." Farragut viewed matters in a more optimistic light, and while the *Chickasaw* was firing on Powell he proposed to Granger that he carry Gaines by assault in a night attack. The general replied that the fort would have to be breached. The next day the *Chickasaw* fired thirty-one rounds at the fort, and early on the 7th the commandant offered to surrender. Farragut says that the garrison was composed of recruits, but the Confederate authorities were incensed at the early surrender.

On this day Farragut issued a characteristic general order: "The admiral desires the fleet to return thanks to Almighty God for the signal victory over the enemy on the morning of the 5th instant."

On the 8th Washington received accurate news of the victory from the Richmond newspapers.

All that remained now was to gather in the remaining spoils of victory at Fort Morgan. Granger landed on the beach east of the fort and commenced regular approaches against it. By the 23d the fort had been made untenable by the fire of shore batteries and the monitors, and, after a brave resistance, surrendered. The United States ensign was hoisted over the fort to the accompaniment of a 100-gun salute and cheers from the fleet.

Farragut's campaign had completely stopped the flow of supplies from the outside world through Mobile, and this contributed toward Sherman's successes in Georgia and the fall of the Confederacy in the following spring.

CHAPTER VII

The Sea of Japan

THE Straits of Tsushima twice before the Russo-Japanese War witnessed momentous struggles vital to the existence of the Japanese empire.

In the thirteenth century the ancestors of the present Japanese and Russian races met in an epic struggle. As early as 1263 Korea was overrun by the Mongols. The next year under Jenghiz Khan they marched down the Nankai Pass and established their capital at Kambaluc, the site of modern Peking. Fifteen years later Kublai Khan completed the conquest of China. As early as 1268 he sent an embassy to Japan suggesting that annual tribute be sent to him as emperor. The Japanese refused even to acknowledge receipt of the envoy's message.

In 1274 Kublai embarked a force of 25,000 Mongols and 12,000 Koreans in 900 vessels, manned by 8000 Korean sailors. This armament first attacked Tsushima, where So Sukekuni with 200 warriors resisted to the end. Ikishima also was captured and the invaders landed on Hakozaki Gulf, where they were attacked by five chieftains. While the Japanese *bushi* fought with their usual bravery, the numbers, tactics, and artillery of the Mongols forced them to retire at nightfall behind their fortifications. Among the interesting facts of this battle was the use of gunpowder in metal tubes. While these ancient cannon are reported to have inflicted heavy losses, it may be assumed that their moral effect upon the surprised Japanese was even greater. The Japanese cavalry was routed by mere noise, their horses getting out of hand when the Mongols raised a din with drums and gongs. Fortunately for the Japanese, that night a gale forced the Mongols to put to sea, where so many ships were lost and damaged that the expedition had to be abandoned. (See Figure on p. 235.)

Seven years later Kublai repeated the attempt on a larger scale. An army of 100,000 Mongols and Chinese embarked from Chinese ports opposite Formosa in a fleet of large seagoing junks. At Tsushima they were to meet a Korean fleet carrying 70,000 Mongol and Korean soldiers. This force was the first to arrive at the meeting place. In May, 1281, it landed on Tsushima, but could not reduce the garrison. A month later the Chinese fleet arrived, Ikishima was captured, and the combined forces landed at Hakozaki Bay. This time, however, the Japanese fortifications were stronger and their forces larger. For fifty-three days the two armies were deadlocked in continual fighting. On August 14 a storm broke over the battlefield and destroyed the greater part of the Mongol fleet; 12,000 Chinese soldiers were made slaves, and Kublai had lost his campaign. This storm was called the *Kamikaze*, or divine wind, by the Japanese.

When the great leader Hideyoshi had subdued Japan he decided to use his great armies to overrun China through Korea. In May, 1592, just four years after the

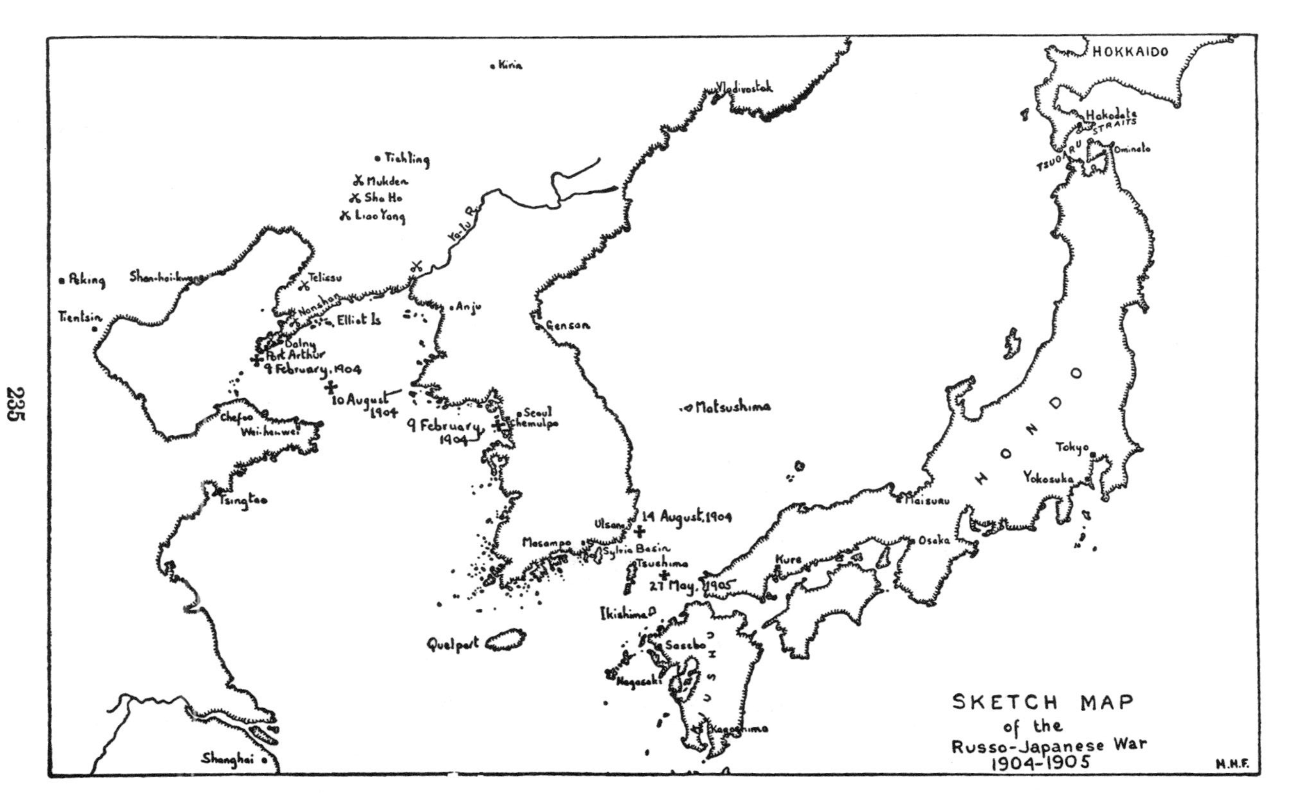
SKETCH MAP
of the
Russo-Japanese War
1904-1905
HOKKAIDO
Hakodate
TSUGARU STRAITS
Ominato
HONDO
Tokyo
Yokosuka
Maizuru
Osaka
Kure
Kagoshima
Sasebo
Nagasaki
Ikishima
Tsushima
27 May, 1905
14 August, 1904
Ulsan
Sylvia Basin
Masampo
Matsushima
Vladivostok
Gensan
Seoul
Chemulpo
9 February 1904
Quelpart
Anju
Ya-lu R.
Kirin
Tiehling
Mukden
Sha Ho
Liao Yang
Telissu
Nanshan
Elliot Is
Dalny
Port Arthur
9 February, 1904
10 August 1904
Chefoo
Wei-hai-wei
Tsingtao
Shanghai
Shan-hai-kwan
Peking
Tientsin
H.M.F.

Spanish Armada, his first corps of 20,000 troops landed on the Korean coast opposite Tsushima, and was soon followed by a second of equal strength. It required only nineteen days for these two corps to march the 270 miles to Seoul, whose walls of 30,000 battlements were found deserted. The Koreans were beaten in several battles and withdrew to the Yalu. By this time the Japanese had been reinforced to a strength of about 200,000 and Korea was being developed as a base for the invasion of China.

But now an unexpected development occurred. The Japanese pirates had long harried the neighboring coasts in their small rowing boats. The Chinese had found that they could not stand up against the Japanese swordsmen in fair fight, for their swords were of incomparable steel and their courage equal to their weapons. The Chinese, therefore, built roofs of heavy timbers over their vessels, so that their archers were inaccessible. The Korean admiral Yi Sun-sin improved upon this scheme by covering the timbers with sheet iron and piercing the ship's sides with loopholes, through which his archers could shoot from positions almost as secure as our modern turrets. With a fleet of eighty such vessels Yi Sun-sin defeated the Japanese in five engagements, in the last of which seventy of their ships were sunk.

Hideyoshi had counted on using oversea transport to bring food directly to his army as it advanced along the coast of the Yellow Sea, just as Xerxes had done twenty-two centuries before. This disaster to his fleet brought the victorious Japanese army to a halt, giving the Chinese the time to place a powerful army in the field and to encourage the Koreans to conduct guerrilla warfare. After a six years' campaign, during which the Japanese regained the command of the sea, they withdrew from Korea without any material gains.

The war with China in 1894 resembled in many respects Hideyoshi's campaigns. The result was due to two marked differences: First, within two months the Japanese had definitely won the command of the sea in two engagements in which six Chinese ships were lost; second, the Koreans offered no resistance. Port Arthur was stormed, and the fall of Wei-hai-wei, with the destruction of the remaining Chinese naval vessels, forced the Dragon flag to be lowered before that of the Rising Sun.

The next ten years was marked by the rapid rise of Russia in the Far East. Not only was Port Arthur strongly fortified and connected with Russia by rail, but a formidable fleet, called the First Pacific Squadron, was based upon it. Japan, realizing that the struggle was inevitable, rapidly developed her army and navy. During the early morning of February 9, 1904, the war commenced with a surprise attack of ten Japanese destroyers on the Russian fleet outside Port Arthur.

The First Pacific Squadron was most unfavorably disposed for war. At Port Arthur was a battle fleet of seven battleships, one armored cruiser, one first class and two third class cruisers, two gunboats, twenty-five destroyers and two minelayers. At Chemulpo were one first class cruiser and one gunboat; at Vladivostok were three armored and one first class cruiser. The Japanese fleet, which was approximately equal to the Russian forces, comprised six battleships, eight armored cruisers, ten second class and seventeen third class cruisers and nineteen destroyers; it had the advantage of being concentrated in one body.

The initial operations of the Japanese took advantage of the scattered dispositions of the Russian forces. In the night attack off Port Arthur two battleships and one cruiser were torpedoed, and the two Russian vessels at Chemulpo were destroyed the same day by overwhelming forces. Leaving a cruiser force to watch the Vladivostok squadron, Admiral Togo established a base in the Elliot Islands, drove in the Russian battle fleet and commenced a close blockade of Port Arthur. The Russians there had a minelayer sunk and at Vladivostok their first class cruiser was wrecked.

The command of the sea being now temporarily secured, the First Army, of three divisions, landed in Korea and on May 1, under Kuroki's leadership, forced the passage of the Yalu into Manchuria. Two days later the Second Army, also of three divisions, landed to the northeast of Port Arthur, on the 26th stormed the Nanshan position, took Dalny, and invested the Russian base. The Third Army, of three divisions, landed at Dalny and under Nogi took over the siege of Port Arthur, while General Oku with the Second Army marched up the railroad toward Liaoyang.

The Russians had sent out the renowned Admiral Makaroff to bring their battle fleet to the proper fighting edge, and he was beginning to accomplish this when a mine carried down the battleship *Petropavlovsk* with him aboard. The Japanese made three attempts to close the entrance to Port Arthur by sinking merchant vessels in it at night, but were only partly successful. If these operations had little material effect, the heroism of the devoted officers and men who eagerly volunteered for this hazardous duty had an inspiring moral effect, not only on the navy but upon all of their chivalrous race. In the last enterprise only forty-four of the 159 officers and men who took part in it returned unhurt. Mines also were responsible for the loss of two Japanese battleships, while a second class cruiser was sunk by collision. On June 15 the Vladivostok squadron suddenly appeared off Tsushima and sank two transports which were carrying the heavy siege guns to be used against Port Arthur.

Just one day before this incident a Russian army pushing down the railroad to relieve Port Arthur was defeated at Telissu and forced back on Liaoyang. The Fourth Army, of two divisions, was landed between Kuroki and Oku, and all three under the superior command of Oyama commenced a concentric advance upon Liaoyang. Nogi meanwhile had been forcing the siege of Port Arthur so strongly that Admiral Vitgeft decided on August 10 to force his way through to Vladivostok. After a long and indecisive engagement two shells struck the bridge and conning tower of the Russian flagship, killing the admiral and jamming the steering gear. The fleet then broke up in confusion; one battleship, three cruisers and five destroyers were lost to the Russians, thus reducing their battle fleet to five battleships, two cruisers and three destroyers, and of these the armored cruiser *Bayan* was in drydock for extensive repairs.

Four days later Vice-Admiral Kamimura brought to action the Vladivostok squadron, sinking the *Rurik* and badly damaging the other two armored cruisers. The end of the *Rurik* was worthy of the old Norse founder of Russia. The command finally devolved upon Lieutenant Iwanof, whose heroism brought laurels to the Russian man-of-war ensign. "All the guns on board," says the ship's chaplain, "were smashed except one; but the brave lieutenant kept on firing as long as there were any shells left to be fired and any gun fit for use. * * * Finding nothing but dismounted guns lying helpless among the heaps of corpses, Lieutenant Iwanof commanded the ship to be blown up and sunk. On being informed that not even a fuse was left on the ship, everything being smashed to atoms, he ordered the sea valves to be opened. * * * Our surviving officers and men—600 in all—raised loud and gallant cheers when they were about to be buried in the ocean with their ship."

The loss of another Russian battleship by a mine on August 28 definitely proved that the First Pacific Squadron could accomplish nothing unless powerful reinforcements were received from Europe.

On September 3 the great battle of Liaoyang terminated in an indecisive victory for the Japanese and in October Kuropatkin took the offensive on the *Shaho*, only to sustain a costly check. On the last day of the year Port Arthur fell, a few days after General Kondratenko, the spirit of the defense, was killed in the

Courtesy Japanese Navy Department

THE JAPANESE FLEET IN THE FIRST PART OF THE ACTION

front lines. General Nogi's army reinforced Oyama, who in March won the battle of Mukden.

On October 15, 1904, Admiral Rozhestvenski had sailed from Libau with the Second Pacific Squadron, consisting of seven battleships, five cruisers, eight destroyers and a number of auxiliaries. Most of these ships had either just been completed or were very old; many had only recently been commissioned; all had poorly organized and untrained crews. Even before leaving, the ships had suffered many material casualties, and the unreliability of their personnel was soon thereafter demonstrated by the Dogger Bank incident, where fire was opened on English fishing vessels mistaken for Japanese torpedo-boats.

The Hamburg-Amerika Company was given the contract for fueling the fleet and no less than seventy colliers left English and German ports to wait for the detachments of the fleet in their appointed ports of call.

At Tangier the squadron separated. Rozhestvenski, with five battleships, three cruisers, five auxiliaries, one hospital ship and one ocean tug, proceeded around the Cape of Good Hope; Felkerzam, with two battleships, two cruisers, four destroyers and nine auxiliaries, went through the Suez Canal. On January 9 the two detachments united in Nosse Be, Madagascar. Two days earlier the admiral, in response to a request for permission to proceed immediately to the Far East, had received orders to wait for the overtaking squadron. This force, consisting of two cruisers, five destroyers (including some left behind by the other detachments) and two auxiliaries, did not arrive until February 14. Rozhestvenski used this time to carry out a program of fleet training; but the tactical exercises resulted only in continual breakdowns for the destroyers, and the target practice was so poor that the admiral did not consider that it justified the expenditure of his service ammunition.

Still further delays ensued because the contractors refused to supply the fleet with fuel as far as the China coast, as their original contract provided. New contracts had to be made. Meanwhile news of the Mukden defeat came in. This and the long delays much reduced the fleet's morale.

On March 16 the Second Pacific Squadron sailed, all ships having heavy deck loads of coal and the destroyers being towed by the auxiliaries. The voyage of this force of forty-five vessels to Kamranh Bay in Indo-China, a distance of 4500 miles, was a really great feat. The squadron was under way continuously for twenty-nine days, coaling from small boats whenever the weather permitted.

At Kamranh and near-by ports Rozhestvenski waited for the Third Pacific Squadron, which, under Rear-Admiral Nebogatov, had sailed from Libau on February 15. This squadron, of one battleship, three coast-defense vessels and four auxiliaries, had originally been rejected by the Russian admiral. But, after successfully holding target practice off the Arabian coast, it made the long cruise to Indo-China in twenty-six days of continuous steaming. On May 9 the junction of the two squadrons greatly raised the morale of the crews and all were resolved to make a supreme effort to reverse the fortunes of war which had set so continually against the Russians.

On May 14 the combined squadrons sailed on their last cruise. Rozhestvenski had before him one of the most difficult problems which had ever confronted a naval commander. Because of the impossibility of supplying his squadron with fuel in Vladivostok, the only naval base now left to the Russians, his only hope lay in seeking an early decision by battle. While the statements as to his intentions are obscure, the fact that he headed directly for the Straits of Tsushima and passed through them in daylight, shows that he realized that battle was necessary; he could, however, have had little confidence in its result.

The composition of the Russian squadrons is shown in the table on page 244.

In addition to these forces the admiral despatched the auxiliary cruisers *Kuban* and *Terek* to show themselves off the eastern coast of Japan, and the *Dnyepr* and *Rion* to operate in the Yellow Sea. It was hoped that the appearance of these vessels would lead the Japanese to disperse their forces. Six additional auxiliaries were sent into Shanghai. As on the 23d, the weather was calm, and sufficient coal was taken on board so that all vessels would have their normal load on the 26th. Admiral Felkerzam died at this time, but his death was concealed from the fleet and his flag left flying from the *Oslyabya*.

On the evening of the 25th Japanese radio was heard. During the next day tactical exercises were held. "Once

First Division (4 first class battleships)	*Second Division* (1 first class and 2 second class battleships and 1 armored cruiser)	*Third Division* (1 second class battleship and 3 coast-defense vessels)
Knyaz Suvorov (Rozhestvenski) Imperator Alexandr III Borodino Orel	Oslyabya (Felkerzam) Sissoi Veliki Navarin Admiral Nakhimov	Imperator Nikolai I (Nebogatov) General-Admiral Apraxin Admiral Seniavin Admiral Ushakov

First Cruiser Division (2 first class and 2 armored cruisers)	*Second Cruiser Division* (1 second class and 2 auxiliary cruisers)
Oleg (Enquist) Avrora Dimitri Donskoi Vladimir Monomakh	Svietlana (Shein) Ural Almaz

First Flotilla (2 third class cruisers and 4 destroyers)	*Second Flotilla* (5 destroyers)
Zhemtshug Izumrud Byedovi Buini Bravi Buistri	Blestyaschi Bezupretshni Bodri Gromki Grozni

Auxiliaries	
Yaroslav (Radlov) Kamchatka (armed) Irtuish (armed) Anaduir (armed) Koreya	Rus (tug) Svir (tug) Kostroma (hospital ship) Orel (hospital ship)

again," writes Semenoff, "and for the last time, we were forciby reminded of the old truism that a 'fleet' is created by long years of practice at sea in time of peace (cruising, not remaining in port), and that a collection of ships of various types hastily collected, which have only learned to sail together on the way to the scene of operations, is no fleet, but a chance concourse of vessels." At the conclusion of the exercises the following general signal was sent to the fleet: "To-morrow at the hoisting of colors battle flags are to be sent up." The long-awaited test of battle was now just over the horizon.

Meanwhile, the main body of the Japanese fleet had been withdrawn during December to home ports for a complete overhaul of three months. On February 27 Admiral Dewa was sent to the southward with a cruiser force and scouted the coasts as far as Singapore. In that port on March 16 news of the departure of the Russian fleet from Madagascar was received and Dewa rejoined the fleet. Early in April the vessels left their home ports and, concentrating at a secret base in Sylvia Bay on the Korean coast, commenced a schedule of tactical exercises and long-range target practice. Vice-Admiral Kamimura laid a field of 715 mines off Vladivostok and then joined Togo with his entire force. Rear-Admiral Shimamura, who had been operating in the Hokkaido area, was ordered to join the fleet with all his force, except a coast-defense vessel, two auxiliary cruisers and a torpedo flotilla in the Tsugaru Straits.

The Japanese forces, omitting torpedo-boats and despatch vessels, were organized as follows:

<table>
<tr><th colspan="6">FIRST FLEET (TOGO)</th></tr>
<tr><td colspan="3">First Division
(4 first class battleships and 2 armored cruisers)</td><td colspan="3">Third Division
(2 second class and 2 third class cruisers)</td></tr>
<tr><td colspan="3">Mikasa (Togo)
Shikishima
Fuji
Asahi
Kasuga
Nisshin (Misu)</td><td colspan="3">Kasagi (Dewa)
Chitose
Otawa
Niitaka</td></tr>
<tr><td colspan="2">First Flotilla
(5 destroyers)</td><td colspan="2">Second Flotilla
(4 destroyers)</td><td colspan="2">Third Flotilla
(4 destroyers)</td></tr>
<tr><th colspan="6">SECOND FLEET (KAMIMURA)</th></tr>
<tr><td colspan="3">Second Division
(6 armored cruisers)</td><td colspan="3">Fourth Division
(2 second class and 2 third class cruisers)</td></tr>
<tr><td colspan="3">Idzumo (Kamimura)
Adzuma
Asama
Tokiwa
Yakumo
Iwate (Shimamura)</td><td colspan="3">Naniwa (Uriu)
Takachiho
Akashi
Tsushima</td></tr>
<tr><td colspan="3">Fourth Flotilla
(4 destroyers)</td><td colspan="3">Fifth Flotilla
(4 destroyers)</td></tr>
</table>

THIRD FLEET (KATAOKA)		
Fifth Division (1 battleship second class and 3 third class cruisers)	*Sixth Division* (4 third class cruisers)	*Seventh Division* (1 battleship third class, 1 coast-defense vessel and 4 gunboats)
Itsukushima (Kataoka) Chinyen Matushima Hashidate (Takedomi)	Suma (Togo) Chiyoda Idzumi Akitsushima	Fuso (Yamada) Tsukushi Takao Maya Chokai Uji
AUXILIARY CRUISERS (OGURA)		
Taichu Maru America Maru Mashu Maru Tainan Maru	Yawata Maru Sadu Maru Shinano Maru	

The opposing fleets may be compared as follows:

Types of ships	RUSSIAN		JAPANESE	
	Number	*Displacement*	*Number*	*Displacement*
Battleships, first class..	5	66,906	4	57,640
Battleships, second class	3	30,278	1	7,220
Battleships, third class.	..	......	1	3,718
Coast-defense vessels..	3	12,378	1	1,750
Armored cruisers	3	20,467	8	73,209
Total armored vessels	14	130,029	15	143,537
Cruisers, first class....	2	13,305	..	......
Cruisers, second class..	1	3,828	7	29,552
Cruisers, third class...	2	6,160	8	23,671
Total cruisers	5	23,293	15	53,223

If we omit from the armored vessels three Russian armored cruisers and the Japanese second and third class battleships and coast-defense vessels, all of which were more than fifteen years old, we find that the Japanese had an advantage of thirteen to eleven in displacement totals of armored ships. The battle speed of the two Japanese armored divisions was fifteen to sixteen knots, against ten knots for the three Russian divisions. The Japanese had a five to two advantage in cruiser displacements and an even greater preponderance in auxiliary cruisers; these advantages would facilitate their obtaining information of the enemy during the battle approach. The Japanese also had a superiority of twenty-one destroyers and forty-five torpedo-boats, against nine destroyers, and this gave them a great advantage in night fighting. The Japanese ships generally were more modern than the Russian and in very much better material condition. The Japanese probably had an advantage in material of two to one.

But it was in personnel that they had an even greater advantage. The Japanese had received the experience of a year's war operations; they had been carefully drilled in tactics and had just completed target practice. Their morale was of the highest. The Russians were without war experience; their tactical training had been elementary; their target practice had been discontinued because it was considered a waste of ammunition. The Japanese had an advantage of at least two to one in efficiency of personnel.

Despite the disadvantages under which they must

fight, the Russians had been greatly encouraged by the junction of the two squadrons, and according to Semenoff "were cheerful and eager for the fray." At least they were prepared, as Russians always have been, to resist to the end.

In order to avoid night attacks by the Japanese torpedo craft, Rozhestvenski had regulated his course and speed to pass to the eastward of Tsushima at noon of the 27th. At sunset of the 26th half the guns' crews were placed on watch, while the other half slept, fully dressed, at their stations. "The night came on dark," says Semenoff. "The mist seemed to grow denser and through it but few stars could be seen. On the dark deck there prevailed a strained stillness, broken at times only by the sighs of the sleepers, the steps of an officer, or by an order given in an undertone. Near the guns the motionless figures of their crews seemed like dead, but all were wide awake, gazing keenly into the darkness. Was not that the dark shadow of a torpedo-boat? They listened attentively. Surely the throb of her engines and the noise of steam must betray an invisible foe?" The admiral at 3 A.M. went to sleep on a chair on the bridge. Fancy the thoughts of this brave old sailor, aged with the terrific responsibility of the last months, as he dropped into a doze.

During the night the Japanese fleet was disposed as follows: The First, Second, and Fourth Divisions were in Douglas Inlet; the Fifth Division, the Sixth Division, less *Akitsushima* and *Idzumi*, and the Seventh Division, less *Fuso*, were in Osaki Bay; seventy miles southwest of Tsushima was a scouting line of four

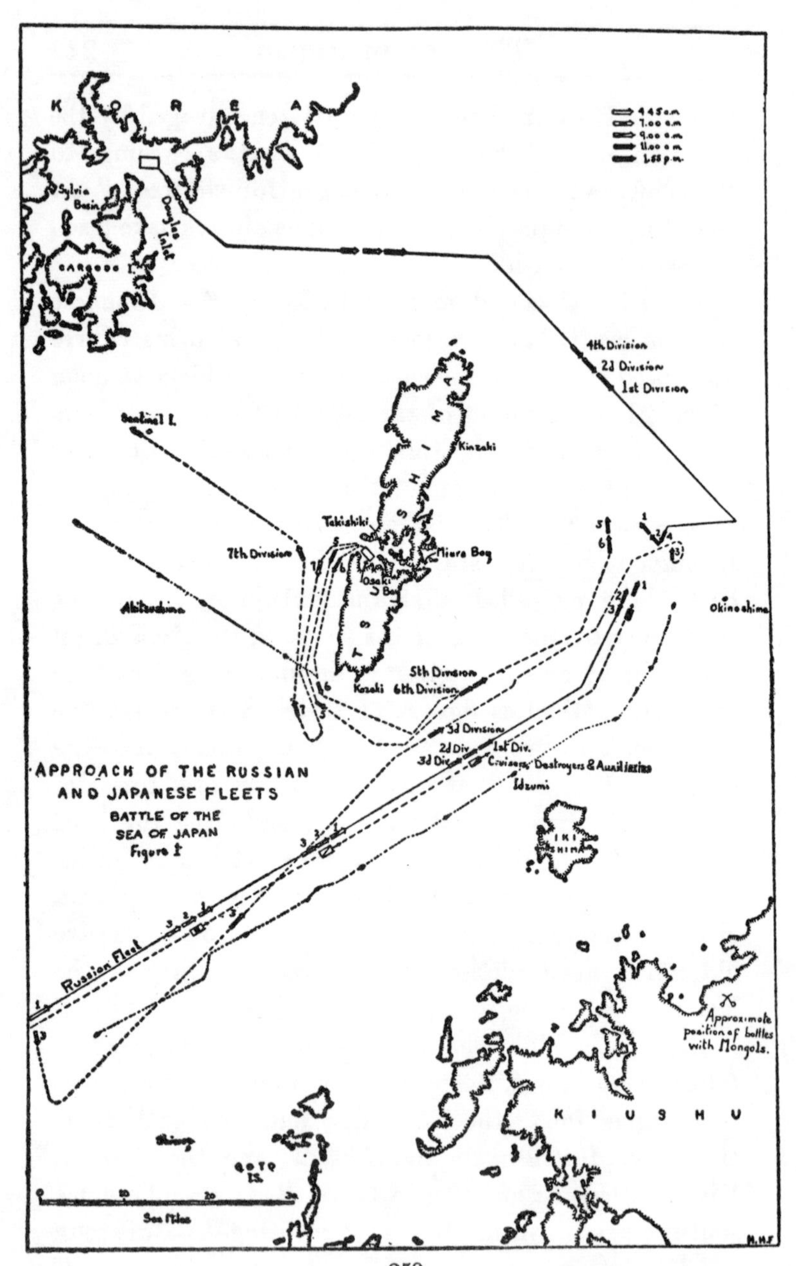
K O R E A
4.45 a.m.
7.00 a.m.
9.00 a.m.
11.00 a.m.
1.55 p.m.
Sylvia Basin
Douglas Inlet
4th Division
2d Division
1st Division
Sentinel I.
Kinzaki
Takishiki
Miura Bay
7th Division
Osaki
Okinoshima
5th Division
Kozaki
6th Division
3d Division
2d Div.
1st Div.
3d Div.
Cruisers, Destroyers & Auxiliaries
Idzumi
APPROACH OF THE RUSSIAN
AND JAPANESE FLEETS
BATTLE OF THE
SEA OF JAPAN
Russian Fleet
Approximate position of battles with Mongols.
K I U S H U
GOTO IS.
Sea Miles
M.H.F.

auxiliary cruisers, and some fifteen miles in rear a second line with the Third Division in the center and the *Akitsushima* and *Idzumi* on the northern and southern flanks respectively. The *Fuso* was patroling off the southern point of Tsushima.

At 2:45 A.M., Japanese time, the auxiliary cruiser *Shinano Maru* sighted a single vessel steaming northeast through the misty moonlight. At about 4:30 A.M. this craft was made out to be a Russian hospital ship; about 4:45 the Russian fleet was sighted, and this important discovery was flashed by radio to the Japanese fleet. The Russian course was reported as east-northeast, and this indicated that they intended to pass to the eastward of Tsushima.

The Third Division, under Vice-Admiral Dewa, steamed to the southeast toward the contact, but missed its objective. The flood of radio despatches indicated to Rozhestvenski that he had been sighted. He recalled the *Svietlana*, *Almaz*, and *Ural* from their advanced position and had them guard the rear of the auxiliaries. At 6:45 the *Idzumi* made contact and broadcasted the Russian position. Dewa, finding himself some twenty-five miles to the southward, turned about toward the reported position. At 7:05 the *Suvorov* made out the *Idzumi* on her starboard beam, and Rozhestvenski allowed her to maintain this position, as he felt he could not risk his two good cruisers in the low visibility, for fear that they might be cut off by superior forces. In consequence Togo received constant reports of the enemy's dispositions, while Rozhestvenski knew nothing of the Japanese forces save what he could see with his own eyes.

Vice-Admiral Kataoka, after taking in the despatch from the *Shinano Maru*, forwarded it on to Togo and ordered the Third fleet to prepare for battle. The *Suma* and *Chiyoda* of the Sixth Division, under Rear-Admiral Togo, stood out to the southward at 5:44, accompanied by eight torpedo-boats. Kataoka quickly followed with the Fifth Division and seventeen torpedo-boats. Apparently the Seventh Division likewise proceeded out to join Rear-Admiral Yamada in the *Fuso*.

At 9:55 Kataoka made contact with the Russian fleet when about seven and one-half miles to the southward of Kozaki. Turning to port with the Fifth Division, he took up a position about five miles on the port bow of the *Suvorov*. The *Akitsushima* returned from her position on the scouting line and joined the Sixth Division. The *Idzumi* also was ordered to rejoin, but her captain, believing that he alone was in contact with the Russian fleet, properly continued to hold his position south of the enemy. Rozhestvenski, believing that the Japanese were preparing to attack his port flank, formed the twelve vessels of his three armored divisions in column, with the cruisers, destroyers, and auxiliaries to the right and rear.

At 10:42 the Third Division, which was coming up from the southward, sighted the Russian fleet and at 11:20 came into position on its port quarter. At 11:42 the *Orel* opened fire on the Third Division at 8000 meters. After the Russians had expended about thirty rounds, fire ceased on signal from the *Suvorov*. The

Third Division, easing out of range, gradually worked up into a position ahead of the Russians. At 12:20 the *Suvorov* headed 23° (true) for Vladivostok. "I happened," says Semenoff, "to look in at the wardroom at the psychological moment. Although the dishes were being handed anyhow, and whatever came nearest was taken, champagne sparkled in the glasses, and every one was standing up, silently listening to the toast proposed by the senior officer, A. P. Makedonsky. 'On this, the great anniversary of the sacred coronation of their Highnesses, may God help us to serve with honor our beloved country! To the health of the Emperor! The Empress! to Russia!' The wardroom resounded with cheers, and their last echoes had scarcely died away ere the alarm sounded on deck."

Meanwhile Togo had been approaching for battle. At 5:05 A.M. he had received the first reports of the enemy and despatched a message which well shows his aggressive temperament: "I have just received the news that the enemy's fleet has been sighted. Our fleet will forthwith proceed to sea to attack the enemy and destroy him!" "All around us," writes Commander Togo of the *Asahi*, "our vessels were emitting clouds of black smoke, and the fleet presented a more than usually grand appearance, which in our eyes already overwhelmed the Russians." At 6:34 Admiral Togo led out the First, Second, and Fourth Divisions, seventeen destroyers, and eleven torpedo-boats. "The one chance in the world had come for us," says Commander Togo, "and the hearts of all officers and men beat high with joyful courage and daring." Reports from his cruisers kept Togo constantly informed of the enemy's movements and dispositions; he headed toward Okinoshima, intending to engage in this vicinity. The W.S.W. wind, of force five, had built up such a rough sea that he had to send the torpedo-boats into Miura Bay. At noon Togo arrived at Okinoshima and at 1:15 sighted the Third Division bearing S.W. by W. and the Fifth and Sixth Divisions to the westward. At 1:39 he sighted the Russian fleet seven miles to the southwest and decided to attack it from the westward, changing course to N.W. by N. at sixteen knots to cross its line of advance.

Soon after the Russian fleet had set its course for Vladivostok at 12:20, the Japanese cruisers dropped out of sight. Wishing to confuse their reports, Rozhestvenski decided to alter his formation, but before his plan was fully executed the Japanese cruisers again appeared. The manœuver was broken off and resulted in the First Division being in a separate column somewhat to the right of that formed by the Second and Third Divisions. This was a satisfactory cruising formation and Rozhestvenski decided to hold it for the present.

By 1:55 the Japanese First and Second Divisions were directly ahead of the Russians. The Third and Fourth Divisions followed them, and the Fifth and Sixth were about seven miles to the westward. The First and Third Destroyer Flotillas kept station on the unengaged side of the First Division; the Second and Fourth took a similar post near the Second Division; the Fourth was near the Third Division. Togo turned

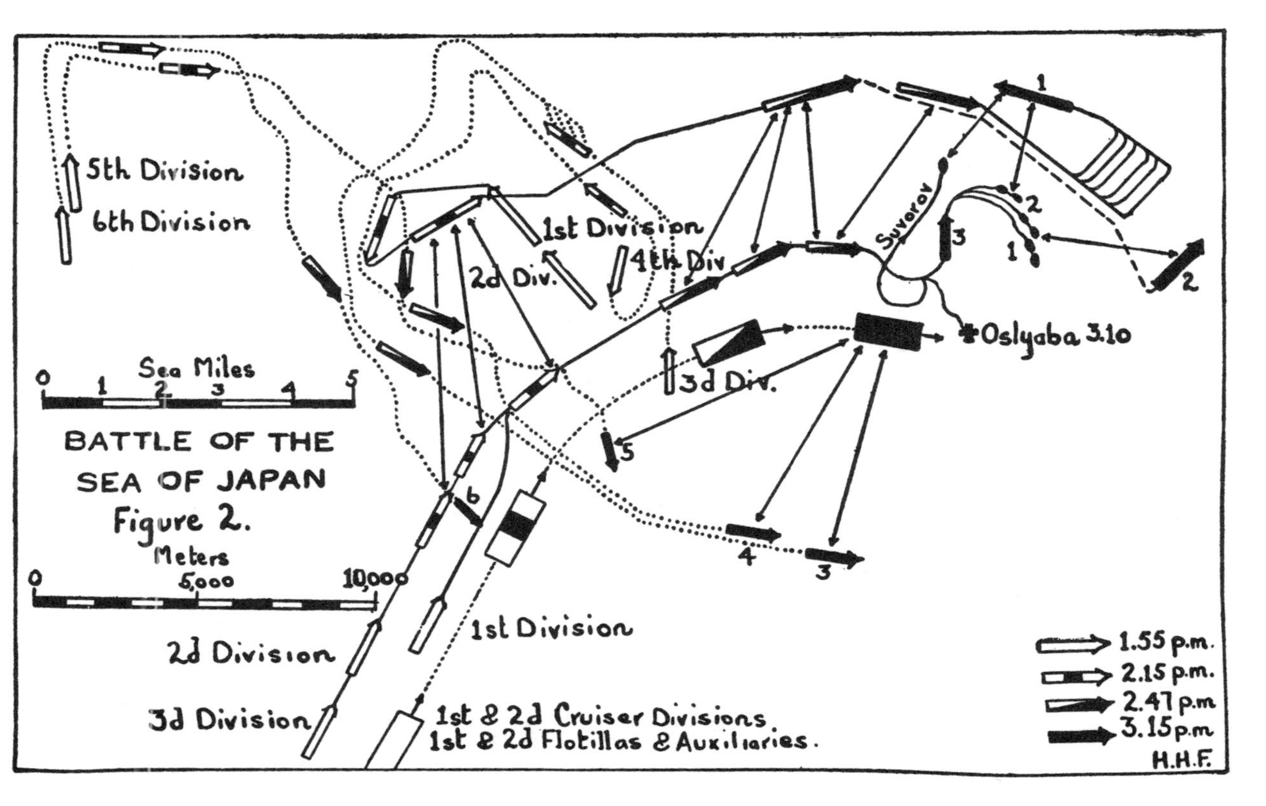

BATTLE OF THE SEA OF JAPAN
Figure 2.

west, battle flags broke out from his mastheads, and on the *Mikasa* signal flags spelled his last signal: "On this battle depends the rise or fall of our empire; do your utmost!"

At this time Rozhestvenski for the first time sighted the Japanese fleet. He headed the First Division slightly to the left and increased speed to eleven knots to take station ahead of the Second Division and thus re-form his battle column of twelve ships. The *Zhemtshug* and *Izumrud* and destroyers of the First Flotilla kept on the starboard beam of the *Suvorov;* the First and Second Cruiser Divisions, the Second Destroyer Flotilla, four auxiliaries and two tugs took station to starboard and rear of the Third Division.

At 2:02 Togo changed course to S.W. by W. and it appeared to the Russians that an action on opposite courses was probable, but four minutes later the *Mikasa* turned sharply to the eastward and steadied on E.N.E. The Russians viewed with "both delight and amazement" this daring manœuver. "Rozhestvenski," says Semenoff, "hastened to avail himself of this favorable opportunity."

Just at 2:08, as the second Japanese ship made the turn, the *Suvorov* opened fire at about 6500 meters. She was quickly followed by the vessels of the First and Second Divisions. By this time single column had been re-formed, and if it was somewhat irregular, this was of no practical disadvantage; certainly the Russians enjoyed an enormous tactical advantage over their enemy.

For two minutes the Japanese did not fire and then

Courtesy Japanese Navy Department

THE RUSSIAN FLEET RECEIVING HEAVY PUNISHMENT DURING THE FIRST PHASE OF THE ENGAGEMENT

only two ships, the *Mikasa* and *Shikishima,* opened up. At 2:11 the *Fugi* joined, followed the next minute by the *Asahi.* Thus, for the first four minutes of the action the Japanese had only from two to four ships firing against eight Russian ships. The range, which had decreased to about 5500 meters, was such as to permit full effectiveness of gunfire. It was not until 2:15 that the *Kasuga* and *Nisshin,* the two rear ships of the First Division, were able to open fire. At that time Togo headed in to close the range, and by 2:18 it had been reduced to 4600 yards and even the 3-inch batteries were in action. Togo then paralleled the enemy.

At 2:15 the *Idzumo,* leading the Second Division, swung about in rear of the First Division and commenced firing, but it required until 2:22 before the last ship of this division could fire. Thus it required some fourteen minutes after the *Suvorov* opened fire for the Japanese to bring their full force into the action. As a slight offset the four very small and weak ships of the Russian Third Division were unable to fire until about 2:18 and then at a range greater than that of the other divisions. From the tactical viewpoint the Russians had a great advantage during this period, and with effective gunnery they might have partly neutralized the Japanese superiority.

But the ineffectiveness of the Russian gunnery justified Togo's acceptance of the temporary tactical disadvantage. While his ships were surrounded by the splashes from Russian projectiles, very few reached their targets and these did not inflict important damage.

Of the six ships in the First Division, four opened on the *Oslyabya* and two on the *Suvorov;* in the Second Division one fired on the *Suvorov,* three at the *Oslyabya* and one at the *Nikolai,* the target of the *Asama* not being stated. The Japanese were somewhat slow in straddling their targets; but once on, their fire became extremely rapid and deadly, being shifted to new targets whenever this would increase its effectiveness. The first hit on the *Suvorov* pierced her side under the center 6-inch turret and set fire to the officers' quarters; the second exploded in the superstructure and wounded many of the after signal party.

"In all seriousness," says Semenoff, "I had intended in the present engagement to note the times and places where we were hit, as well as the damage done. But how could I make detailed notes when it seemed impossible even to count the number of projectiles striking us? I had not only never witnessed such a fire before, but I had never imagined anything like it."

As early as 2:26 the *Oslyabya* and *Navarin* were burning and a few minutes later the *Borodino* caught fire. As the Japanese were making sixteen knots to ten for the Russians, they drew ahead rapidly; and their Second Division, coming abreast of the *Suvorov* at 2:35, concentrated on her and the *Alexandr,* shooting both into flames. In order to reduce the range as much as possible because of his wrecked range-finders and fire-control system, Rozhestvenski had held his converging course; but at about 2:40, in order to keep his broadsides bearing, he was forced to steer a curving course to the right. Semenoff thus dramatically paints the situation in the conning-tower: "Instead of two dead bodies, five or six were now lying in the conning-tower. The man at the wheel having been incapacitated, Vladimirsky had taken his place. The latter's face was covered with blood, but his mustache was smartly twisted upward and he wore the same self-confident look as he had in the wardroom when discussing the future of gunnery."

Despite the comparative ineffectiveness of the Russian fire, every Japanese ship had been hit and had received casualties. The *Mikasa* was struck by no less than ten heavy projectiles, while the *Asama* was forced to leave the line due to three hits aft on the water-line, which caused severe leaks and temporarily wrecked the steering gear. This ship followed some distance in rear of her division, rejoining it later in the action.

At about 2:50 a double catastrophe occurred to the Russian fleet. The *Oslyabya* had a great hole knocked in her port side abreast of the forward turret by three shells, and water poured in so rapidly that she was forced to leave the line; her masts and stacks were shot down and not a single gun of her port battery remained in action. Fifteen minutes later she capsized. After the destroyers *Bravi* and *Buini* had picked up about 400 men they were driven off by gunfire, the former ship being hit and reduced to eleven knots.

But even this was not the worst. The heroic *Suvorov,* which was fought this day in a way that would have brought pride into the face of her illustrious namesake, had been receiving a terrific fire. She was literally shot to pieces; but her resolute crew kept every undamaged gun in action which the raging fires would permit them to approach. Rozhestvenski continued to lead the fleet in the most gallant manner until shell fragments came in under the mushroom roof of the conning-tower, wrecked most of the instruments, broke the compass, wounded the admiral himself in three places very severely and disabled the steering gear. Circling to starboard, the ship endeavored to follow the line. "The *Suvorov*," according to a Japanese account, "subjected to the fire of both our squadrons, left the line. Her upper works were riddled with holes and she was entirely enveloped in smoke. Her masts had fallen and her funnels came down one after the other. She was unable to steer, and her fires increased in intensity every moment. But even outside the fighting line she still continued firing, so that our bravest sailors credited her with making a plucky resistance."

Meanwhile, the four Japanese cruiser divisions, having at about 2:25 concentrated to the northwestward of their battle-line, came down on southeasterly courses toward the Russian rear. By 2:50 they had gained the desired position and began to engage the Russian cruisers at long range.

Shortly after the *Suvorov* left the line the *Alexandr*, Captain Bukrostov, took the lead; but she also soon had to leave the line. The *Borodino*, Captain Serebryanikov, at about 2:55 turned sharply to the left and northward. This was a good move, as it threatened the Japanese rear and brought the undamaged starboard batteries of the Russian ships into play. At 2:58, to counteract this manœuver, Togo turned the First Division to the left 90° together and at 3:05 repeated this manœuver, thus placing his six ships in column on a northwesterly course, with the *Nisshin* leading. The Second Division did not manœuver with the First but kept on to the southeast, thus masking its fire for some time. The Russians, however, were able to profit little by this respite, for the Second Division closed the range to 3000 meters and poured in a very heavy fire. Also the despatch vessel *Chihaya* fired two torpedoes at the *Borodino.* At about 3:05 the Russians, instead of fighting on a northerly course and easing off to the left as necessary, began to turn to the right in a wide circle to an easterly course. This headed them for a time directly at the First Division, which at 3:07 poured a devastating fire into them at 5000 meters. Range came down as low as 3000 meters and the Russians received terrible punishment. The *Alexandr* resumed the lead and received a series of hits on her bridge and forward port 6-inch turret; she continued to circle toward the southward.

At 3:10 the Japanese Second Division began countermarching to port to follow the First Division. As it steadied on a northwesterly course at 3:16 fire was reopened, this time with port batteries, on the Russians, who were now passing to the southward on opposite courses in a most confused formation. The *Alexandr*

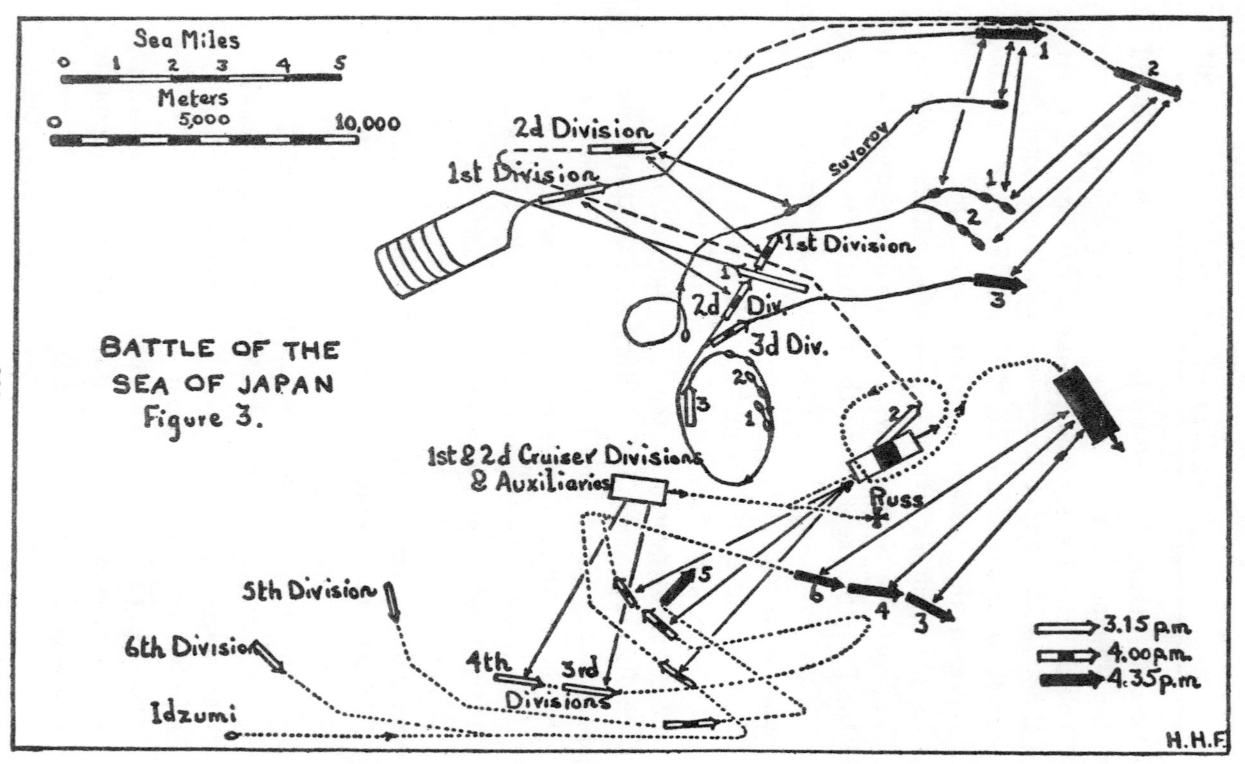

BATTLE OF THE SEA OF JAPAN
Figure 3.

continued her turn to the right until at 3:30 she was proceeding again on a northerly course toward the *Suvorov*, having completed a circle. At this time the mist and smoke gave the Russians a temporary respite and the action ceased. The Japanese already considered the battle won. The executive officer of the *Asahi* writes: "I took another tour of inspection through the batteries, when I was unanimously greeted with 'Best congratulations, Commander.' And certainly we were to be congratulated on the issue of that day's battle. Similar greetings were exchanged all over the ship; we felt as if it were New Year's day. The next duty I undertook was to visit the wounded at the dressing station on the lower deck. Some of them had their throats shot through and could scarcely breathe, yet cried out faint *Banzais*."

Meanwhile on the *Suvorov* fires had compelled the conning-tower to be abandoned. The admiral was again painfully wounded in the left leg and was carried into a 6-inch turret. The rudder had been repaired, but all wheel-ropes had been shot away and there were left no voice-tubes or telephones which could be used to communicate with the steering-engine-room from above. At 3:34 the Second Division was encountered, which concentrated a terrific fire from their port batteries upon the *Suvorov;* by this her forward turret was destroyed, and only a weak reply could be made with the secondary battery. The Fifth Destroyer Flotilla dashed in to about 600 meters and each of the four boats fired a torpedo, for two of which the Japanese claimed hits; the flotilla was driven off by the gunfire of the Russian fleet, the flagboat receiving two hits. The *Chihaya* fired two torpedoes at 1600 meters and in turn was hit three times.

At 3:42 Togo went 90° left together with the First Division and at 3:49 repeated the manœuver, thus resuming the lead with the *Mikasa*. At the same time Kamimura countermarched to starboard and took station ahead of the First Division. The Russian fleet was likewise steaming to the northeast on a converging course. At 4:01 the First Division reopened fire at 6500 meters, followed a minute later by the Second at 5000 meters. The Russians again received severe injuries; the *Alexandr* left the line and the *Borodino* again took the lead. The *Suvorov* was proceeding between the lines and again received the concentrated Japanese fire. "The *Suvorov*," says their official account, "presented a pitiful sight. All her upper works were swept away and black smoke covered her hull and gushed from her gunports."

By about 3:10 the Japanese Third and Fourth Divisions had reached a position south of the Russian fleet and an engagement with their cruisers and auxiliaries on parallel courses took place, the range gradually decreasing to 5000 meters. By about 3:35 the converted cruiser *Ural* and several auxiliaries had been badly hit and set on fire; the cruisers *Oleg*, *Avrora*, and *Donskoi* countermarched to the left to protect them and come to the assistance of the *Suvorov*. At the same time the Japanese Third and Fourth Divisions countermarched to the left; a number of their ships had been hit, the *Kasagi* below the water-line; the *Takachiho* had left the Fourth Division because of a jammed steering gear. The range between the opposing cruisers increased to 10,000 yards, and the *Anaduir* took advantage of this to rescue 330 men from the *Ural.* It appears that a few men remained on board at this time and that the ship continued to follow the fleet at very slow speed. The Japanese cruisers gradually closed in to the northward and several Russian cruisers burst into flames under their fire. At about 3:50 the *Oleg*, *Avrora*, and *Donskoi* countermarched to the left to their original course, having completed a long ellipse, which for the sake of clarity has not been shown on the sketches. At 4:07 the Third and Fourth Divisions likewise countermarched to the right to southeasterly courses and renewed the action with their port batteries. At 3:40 the *Idzumi* rejoined the Sixth Division and at 4:00 this unit entered the action, following the Fourth Division. The Fifth Division had kept off to the southward for some unexplained reason and did not even sight the others until 4:10 P.M.

The Russian fleet in great confusion kept turning in a wide circle to the right, until at 4:35 they were heading southeast. "The enemy," says the Japanese official account, "turning more and more to starboard, there was some doubt whether they would cross astern of the Japanese ships or escape to the northward." For this very unconvincing reason Togo with the First Division went left 90° together, so that another similar turn could be used to place it on a westerly course. However, it soon became apparent that

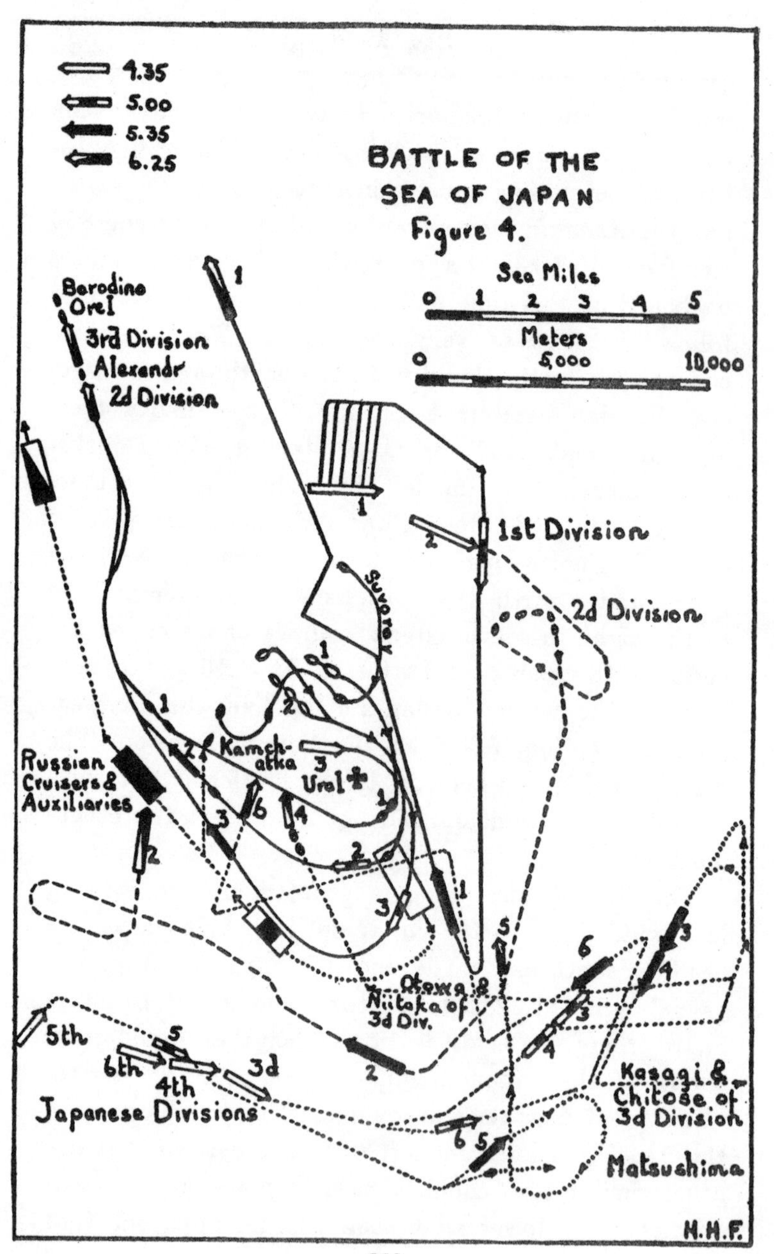
4.35
5.00
5.35
6.25
BATTLE OF THE SEA OF JAPAN
Figure 4.
Sea Miles
0 1 2 3 4 5
Meters
0 5,000 10,000
Borodino
Orel
3rd Division
Alexandr
2d Division
1st Division
2d Division
Suvorov
Kamchatka
Ural
Russian Cruisers & Auxiliaries
Otowa &
Niitaka of 3d Div.
5th
6th
4th
3d
Japanese Divisions
Kasagi &
Chitose of 3d Division
Matsushima
H.H.F.

the Russians were keeping on to the southward instead of going north, and Togo's manœuver resulted in his completely losing contact with them. At 4:43 Togo came back into column and steered to the southward, ordering the Fourth Flotilla to attack. Togo's manœuver also had an unfavorable effect on the Second Division, for it also at 4:43 countermarched to the northwest toward him, likewise losing contact with the enemy. When the First Division was again seen coming to the southward the Second turned so as to take position on its port bow; both kept on to the southward, where the Fourth Flotilla was attacking the *Suvorov* and the Third and Fourth Divisions had become engaged with the Russian battle fleet.

At 5:05 the Fourth Flotilla, with three boats in column, approached the Russian flagship to within 600 meters and fired torpedoes; then reversing course they came past her again at a range of 300 meters. On the *Suvorov* there were but two 3-inch guns intact and one of these was on the unengaged side. With the other gun, the Russians beat off the destroyers, hitting one of them.

We left the cruisers at 4:10 heavily engaged on easterly courses. The *Ural* and three auxiliaries continued to be heavily hit and the Russians turned toward their battle fleet in the northeast. The Japanese cruisers continued the pursuit in that direction, sinking the tug *Russ* and continuing to hit the *Oleg*, *Avrora*, *Izumrud*, *Kamchatka*, and *Irtuish*. At about 4:40 the Russian cruisers joined their battle fleet and twenty minutes later their Third Division emerged from the mist and covered the Japanese Third and Fourth Divisions with a heavy fire at 6000 meters, hitting the *Naniwa* on the water-line and slightly damaging most of the other vessels, which made off to the eastward.

While cruising to the southward the First Division fired on two battleships on an opposite course and some isolated cruisers and auxiliaries. At about 5:20 both First and Second Divisions intervened between the Japanese cruisers and the Russian Third Division, driving off the latter to the westward.

At 5:27 the First Division countermarched to the north, sank the *Ural* with a torpedo and fired on the *Kamchatka* and *Suvorov.* The latter ship returned the fire with her 3-inch guns and a shell struck the *Asahi.* "Quartermaster K. Yaginuma," says her executive officer, "whilst engaged in steering inside the tower, had his right shoulder pierced by one of these splinters. Quite undismayed, he held the wheel in his left hand and asked the torpedo lieutenant standing by him to look at his shoulder. The latter turned round and inspected his wound. It was big enough to put a finger in and his face was already paling under the severity of the shock. In spite of all, however, he held on to the wheel with his left hand, keeping the ship on her course so as not to hamper her evolutions, and waited to be relieved before he went to the dressing station."

At about 5:30 the *Buini,* with 200 survivors of the *Oslyabya* on board, approached the *Suvorov* while under a heavy fire. Preparations were made to bring

Rozhestvenski to the destroyer on a raft, when her captain, Kolomeytseff, performed a wonderful feat in bringing his boat alongside the battered flagship, from whose side projected injured guns and broken torpedo-net booms. The admiral was lowered on board and a few of his staff jumped after him, amid the cheers of the few men who remained of the *Suvorov's* crew. Semenoff, who had boarded the *Buini*, thus describes the condition of the flagship: "The mainmast was cut in half. Her foremast and both funnels had been completely carried away, while her high bridges and galleries had been rent in pieces; and instead of them, shapeless piles of distorted iron were heaped upon the deck. She had a heavy list to port, and, in consequence of it, we could see the hull under the waterline on her starboard side reddening the surface of the water, while great tongues of flames were leaping out of numerous rents." Rozhestvenski had been so badly wounded that he could only say that Nebogatov should take command and steer toward Vladivostok. The destroyer *Bezupretshni* delivered this message to the *Nikolai* at about 7:00 P.M.

At 6:00 the First Division again sighted the Russians to the W.N.W. and concentrated their fire on the *Alexandr*, which then was in the lead, at 6300 meters. Meanwhile the Second Division, instead of following the First, had gone to the westward. As darkness came on, Kamimura at 6:03 thought it necessary to turn to the southward away from the enemy, and for some unexplained reason it was not until 6:15

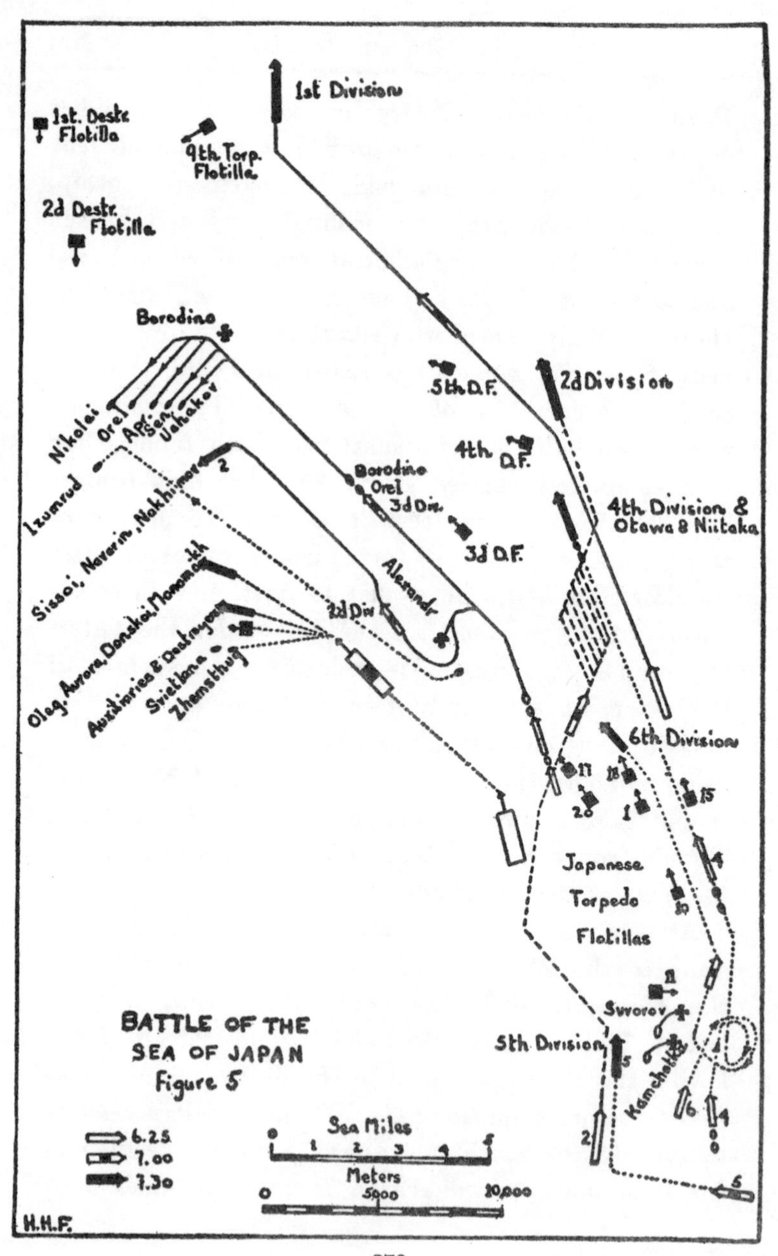
1st Division
1st. Destr. Flotilla
9th. Torp. Flotilla
2d Destr. Flotilla
Borodino
Nikolai
Orel
Apr.
Sen.
Ushakov
Izumrud
Sissoi, Naverin, Nakhimov
Oleg, Aurora, Donskoi, Monomakh
Auxiliaries & Destroyers
Svietlana
Zhemstchug
5th D.F.
2d Division
4th D.F.
Borodino
Orel
3d Div.
3d D.F.
4th Division & Otowa & Niitaka
Alexandr
2d Div
6th Division
Japanese Torpedo Flotillas
Suvorov
5th Division
Kamchatka
BATTLE OF THE SEA OF JAPAN
Figure 5
6.25
7.00
7.30
Sea Miles
Meters
H.H.F.

that he again headed toward them. This delay prevented him from taking any further effective part in the battle.

By 6:25 the First Division was abreast of the Russian battleships at 5500 meters. The Russians still had ten ships in line, against six for the Japanese. Many of the Russian vessels, however, had been heavily hit and they continued to receive severe injuries under the effective Japanese fire. At 6:50 the *Alexandr* turned out of the line and capsized. The *Izumrud* endeavored to save her crew, but was driven off by the Japanese fire. The Second Division now opened up at 8000 meters on the rear of the Russian line, but its fire at this range could not have been effective. At 7:10 Togo brought the action to a close, and the last shot from the *Fuji* is supposed to have exploded the magazine of the *Borodino*, which immediately heeled over and sank just as darkness came on. An officer of the *Zhemtshug* writes: "The end of the *Borodino* was heroic. Never leaving the line, notwithstanding all the damage she had suffered and the fires which had broken out on board, she still struck back at the enemy's vessels. Already heeling over to starboard, she kept on firing, and at the very moment of turning over on her side she got away a shot from her after turret." Only one man of her gallant crew was saved.

We left the Japanese cruisers when the First and Second Divisions intervened between them and the Russians at 5:20. Five minutes later the Third, Fourth, and Sixth Divisions turned again to the westward toward the enemy; at 5:40 the Sixth Division turned north to attack the *Ural,* but, as this vessel sank before fire could be opened, the division turned again to the west. The Fifth Division was to the southward of the Russians. By this time the lightly protected cruisers were showing the effect of the Russian fire. At 5:40 the *Naniwa,* of the Fourth Division, had taken in so much water that she had to slow down to make repairs; this done, she followed her division. At 5:30 the *Matsushima,* of the Fifth Division, left the line with an injured steering gear and did not rejoin until three hours later. By about 5:50 the *Kasagi,* flagship of the Third Division, was in a dangerous position due to a previous under-water hit, and Admiral Dewa turned his divison away from the enemy. Ten minutes later he ordered the *Otawa* and *Niitaka* to join Admiral Uriu's Fourth Division, while the *Kasagi,* escorted by the *Chitose,* proceeded toward the nearest land.

As the two main fleets proceeded to the northward the injured Russian vessels remained behind at the mercy of the Japanese cruisers, which at about 6:10 set their courses to the northward. At that time the *Otawa* and *Niitaka* joined the Fourth Division and ten minutes later the *Takachiho,* which had previously left the line, also joined, bringing the division's strength up to six cruisers. The Fifth Division now numbered three and the Sixth Division four cruisers; thus a total of thirteen cruisers passed over the battlefield. The three divisions attacked the *Kamchatka* and *Suvorov* at close range. The former went down at 7:00, but the *Suvorov,* with only a few guns in action, fought off the concerted attack of the thirteen cruisers. Admiral Kataoka ordered the Eleventh Torpedo Flotilla to attack. "At 7:20," reads the official account, "approaching to about 300 meters, the four boats delivered a torpedo attack and saw at least three torpedoes hit. The *Suvorov*, wrapped in black smoke and flames, turned turtle and for a while floated bottom up, but at 7:30 P.M., her bow rising high in the air, she suddenly disappeared below the surface of the sea. Smoke, drifting over the water, was all that was visible."

Thus ended the day action. The Russians had lost four battleships and three auxiliaries; three more battleships had been severely damaged; all their other ships had been hit. Against these losses a total of 144 hits had been made on the twelve vessels of the Japanese battle-line, the *Mikasa* alone receiving thirty-two; all the Japanese cruisers had been hit, and two were temporarily out of action. The victory had been decided; it remained to gather the spoils.

At 7:30 P.M., as the Russian fleet was withdrawing in a southwesterly direction, Nebogatov in the *Nikolai* took the lead, and the remaining vessels of the battle-line fell in astern of him in the following order: *Orel, Apraxin, Seniavin, Ushakov, Sissoi, Navarin*, and *Nakhimov;* the *Izumrud* proceeded with the column. On their port hand Enquist led a column of four cruisers —*Oleg, Avrora, Donskoi*, and *Monomakh*. To the left of this column was the *Svietlana*, followed by the *Zhemtshug;* to its rear were the *Almaz*, the destroyers and the remaining auxiliaries.

All Japanese divisions withdrew toward Matsushima,

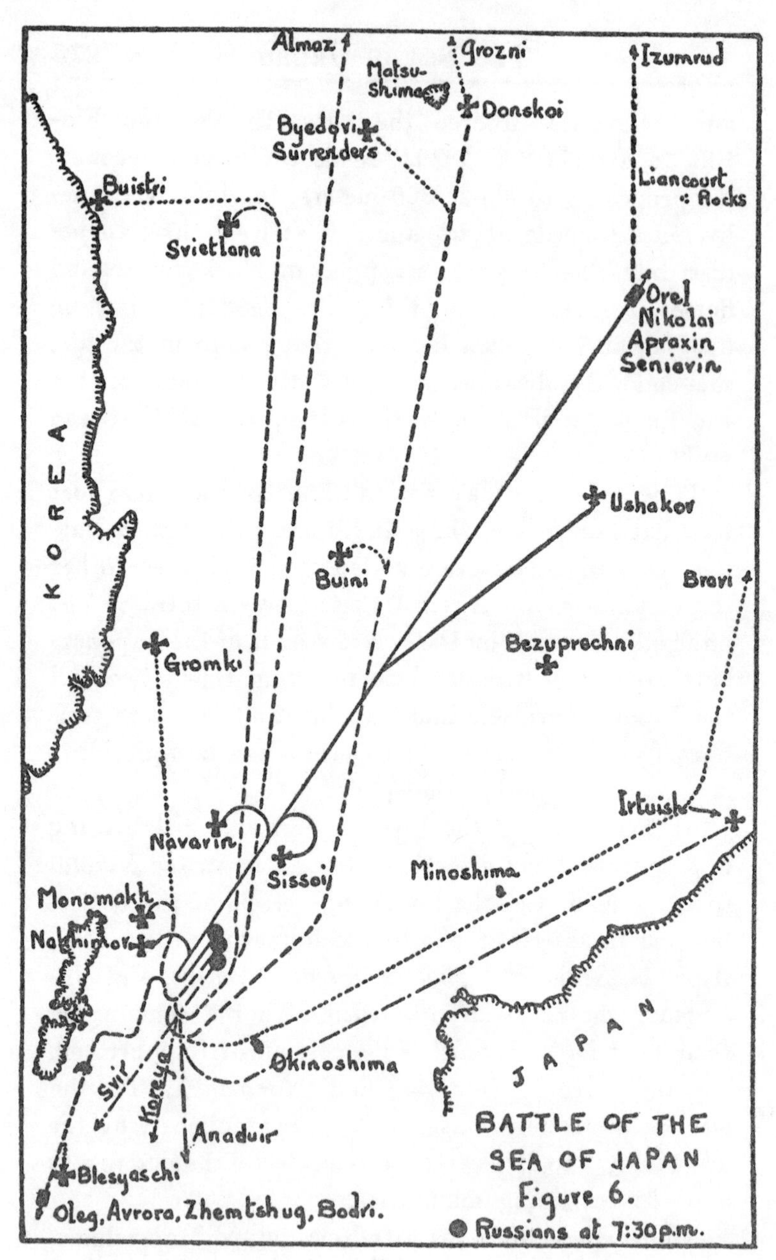

BATTLE OF THE SEA OF JAPAN
Figure 6.

200 miles to the northward, where they were to concentrate the next morning in the line of advance toward Vladivostok. The Japanese destroyers and torpedo-boats, which had grouped themselves to northward and eastward of the Russian fleet, received the order to attack. The night was clear; the wind had dropped somewhat. However, the sea was still rough and the boats rolled heavily. As darkness came on they crept in on their objectives. Throughout the night they attacked with great gallantry and fair results. The accompanying table of their operations has been compiled from the Japanese official account and gives a condensed description of their activities. Unfortunately, it has not proved possible to connect their operations up with the narratives of the Russian vessels so that the vessels they attacked could be identified.

At about 8:30 Nebogatov countermarched to the northward, being followed by the vessels in his column and the *Izumrud*. As it was now very dark, the other vessels apparently did not see this manœuver and kept on to the southwest. Only the cruiser *Almaz* decided to act on her own and soon after 8:30 headed for Vladivostok, which she succeeded in making. Nebogatov increased speed to twelve knots and the three badly-damaged vessels of the Second Division soon lost contact. The *Ushakov* also gradually fell astern. Only the *Orel*, *Apraxin*, and *Seniavin* were able to follow the *Nikolai*. These four ships successfully beat off the attacks of the Japanese torpedo craft and by 11:00 P.M. were clear. The *Ushakov* also was able to avoid being torpedoed.

On the Second Division fell the full force of the Japanese blow. In manœuvering to avoid torpedoes the *Sissoi*, *Navarin*, and *Nakhimov* lost contact with each other. The *Sissoi* had been hit on the water-line by a heavy shell and had taken in much water. After avoiding many torpedoes, she was hit by one which destroyed her rudder and one propeller. After daylight Tsushima was seen in the distance and her captain headed in that direction. Three Japanese auxiliary cruisers arrived just in time to rescue her crew as she went down.

The *Navarin's* hull had been pierced by four shells in the day action; she was leaking so badly that she could only creep through the water; often it was necessary to stop. Between 11:00 P.M. and 1:00 A.M. she was hit by four torpedoes and capsized with the loss of all but three men.

The *Nakhimov* was hit with a torpedo about 9:00 P.M. and continued to beat off attacks until midnight. By daylight the ship had taken in so much water that her captain headed toward Tsushima to save the crew. At 9:20 A.M. the Japanese destroyer *Shiranubi* and the auxiliary cruiser *Sadu Maru* appeared; the Russians opened the sea valves and went down with flags flying. The *Sadu Maru* saved the greater part of the crew, but her brave captain was in the water for seven hours until saved by fishermen.

Admiral Enquist, as he proceeded to the southward, increased speed to eighteen knots. Only the *Avrora* and *Zhemtshug* could keep up with the *Oleg* at this speed and the *Svietlana*, *Donskoi*, and *Monomakh* fell to the rear. At 8:30 Enquist was attacked by torpedo craft and says that he avoided no less than seventeen torpedoes. He made several attempts to break through to the northward, but each time turned back on making contact with torpedo craft. At 1:00 A.M. he decided to proceed to the southward, and eventually his three cruisers were interned at Manila.

The other three cruisers soon became separated. The *Svietlana* and *Donskoi* broke through to the northward. The *Monomakh* saw a vessel which made the Russian recognition signal and this proved to be the destroyer *Gromki.* Three torpedo attacks were beaten off and again the Russian signal was seen. This time it was a Japanese boat, which scored a torpedo hit. Further attacks continued until 2:00 A.M., and while these were avoided, the necessity for running at high speed sent so much water into the ship that she was in a sinking condition. At daylight she was headed for Tsushima, but ran into the sinking *Nakhimov*, the *Shiranubi*, and the *Sadu Maru.* The *Monomakh* went down at 10:20, her crew being saved by the *Sadu Maru.*

The *Gromki* endeavored to escape, but was pursued by the *Shiranubi* and a torpedo-boat. After a two hours' chase the Japanese vessels opened fire and a desperate action at close range took place. Even after their boilers had been damaged and hits below the water-line had flooded the magazines, the Russians kept on fighting. It was not until 12:50 P.M. that the *Gromki* went down with flag flying, having lost two-thirds of her crew. The Japanese rescued the remainder and also the wounded.

At daylight Nebogatov, relieved to find the horizon clear, continued toward Matsushima, but Kataoka with the Fifth Division soon made contact with him and tracked the Russians at a distance of seven miles. At 5:20 Togo with the First and Second Divisions was about fifteen miles south of Matsushima; the Fourth and Sixth Divisions were about twenty more miles to the southward. At 6:00 Togo, receiving news of Nebogatov, countermarched to the southward and at 7:30 went to the eastward, ordering the Fourth and Sixth Divisions to concentrate on the enemy. At 8:30 the latter divisions made contact and an hour later the Russians sighted the First and Second Divisions on the port bow standing across their course. At 10:30 the Japanese opened fire and the *Nikolai* hoisted the signal indicating surrender. The *Nikolai* and *Orel* were in such condition that they could have made little resistance, the latter having been hit some seventy times; the *Apraxin* and *Seniavin*, although little damaged, were such small vessels that they also could have accomplished little. While Nebogatov had little chance of inflicting damage on the enemy, by resisting for several hours he might have given other Russian vessels a better chance to escape; to have maintained the prestige of his nation and service he should at least have opened his sea valves to deprive the enemy of four such fine trophies. The *Izumrud* put on full speed and escaped; later, in trying to enter Vladivostok in a fog, she grounded and was wrecked.

At about 3:30 P.M. the Japanese were still securing their prizes, when the unlucky *Ushakov* came on the scene. When Captain Miklukha saw two armored cruisers, the *Iwate* and *Yakumo*, standing down upon him, he called a council of his officers. Their decision to resist to the end was gloriously executed. The Japanese, having double the speed of their crippled opponent, kept outside the range of his 4.7-inch guns, and after half an hour's fight the *Ushakov* had such a list that her turret guns could not be elevated enough to reach their targets. The sea valves were then opened and the ship went down with colors flying. The survivors were rescued, but the brave captain went down with his ship.

The cruiser *Svietlana* at daylight was joined by the destroyer *Buistri* in a position a little to the westward of Nebogatov. She was sighted by the Fifth and then the Fourth Division. Admiral Uriu, commanding the latter division, detached the cruisers *Otawa* and *Niitaka* and the destroyer *Murakumo* after the Russians. The *Svietlana* had been hit by a heavy shell during the main action; two of her magazines were flooded and her speed so reduced that there was no possibility of escape. Her brave captain fought the ship until all the ammunition was expended and then opened the sea valves. At 11:00 she went down with flag flying; two-thirds of her crew were saved. The *Buistri* was run aground on the Korean coast.

The *Donskoi* had taken a leading part in the defense of the auxiliaries during the main action and her upper works had been considerably shot up. Early on the 28th she found herself in company with three destroyers, *Buini*, *Byedovi*, and *Grozni*. On the *Buini* were

Rozhestvenski and his staff, but the admiral was incapable of giving any orders. As the *Buini* had been damaged, he was transferred to the *Byedovi.* The *Buini* soon afterward broke down completely and her crew and the men she had rescued from the *Oslyabya* were sent to the *Donskoi.* At 7:20 the *Chitose* passed without opening fire, being headed toward Nebogatov's detachment. The *Donskoi* headed toward Matsushima at eleven knots and was not sighted until 5:20 P. M., when she ran into the *Otawa* and *Niitaka,* returning from their encounter with the *Svietlana.* These ships approached on the port beam, and soon afterward all four ships of the Fourth Division appeared to starboard. At 6:50 the *Otawa* and *Niitaka* commenced firing, being joined half an hour later by the Fourth Division. The *Donskoi* put up a splendid fight with her six opponents, who seem to have shown little energy and withdrew as darkness came on. The Second Destroyer Flotilla then made an unsuccessful night attack. By this time the *Donskoi* had received serious damage; her speed was much reduced; her captain mortally wounded; one-third of her crew were killed or wounded and the remainder completely exhausted by the events of the last thirty-six hours. The ship was taken in close to Matsushima and the crew transferred to the island during the night. In the morning a few men took the ship into deep water and sank her. The *Donskoi's* story is an epic of the sea. The destroyer *Byedovi,* with Rozhestvenski on board, surrendered without resistance and the *Grozni* escaped to Vladivostok.

Of the remaining destroyers the *Bezupretshni* was sunk with all hands, the Japanese withholding all details of the action. The *Bravi,* though badly damaged, got to Vladivostok. The *Blestyaschi* was sunk by her own crew. The *Bodri* was towed into Shanghai; the auxiliaries *Svir* and *Koreya* interned in Shanghai. The *Irtuish* had been so badly damaged in the main action that her crew ran her aground on the Japanese coast. The *Anaduir* a month later put into Diego Suarez with 336 of the *Ural's* crew.

Togo's victory was one of the most complete of history. On October 22 he reported in person to the emperor, saying: "Today, peace being restored, we, your Majesty's humble servants, after discharging our duties, are able to return in triumph to the capital. This is due solely to the illustrious virtues of your Majesty, for which we are very thankful."

JAPANESE NIGHT TORPEDO ATTACKS

Flotilla Attacking	*Ships of Flotilla*	*Time of Attack*	*Range in Meters*	*Torpedoes Fired*	*Hits by Enemy*	*Remarks*
2d Destroyer Flotilla	Oboro	8:10	550	1	Yes	1 killed; 4 wounded
	Ikazuchi	8:10	550	1	Yes	13 casualties; badly hit
	Inazuma	8:10	550	1	2	Slight damage
	Akebono	8:10	550	1	Yes	4 wounded
1st Destroyer Flotilla	Harusame	Did not locate enemy; collided with Yugiri				
	Fubuki	Did not locate enemy				
	Ariake	9:08	400	1	No	
	Arare	9:08	400	1	Yes	1 wounded
	Akatsuki	Did not locate enemy; collided with T. B. 69				

Flotilla Attacking	*Ships of Flotilla*	*Time of Attack*	*Range in Meters*	*Torpedoes Fired*	*Hits by Enemy*	*Remarks*
3d Destroyer Flotilla	Shinonome	9:02	500	1	No	
	Usugumo	9:02	300	1	Yes	1 wounded
	Kasumi	9:02	300	1	3	
	Sazunami	9:02	400	1	No	
5th Destroyer Flotilla	Shiranubi	10:30	...	1	No	
	Murakumo	8:30	...		1	
	Yugiri	8:30	600	1	No	Collided with Harusame
	Kagero	8:30	500	1	No	
4th Destroyer Flotilla	Asagiri	2:30	...	1	No	
	Murasame	Damaged in day action; proceeded to port				
	Asahio	2:30	...	1	No	
	Shirakumo	2:30	...	1	No	
9th Torpedo Flotilla	Aotaka	9:20	800	1	No	
	Karigane	9:20	800	1	No	Saved 25 men from T. B. 69
	Tsubame	9:10	450	1	Yes	1 wounded
	Hato	9:10	600	1	No	
1st Torpedo Flotilla	T. B. 69	Sank at 10:45 after collision with Akatsuki; 2 drowned				
	T. B. 68	9:15	300	1	30	4 killed; 6 wounded
	T. B. 70	Jammed steering gear; did not attack				
	T. B. 67	9:20	250	1	No	
10th Torpedo Flotilla	T. B. 43	Collided with Sagi; did not attack				
	T. B. 40	9:30	500	1	No	
	T. B. 41	9:30	...	1	No	
	T. B. 39	9:30	...	1	No	
15th Torpedo Flotilla	Hibari	10:10	600	1	No	
	Uzura	Did not locate enemy				
	Hashitaka	Did not locate enemy				
	Sagi	Collided with T. B. 43 and just escaped sinking				
17th Torpedo Flotilla	T. B. 34	9:10	250	1	Yes	Sunk by gunfire
	T. B. 31	9:10	600	1	No	Saved 20 men from T. B. 35
	T. B. 32	9:30	500	1	No	
	T. B. 33	9:23	250	..	3	1 killed; 7 wounded
18th Torpedo Flotilla	T. B. 36	Did not attack			1	4 wounded
	T. B. 60	9:00?	450	1	No	
	T. B. 61	Steering gear jammed; saved crew of T. B. 34				
	T. B. 35	9:00	200	1	Yes	Sunk by gunfire

CHAPTER VIII

Jutland

ENEMY in sight!" This was the meaning of a hoist of flag signals which fluttered from the *Galatea's* signal yard at 2:20 P.M., May 31, 1916. Seven minutes later the *Elbing's* searchlight was flashing out the dots and dashes which spelled: "Enemy battle cruiser in sight west by north." These two signals raised the curtain on one of the most thrilling dramas in history; for the next twelve hours the fate of Europe hung in the balance. "The Day" for which Briton and Teuton had waited a quarter of a century had arrived.

The battle itself was worthy of the great stake for which the two fleets were playing. Its entire course was replete with thrill after thrill. One unexpected development followed another. Now fortune placed opportunities in the hands of one leader; now the goddess, fickle as ever, reversed her favors. In the dim visibility toward the end of the day the Germans blundered twice into positions which by every principle of tactics meant the destruction of their fleet, but each time their resolute admiral saved the situation by manœuvers so remarkable that until long after the war the British never credited them as being possible.

No battle was fought before on such a large scale.

Thirty-seven huge battleships and battle cruisers of the first line flew the white ensign from every masthead, while twenty-one equally imposing vessels showed the red, white and black man-of-war flag of Germany. These large ships were supported by cruisers, second line battleships, light cruisers and destroyers so as to literally fill the sea for miles with gigantic swells and thick smoke-clouds. While the entire forces were not constantly engaged during the twelve hours which the battle lasted, there were few moments free from some desperately contested fighting and none when the moral strain of impending battle was absent.

The battle, from the viewpoint of the individual officer and man, will never cease to be an inspiration to those who delight in deeds of heroism and realize that in the last analysis no country can endure whose citizens are unwilling to trade their lives for its security. The conduct of officers and men in both fleets was magnificent, a triumph of naval organization and discipline. You might have seen, had you been present, the crew of the *Nestor* in their boats cheering their ship as she sank under the fire of the German battle fleet; you might have heard, had you waited until after night had fallen, a terrific explosion in the little *Frauenlob*, followed by three "hurrahs" for their Kaiser and fatherland before the entire crew was carried down by the ship.

A battle is important not in itself but in the effect it actually had or might have had upon the course of the war. A tactical victory not always has a favorable effect upon the general situation. After completely defeating Frederick at Kunersdorf, the Russians did nothing further the entire campaign; their leader was heard to say: "Let me fight but another such victory, and I may go to Petersburg myself with the news of it."

To get the proper setting for Jutland we must picture the naval and military situations then existing. The year 1915 had been a successful one for the Central Powers. On the eastern front the Russians had been crushingly defeated with a decisive effect only recently revealed. Bulgaria had entered the war. Serbia had been overrun; Italy had been checked; and the British and French had been compelled to admit final defeat on Gallipoli; on the western front the Allies had purchased their meager successes at far too heavy a price.

At the beginning of 1916 the Central Powers, as a result of these successes, had strategic reserves with which to launch further offensives: the Germans against Verdun; the Austrians in the Trentino; the Turks at Kut-el-Amara. Each of these operations, by a remarkable coincidence, commenced with striking successes, but ended only in consuming the reserves of the Central Powers. The Allies, with a great superiority of men and equipment, prepared to seize the initiative with a great simultaneous attack on all fronts.

Already the Russians had overrun Armenia; in Mesopotamia the British were building up their armies for another advance on Bagdad; the Saloniki front was being prepared for a sortie against the Bulgarian armies; the Italians were making ready for a new

Isonzo battle; astride the Somme the British and French were preparing for a thrust on a scale hitherto unheard of; on the Russian front Brusiloff's offensive was about to commence its inundation of Austrian territory; Roumania at last had decided that the time to get the richest spoils with the least effort was approaching. Hindenburg and Ludendorff were soon to be brought to the helm as a last recourse to remedy a situation which the latter described as "very critical."

During the winter of 1914-15 the High Sea Fleet had made a number of sorties well out into the North Sea, but the loss of the *Blücher* in the action on the Dogger Bank had discouraged further operations of this kind, and in February, 1915, their principal efforts were devoted toward the prosecution of submarine warfare. At first this had only moderate success, and as it developed more successfully for the Germans, the results were kept down by the increasing restrictions which neutral protests forced Germany to accept. From the middle of 1915 to the middle of 1916 a constant level of shipping losses was maintained.

During 1915 the High Sea Fleet limited its operations to the control of the Baltic, the Cattegat, a part of the Skagerrak and a small area off Helgoland which permitted the submarines to gain the sea. In the Baltic they kept open communications with the Scandinavian powers and allowed the German armies in Courland to be supplied by water through Libau, but they were unable to gain the control of the gulfs of Riga and Finland. Meanwhile the Grand Fleet consolidated its position in the North Sea and commenced to exert pressure by adding to the contraband list and placing restrictions on the trade of neutral nations adjacent to Germany. A large organization to meet the German submarines was gradually built up.

In February, 1916, Vice-Admiral Scheer assumed command of the High Sea Fleet; as the submarine campaign had not produced the necessary results with the numerous and complicated restrictions placed on the captains, Scheer was allowed a free hand to see what he could accomplish with the High Sea Fleet. He commenced a series of advances toward the English coast with the hope of bringing inferior forces to action, while taking precautions against being forced to fight the greatly superior Grand Fleet.

On February 11 three destroyer flotillas led by a light cruiser sank the British ship *Arabis* in a raid over the Dogger Bank. On March 5 the entire High Sea Fleet advanced well into the approaches to the English Channel without sighting hostile forces.

Meanwhile the Russians had been bringing pressure upon the Admiralty to attempt an advance into the Baltic, an operation which, if successful, would practically have decided the war. The British rightly replied that this was impracticable until the High Sea Fleet was defeated, but agreed to adopt more aggressive measures to accomplish this task. Consequently, on March 25 the Harwich Force, supported by the Grand Fleet, launched a seaplane attack on the airship hangars just south of the Danish frontier; while the air attack was without result, a number of contacts occurred between the light forces, in which each side lost a destroyer and the British had two light cruisers damaged by collision.

The Germans retaliated with an advance of the High Sea Fleet on April 25; Lowestoft and Yarmouth were heavily bombarded and a fleet engagement was narrowly missed. Each side lost a submarine; the British had two light cruisers and a destroyer put out of action, while the German battle cruiser *Seydlitz* was damaged by a mine. The British came back with another seaplane attack, during which a German airship was shot down by light cruisers.

This manœuvering of the two fleets was certain to result in a clash between them. In fact, the next sortie of the High Sea Fleet was to bring this to pass.

This operation was planned by Admiral Scheer as an attack on the English coast at Sunderland. As submarine warfare about the British Isles had been suspended after the *Sussex* incident, he was able for the first time to use his submarines in conjunction with the fleet; twelve of them took up their stations off the British bases on May 22, with orders to remain until the end of the month. On the 29th all was in readiness for the movement, but it had to be postponed because the weather was unsuited for airship scouting. As it continued unfavorable the next day, Admiral Scheer reluctantly substituted a movement into the Skagerrak, which was considered less dangerous. About 5:00 P.M. on the 30th the operation signal "31 May Gg 2940" was sent to the fleet by radio, indicating that the plan would be executed on the 31st.

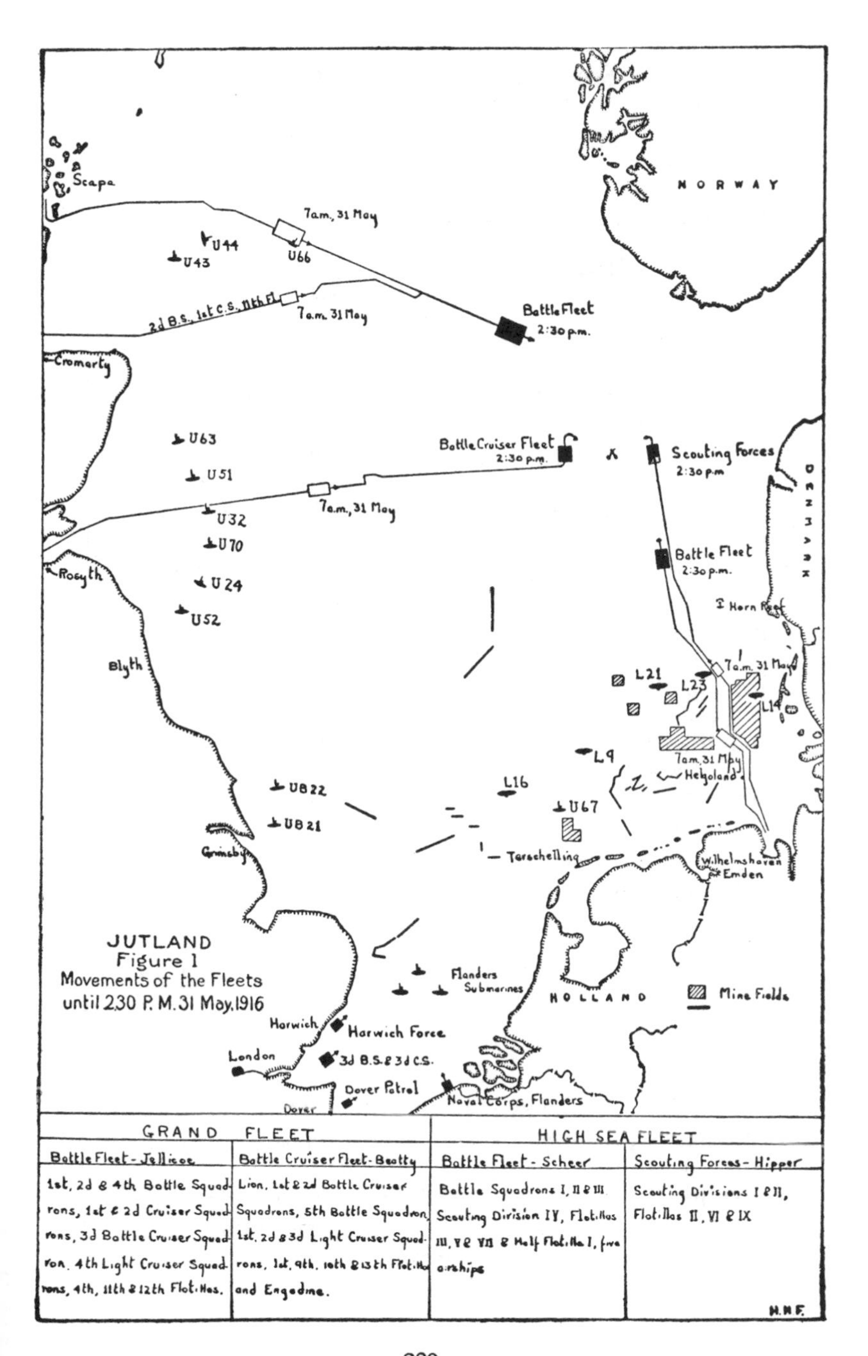

JUTLAND
Figure 1
Movements of the Fleets
until 2.30 P. M. 31 May, 1916

GRAND FLEET		HIGH SEA FLEET	
Battle Fleet - Jellicoe	Battle Cruiser Fleet - Beatty	Battle Fleet - Scheer	Scouting Forces - Hipper
1st, 2d & 4th Battle Squadrons, 1st & 2d Cruiser Squadrons, 3d Battle Cruiser Squadron, 4th Light Cruiser Squadrons, 4th, 11th & 12th Flotillas.	Lion, 1st & 2d Battle Cruiser Squadrons, 5th Battle Squadron, 1st, 2d & 3d Light Cruiser Squadrons, 1st, 9th, 10th & 13th Flotillas and Engadine.	Battle Squadrons I, II & III Scouting Division IV, Flotillas III, V & VII & Half Flotilla I, five airships	Scouting Divisions I & II, Flotillas II, VI & IX

The opposing fleets were composed as follows:

GRAND FLEET (JELLICOE)	HIGH SEA FLEET (SCHEER)
Battle Cruiser Fleet (Beatty)	*Scouting Forces* (Hipper)
Lion, flagship (battle cruiser)	Scouting Division I (5 battle cruisers)
1st Battle Cruiser Squadron (3 ships)	Scouting Division II (4 light cruisers)
2d Battle Cruiser Squadron (2 ships)	Regensburg, flagship of destroyers (light cruiser)
5th Battle Squadron (4 battleships)	Flotilla II (10 destroyers)
1st Light Cruiser Squadron (4 ships)	Flotilla VI (9 destroyers)
2d Light Cruiser Squadron (4 ships)	Flotilla IX (11 destroyers)
3d Light Cruiser Squadron (4 ships)	
1st Flotilla (1 light cruiser and 9 destroyers)	
13th Flotilla (1 light cruiser and 10 destroyers)	
9th Flotilla (4 destroyers)	
10th Flotilla (4 destroyers)	
Engadine (aircraft tender)	
Total: 6 battle cruisers, 4 battleships, 14 light cruisers, 27 destroyers, and 1 aircraft tender.	*Total:* 5 battle cruisers, 5 light cruisers and 30 destroyers.
Battle Fleet (Jellicoe)	*Battle Fleet* (Scheer)
2d Battle Squadron (8 battleships)	Battle Squadron III (7 battleships)
4th Battle Squadron (8 battleships)	Friedrich der Grosse, flagship (battleship)

Opposing Fleets—Continued

Battle Fleet (Jellicoe) —*Continued*	*Battle Fleet* (Scheer) —*Continued*
1st Battle Squadron (8 battleships)	Battle Squadron I (8 battleships)
3d Battle Cruiser Squadron (3 ships)	Battle Squadron II (6 battleships, second line)
1st Cruiser Squadron (4 ships)	Rostock, flagship of destroyers (light cruiser)
2d Cruiser Squadron (4 ships)	Flotilla I (4 destroyers)
4th Light Cruiser Squadron (5 ships)	Flotilla III (7 destroyers)
12th Flotilla (2 destroyer leaders and 14 destroyers)	Flotilla V (11 destroyers)
11th Flotilla (1 light cruiser, 1 destroyer leader and 14 destroyers)	Flotilla VII (9 destroyers)
4th Flotilla (2 destroyer leaders and 17 destroyers)	Scouting Division IV (5 light cruisers)
Attached vessels (6 light cruisers, 1 destroyer and 1 minelayer)	
Total: 24 battleships, 3 battle cruisers, 8 cruisers, 12 light cruisers, 5 destroyer leaders, 46 destroyers and 1 minelayer.	*Total:* 16 battleships, 6 battleships second line, 6 light cruisers, 31 destroyers.

The Grand Fleet had a superiority over the High Sea Fleet in the ratio of 1.75 to 1.00.

At noon on the 30th the Admiralty warned Admiral Jellicoe, commander-in-chief of the Grand Fleet, that the High Sea Fleet was assembling in the outer roads. At 5:40 P.M., when the German operation signal was intercepted, the Admiralty ordered the entire Grand Fleet to concentrate in the approaches to the Skagerrak "to await eventualities." By 10:30 P.M. the battle fleet had left Scapa and Cromarty, while the battle cruiser fleet had stood out from the Firth of Forth. It was not until three hours later that the High Sea Fleet proceeded from its anchorages. The skill of the British Intelligence Service had again given the Grand Fleet an incalculable advantage.

Chance drew the two fleets toward the Skagerrak. While two German submarines sighted some vessels of the Grand Fleet, their reports were not definite enough to disclose the British intentions to Admiral Scheer. Possibly had the weather been more suitable for airship scouting he might have received news of the approach of the Grand Fleet, but it was not until 11:30 A.M. that the five airships were able to take the air, and even then the low-lying clouds at 900 feet restricted their field of vision.

The Germans had the station ship at Wilhelmshaven employ the radio call letters ordinarily used by their fleet flagship, and this led the British to believe that the fleet was still in port. At 2:30 P.M. the forces had reached the positions shown in Figure 1, each fleet entirely unsuspecting that contact was about to occur.

Admiral Beatty's instructions required him to change course toward his battle fleet at 2:00 P.M., but as he was still somewhat in rear of his assigned position, he did not execute the signal to steer north until 2:15. At 2:00 the light cruiser *Elbing*, on the western flank of the screen guarding the German scouting forces, sighted a Danish freighter and sent two destroyers, *B-109* and *B-110*, to search it. At the same time this merchant vessel was sighted by the light cruisers *Galatea* and *Phaeton*, the easternmost vessels of Beatty's screen, and they headed toward it. *B-109*, sighting their smoke, flashed a searchlight signal to the *Elbing*, which headed in their direction at full speed. At 2:20 the *Galatea* saw the destroyers and reported by flags "Enemy in sight!" Seven minutes later the *Elbing* reported by radio a hostile battle cruiser to the westward and at 2:28 *B-109* reported "scattered enemy forces in square 164yIV" of the secret German position chart. At this instant the *Galatea* and *Phaeton* opened fire and soon their salvos were straddling the destroyers. The *Elbing* quickly came to their assistance, and as her first hit landed aboard the *Galatea* from a distance of 14,000 yards, the two British cruisers drew off.

Upon receipt of the contact reports Beatty and Hipper had turned their forces toward the scene of action to locate the hostile forces and report their strengths and dispositions to their respective commanders-in-chief. On the German side Scouting Division II gradually assembled its four light cruisers toward the northwest, while the three flotillas concentrated for attack. On the British side the First and Third Light Cruiser Squadrons gradually concentrated to the northwest against Scouting Division II, while Beatty proceeded with his main body to the eastward. This force was separated into three main divisions, the Second Battle Cruiser Squadron being some three miles east of the *Lion*, in which Beatty led the First Battle Squadron, while five miles north of the *Lion* was the Fifth Battle Squadron. The latter squadron had difficulty in making out Beatty's flag signal to turn to the eastward, and opened out their distance to about ten miles. The Second Light Cruiser Squadron assembled near the battle cruisers.

At 3:07 the aircraft tender *Engadine* hoisted out a seaplane which took off a minute later to scout toward the northward; it reported the movements of the German light cruisers until engine failure at 3:45 forced a landing.

At about 3:25 the hostile battle cruisers sighted each other. Hipper was steering northwest and Beatty had the option of engaging him on a parallel or opposite course. He elected the latter at 3:30 and this forced Hipper to countermarch to the southward to parallel him. This unexpected development placed the First and Third Light Cruiser Squadrons and Scouting Division II so far in rear that they took no part in the battle cruiser action. Even though Hipper slowed five knots he was unable to get his light cruisers into the van, but except for this his dispositions were admirable; hoisting the signal "Fire distribution from the left," he gallantly closed in on his more powerful opponent. Commander Paschen, the gunnery officer of the *Lützow*, says that he sighted in the distance the ships of the Fifth Battle Squadron, but it is improbable that Admiral Hipper did so, for his despatches to Admiral Scheer make no mention of this squadron, and it was not until 4:12 that the commander of Scouting

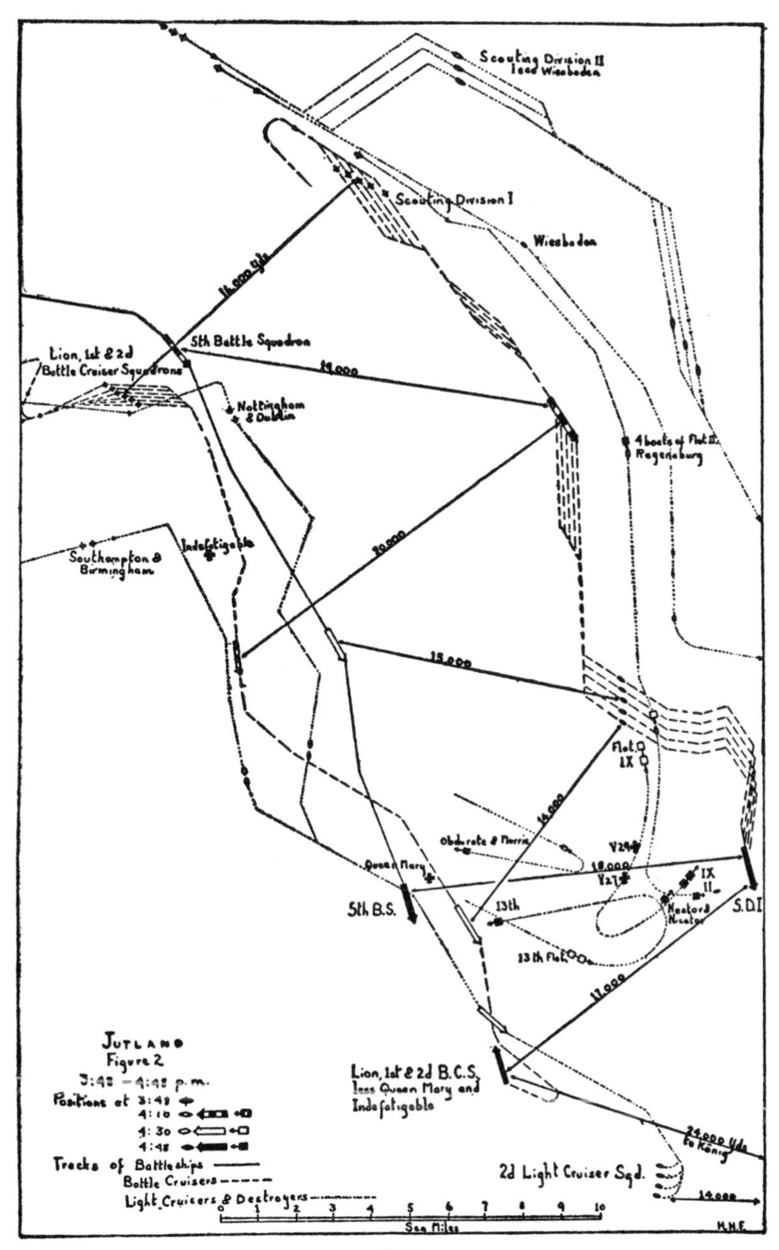

Scouting Division II
lead Wiesbaden
Scouting Division I
Wiesbaden
16,000 Yds
5th Battle Squadron
Lion, 1st & 2d
Battle Cruiser Squadrons
19,000
Nottingham
& Dublin
4 boats of Flot II.
Regensburg
Southampton &
Birmingham
Indefatigable
20,000
15,000
Flot.
IX
14,000
Obdurate & Morris
V29
18,000
V27
IX
II
Queen Mary
5th B.S.
13th
Nestor &
Nicator
S.D.I
13th Flot.
17,000
Jutland
Figure 2
3:48 – 4:48 p.m.
Positions at 3:48
4:10
4:30
4:48
Lion, 1st & 2d B.C.S.
less Queen Mary and
Indefatigable
24,000 Yds
to König
Tracks of Battleships
Battle Cruisers
Light Cruisers & Destroyers
2d Light Cruiser Sqd.
14,000
0 1 2 3 4 5 6 7 8 9 10
Sea Miles
M.H.F.

Division II reported their presence to the commander-in-chief.

The British dispositions were not so fortunate. The First and Third Light Cruiser Squadrons were even farther to the rear than the German light cruisers. The Fifth Battle Squadron was 7.5 miles in rear of Beatty and its effective entry into the battle was long delayed; it must be realized, however, that Beatty still had a good superiority without these four most powerful battleships afloat, and had they been present Hipper would hardly have accepted the gage thrown down to him. But still further, Beatty did not unite his two battle cruiser squadrons until a short time before the action commenced; at 3:45 he was compelled to signal another manœuver to get his own smoke out of the line of fire. Only three minutes later, while in the midst of this manœuver, streaks of flame rippled down the *Lützow's* side against a background of brown smoke puffs, announcing that four 12-inch shells were hurtling toward their target. Beatty immediately hauled down the flag signal "Open fire and engage the enemy!" Tall pillars of water arose majestically about the war-gray ships. For some minutes the two rear British vessels could not join in the action, and the others, due to failing to receive correctly the fire distribution signal, concentrated on the first and third hostile vessels, leaving the second vessel able to fire under target-practice conditions. The British destroyers, scattered about the battleships and battle cruisers to protect them against submarines, had not been ordered to concentrate into flotillas until shortly before fire was

Courtesy U. S. Navy Department

THE GRAND FLEET IN CRUISING FORMATION

opened, and as their speed only slightly exceeded the twenty-five knots at which the battle cruisers were bowling along, they could not prevent their dense smoke from interfering with the British gunnery. Even the atmospheric conditions favored the Germans.

Under these conditions the German fire was remarkably accurate and deadly; soon the dull red glows, indicating hits on British ships, encouraged the German observers. In the first twelve minutes of firing no less than eleven heavy shells crashed into the British battle cruisers. One pierced the *Lion's* amidship turret and killed all but two men. The dying turret officer, Major Harvey, V. C., Royal Marines, used his last energy to order the magazine doors closed, and this saved the ship when powder in the turret caught fire and raged to the magazine doors. One turret on the *Princess Royal* and two on the *Tiger* also were put out of action. On the other hand, the British fire, for the reasons already described, was ineffective and only three hits were made; one shell from the *Queen Mary* put a turret on the *Seydlitz* out of action.

Beatty now began to open the range, but the German gunnery became more and more deadly. At 4:03 two successive salvos from the *von der Tann's* 11-inch, directed by Commander Mahrholz, fell squarely on the *Indefatigable.* A great pall of smoke rose above her, a picket boat flew high in the air, and in a minute's time over a thousand men had been carried down with their ship. German destroyers later picked up the only two survivors. The fire of the *Lützow* was beautifully directed by Commander Paschen, who chalked up six hits on the *Lion* in four minutes. The after turret of the *Princess Royal* was put out of action. At 4:06, however, the range became so great that the action decreased in intensity and soon ceased completely. During the ten-minute period ending at 4:10 the British received about eleven hits, while the Germans seem to have been unhit.

As the battle cruiser action died out, the Fifth Battle Squadron opened fire on the German battle cruisers. "We then began to get quite jubilant," writes a midshipman of the *Malaya*, "so much so, that when a German shell landed abreast us on the port side about 500 yards short, there was a positive cheer from the *Malaya*. Then we heard the other ships of our own squadron open fire, one after the other ahead of us, each salvo helped on its way by a cheer." Within a few minutes these powerful battleships, mounting 15-inch against the 11- and 12-inch guns on the German ships, began to make their weight felt, a shell hitting the *von der Tann* near the stern and allowing 600 tons of water to leak into the ship.

At 4:12 Beatty, noting the entry into action of this powerful reinforcement, commenced closing the range and the battle between the cruisers was reopened. Two of the *von der Tann's* turrets were damaged, but at 4:26 the *Queen Mary* blew up with a loss of over 1200 men under the concentrated fire of the *Derfflinger* and *Seydlitz*. This splendidly-drilled British ship had already contributed three hits and her crew behaved most heroically in the terrible disaster which overtook them. "P. O. Stares was the last I saw coming up from the working chamber," writes a gunner's mate of "X" turret, "and I asked whether he had passed the order to the magazine and shell room, and he told me it was no use, as the water was right up the trunk leading from the shell room, so the bottom of the ship must have been out of her. Then I said, 'Why didn't you come up?' He simply said, 'There was no order to leave the turret.' " During the twenty-minute period ending at 4:30 the British received about thirteen hits to eight for the Germans; two of the latter were scored by the Fifth Battle Squadron.

As early as 5:09 Beatty had ordered the twelve destroyers of the Ninth, Tenth and Thirteenth Flotillas, which had concentrated in the van, to attack. As the *Queen Mary* sank, Commander Bingham, V. C., led them toward the German battle cruisers. At the same time Commander Goehle, seeing that the fire of the Fifth Battle Squadron was placing his admiral in a critical position, led the eleven boats of Flotilla IX in four groups against the British battle cruisers. The destroyers engaged in a sharp fight at point-blank range between the lines, in which the larger and more heavily armed British boats had the advantage. The *V-29* was sunk by a torpedo, while *V-27* had her main steam line shot away. The *V-26*, beautifully handled by Lieutenant-Commander Hans Koehler, ran alongside *V-27* under a heavy fire and rescued her crew, including the wounded; after sinking *V-27* to prevent her from falling into the hands of the enemy, he then rescued the greater part of the crew of *V-29*, the remainder being saved by *S-35*. After firing ten torpedoes at very long range the German boats withdrew, their retirement being covered by the light cruiser *Regensburg* and four boats of Flotilla II.

The British attack had been partly countered by the German destroyers; the *Nomad* was brought to a stop with hits in her engine room. Commander Bingham, however, led the *Nestor* and *Nicator* with utmost gallantry against the German battle cruisers, which turned away sharply and covered him with barrages from their secondary batteries. The two attacking boats each fired two torpedoes at the close range of 5000 yards, and Hipper was able to avoid them only by making further changes of course. These manœuvers were not without advantage to the Germans, because they disengaged the battle cruisers from both the British battle cruisers and the Fifth Battle Squadron. At this time Hipper was glad to make out his own battle fleet coming up from the southward and he headed toward it.

Commodore Goodenough had been scouting ahead of the British battle cruisers with the Second Light Cruiser Squadron. At 4:30 he reported a light cruiser to the southeast and three minutes later his searchlight flashed to Beatty the laconic message "Battleships southeast!" At 4:38 he broadcast by radio his contact with the German battle fleet. Soon Beatty was able to see it for himself, and recalling his destroyers he ran up the general flag signal "Alter course in succession sixteen points to starboard."

While Beatty countermarched to the northward the Second Light Cruiser Squadron kept on until the dis-

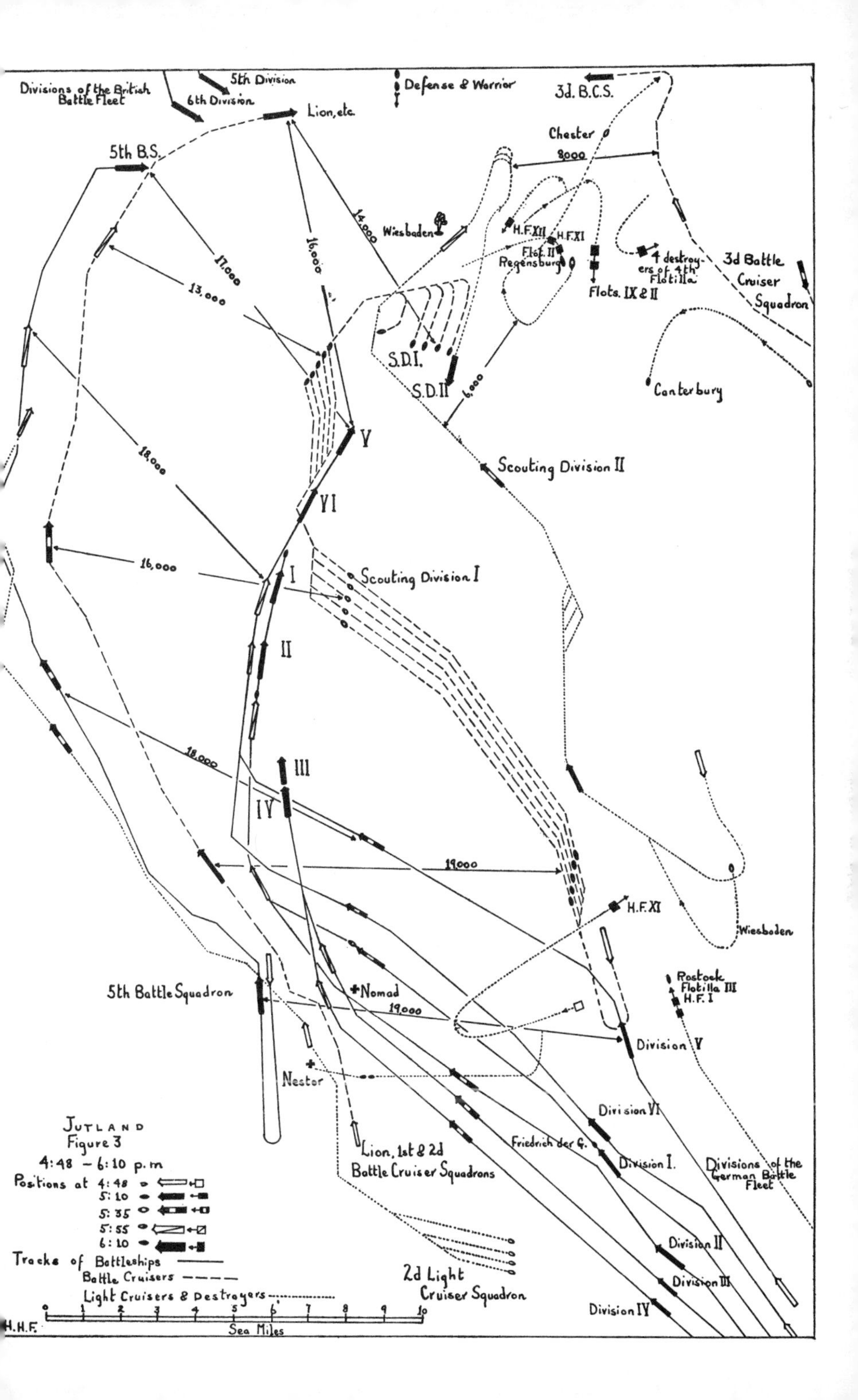
Divisions of the British Battle Fleet
5th Division
6th Division
Defense & Warrior
3d. B.C.S.
Lion, etc.
Chester
8000
5th B.S.
14,000
16,000
17,000
13,000
Wiesbaden
H.F.XII
H.F.XI
Flot. II
Regensburg
Flots. IX & II
4 destroyers of 4th Flotilla
3d Battle Cruiser Squadron
S.D.I.
S.D.II
6,000
Canterbury
V
Scouting Division II
18,000
VI
16,000
I
Scouting Division I
II
18,000
III
IV
19000
H.F.XI
Wiesbaden
Rostock
Flotilla III
H.F.I
5th Battle Squadron
Nomad
19,000
Division V
Nestor
Division VI
Friedrich der G.
Division I.
Divisions of the German Battle Fleet
JUTLAND
Figure 3
4:48 – 6:10 p.m
Positions at 4:48
5:10
5:35
5:55
6:10
Lion, 1st & 2d Battle Cruiser Squadrons
Tracks of Battleships
Battle Cruisers
Light Cruisers & Destroyers
2d Light Cruiser Squadron
Division II
Division III
Division IV
0 1 2 3 4 5 6 7 8 9 10
H.H.F.
Sea Miles

positions of the German battle fleet could be clearly made out. At 4:45 Goodenough turned off under a tornado of fire, which his ships skilfully avoided by frequent changes of course.

During the fifteen-minute period ending at 4:45 the British received one hit, while the Germans were unhit. As this time marks the close of the battle cruiser action, it is interesting to note that the British received about thirty-six hits against about eleven for the Germans. This surprising result in an action where he was greatly inferior in fighting strength reflects the highest credit upon Admiral Hipper and his well-trained forces.

During the battle cruiser action the German battle fleet had been steaming to the northward and westward with the twenty-two battleships in one long column. As early as 4:30 the *König*, leading the column, had sighted flashes of gunfire on the horizon. At 4:45 Scheer signaled for his divisions to change course toward the enemy and a minute later hauled down the signal to open fire. The four leading ships fired on the battle cruisers, while other vessels fired at the Second Light Cruiser Squadron, but no hits on either target were made.

After firing half his torpedoes against the German battle cruisers, gallant Bingham with the *Nestor* and *Nicator* fired the rest at the German battle fleet at the incredibly short range of 3000 yards. A barrage of secondary gunfire sent down the *Nestor*, her crew singing "God save the king" as she stood on end and disappeared beneath the waves. The *Nomad* was also sunk. German destroyers saved the greater part of their crews. The *Nicator* was enabled to make an almost miraculous escape by dodging the German salvos. "Luckily," says one of her officers, "we had a reserve of speed over the *Nestor*, our next ahead, so we were able to do this salvo dodging without dropping astern of station at any appreciable extent. Throughout the whole action the captain was leaning coolly against the front of the bridge, smoking his pipe, and giving his orders to the helmsman."

When Hipper had approached to within five miles of the *König* he countermarched at 4:50 to the northward, took station in the van of the High Sea fleet and renewed his action with Beatty. As he turned, the *Petard*, *Turbulent*, *Nerissa*, and *Termagant*, which had been delayed in their attack, fired a total of ten torpedoes, one of which hit the *Seydlitz;* the damage inflicted, however, was so slight that she was able to remain in formation until the end of the action. At the same time six destroyers of Flotilla VI launched seven torpedoes at the British battle cruisers. The range, however, was very great, 9000 yards, and all of them missed.

Admiral Evan-Thomas had not been able to make out the *Lion's* signal to countermarch and apparently had not picked up Commodore Goodenough's radio contact report of the German battle fleet. Consequently he continued to lead the Fifth Battle Squadron to the southward. At 4:48 the *Lion* directed him again to countermarch and at 4:50 the signal was correctly made out by the *Barham*, just as that vessel passed the *Lion* on an opposite course. It was not until six minutes later that Evan-Thomas commenced his turn, just as the *Barham* received her first hit from the German battleships.

A running fight now commenced; the *Barham* was under a heavy concentration of fire and in the next few minutes received five more hits. In return Evan-Thomas scored two hits on the German battleships. The German battle cruisers had rather the better of the argument with Beatty at this time, receiving three hits on the *Seydlitz* against four on the *Lion* and *Tiger*. During the twenty-five-minute period ending at 5:10 the British received nine hits to five for the Germans.

For the next twenty-five minutes Evan-Thomas, unsupported by Beatty, continued the action single-handed against Hipper and the leading division of German battleships under Rear-Admiral Behncke. Although in a most critical position, the Fifth Battle Squadron was able to return thirteen hits for the equal number it received. The *Seydlitz* and *Malaya* each received seven hits. "They had no thought," writes a turret officer of the latter ship about his crew, "that we should come off worse than the enemy, but only wanted to know how many German ships were left requiring to be finished off. They were full of confidence that every shell was doing its bit, and many and varied were the benedictions they sent with each round fired. When things were at their hottest I heard one man in the gun-house call out to the others, 'Don't get rattled—you're putting your —— feet all over the —— paintwork.' "

By this time all the *von der Tann's* turrets were out

of action due to hits or accidents, but Captain Zenker kept her in the battle-line for the remainder of the day to draw the enemy's fire off his comrades; by zigzagging his course he was able to avoid being hit, and several hours later was able to get two turrets into action again in the last combat of the day. The after turret of the *Seydlitz* was put out of action.

At 5:35 the tide of battle turned for the first time in favor of the British. The visibility conditions for the first time now favored them. The Fifth Battle Squadron, with their twenty-five knots' speed, had run out of range of the German battleships and were able to bring a greatly superior fire against Hipper. Beatty, after having repaired damages and rested his crews, re-entered the action at 5:42. As a consequence, in the twenty-minute period ending at 5:55 the Germans received five hits against none for the British. The *Lützow's* radio was wrecked. The Fifth Battle Squadron had performed wonders.

Admiral Jellicoe meanwhile had been proceeding toward the scene of action with his battle fleet. His twenty-four battleships were formed in six parallel columns of four ships each, screened against submarines by three destroyer flotillas. Three miles ahead was a line of five vessels of the Fourth Light Cruiser Squadron. Some seven miles ahead of the light cruisers was a line composed of the First and Second Cruiser Squadrons, while some ten miles still farther ahead was Rear-Admiral Hood with the three vessels of the Third Battle Cruiser Squadron, two light cruisers and four destroyers. As news of the proceedings came in

Courtesy U. S. Navy Department

THE THIRD BATTLE CRUISER SQUADRON

H.M.S. "Australia," the leading ship, did not take part in the action. The second ship is the *New Zealand*. The third ship, in the foreground, is the *Indefatigable,* which was sunk fifteen minutes after fire was opened from time to time, the admiral took the necessary measures to bring his fleet to the assistance of Beatty. At 3:10 speed was increased to eighteen knots and the cruisers were ordered to increase their distance ahead of the battleships from ten to sixteen miles, but as the latter's speed was further increased to twenty knots, they did not have sufficient excess speed to execute the order. At 4:05, in accordance with orders from Jellicoe, Hood proceeded at twenty-five knots to support Beatty.

During the battle cruiser action both Beatty and Goodenough had reported their positions from time to time, but because of the high speeds and frequent changes of course these were considerably in error. Thus, instead of making contact with Beatty, Hood brought up some fifteen miles east of him and on the other side of the High Sea Fleet. At 5:35 the light cruiser *Chester*, which was guarding Hood's western flank, sighted in the mist to the southward the four light cruisers of Scouting Division II, which were then stationed ahead of Hipper. The German vessels, using British recognition signals, approached the *Chester* to within 6000 yards and then covered her with a hail of projectiles; seventeen hits disabled three guns and caused heavy personnel losses; the *Chester* turned quickly toward her supporting battle cruisers. These countermarched to the northwest and at 5:55 their salvos took the German light cruisers completely by surprise; the *Wiesbaden* received a hit in the engine room which brought her to a complete stop.

Rear-Admiral Boedicker, commanding Scouting

Division II, was now in a critical position, particularly as the cruisers *Defense* and *Warrior*, in advance of the British battle fleet, fired at him from the northward. He quickly turned to the southward and got off without further damage, except for a 12-inch hit on the *Pillau*, which damaged four boilers and reduced her speed to twenty-four knots. In the uncertain visibility Boedicker at 6:00 reported to both Hipper and Scheer: "Am under fire from enemy battleships." This unfortunate though excusable error greatly confused the situation.

The flotillas proceeding in company with Scouting Division II likewise mistook Hood's forces for the van of the British battle fleet and, in order to relieve their battle fleet from what seemed to be a dangerous situation, advanced to the attack. They ran directly into Hood's four destroyers which Commander Loftus Jones, V. C., was leading in the *Shark*. The *Canterbury* assisted the British destroyers, while the *Regensburg* entered the action on the other side. In the prolonged close fighting which ensued the *Shark* was literally shot to pieces and sunk by a torpedo, her heroic captain fighting her to the end. "Several of the enemy destroyers came very close to us," reports a survivor; "in line formation, the range being about 600 yards, we were still firing our only gun; by this time the gun's crew consisted of three men, the midshipman, T. Smith, R. N. R., J. Howell, A. B., Gunlayer II., and C. Hope, A. B. The captain was then slightly wounded in the leg, but he managed to control the gun." Only six men were saved when the ship was lost. The *Acasta* was also severely damaged. The German destroyers fired a number of torpedoes; while these would have been effective when fired at a long line of ships, the Third Battle Cruiser Squadron presented such a small target that it avoided all of them. The premature engagement of the destroyers had very unfavorable effects for the Germans, as the flotillas could not be reassembled for an attack when an excellent opportunity occurred about thirty minutes later.

At 5:55 Beatty sighted, distant about five miles to the northward, Jellicoe's southernmost battleship division standing at right angles across his course from left to right. Accordingly he changed course to the right and increased speed to twenty-five knots to take station ahead of the battleships. As the Fifth Battle Squadron was following him and as Hood had already entered the action from the eastward, a powerful concentration against Hipper was effected; the latter's position was further embarrassed by the attack of the *Shark's* division and a particularly gallant advance of the *Onslow* from a position on the *Lion's* engaged bow. The *Derfflinger* was severely damaged by a shell which hit her forward torpedo room, while the *Seydlitz* received two more hits. The visibility conditions were so unfavorable to the Germans that they could not see the vessels firing upon them. Hipper therefore followed the light cruisers back toward the battle fleet. During the fifteen-minute period ending at 6:10 the Germans received five heavy hits to one for the British.

During the pursuit of Beatty's force by the High Sea Fleet Jellicoe had been receiving information concerning its course, speed, and formation. Beginning at 4:38, Goodenough had sent in five detailed and generally accurate reports from the *Southampton*. In all of them, however, his own positions were greatly in error. The Admiralty furnished the British commander-in-chief with deciphered German radio despatches and the radio compass positions of the vessels sending them. Thus, at 5:00 he received the correct course and speed and the position correct to four miles of the German battle fleet at 4:09. At 5:53 he received similar information as of 5:30, the position being in error only three miles. At 5:42 the cruiser *Black Prince* reported the position of the German battle cruisers, while the First Cruiser Squadron, the First Battle Squadron and the *Calliope* reported gun flashes and ships in action to the southward. Goodenough's last report, at 5:50, unfortunately stated that the German battle cruisers were in rear of their battleships. All this information was so delayed in transmission and so conflicting that Jellicoe could deduce no certain facts from it, and the low visibility prevented him from seeing anything for himself.

In response to a query made at 5:55 Admiral Burney, leading the southernmost battleship division, reported the positions of Beatty and Evan-Thomas. At 6:00 he hoisted the signal to his squadron, "Enemy in sight S.S.E. battle fleet," but this does not appear to have reached Jellicoe, for at 6:01 he asked Beatty, "Where is enemy's battle fleet?" At 6:03 Goodenough reported the German battle cruisers, but said that he had lost their battle fleet; at 6:06 Beatty also reported the battle cruisers. At 6:10 Evan-Thomas was the first to report the German battle fleet, followed four minutes later by a report from Beatty.

It was not, therefore, until from 6:10 to 6:14 that Jellicoe received information upon which he could base his deployment. The British formation of six divisions abreast was designed for use when the enemy could be brought 90° from the line drawn through the division flagships; in this case all six flagships could change course simultaneously 90° to the right or left, followed in succession by the remaining three ships of their divisions; this would place twenty-four ships in one long column in about three minutes, with the enemy abeam, a direction which would allow the full battery to be brought to bear and in which the change in range and bearing of the enemy would usually be least.

But Jellicoe, instead of finding the enemy at 90° to the line through his division flagships, saw that they must be about 45° to this line; as salvos began to fall among his right flank divisions, immediate decision was necessary. A discrepancy of about eleven miles between the positions reported by Beatty and Jellicoe to each other caused this condition. It also was responsible for the fact that Beatty, instead of being east of Jellicoe when the junction was made, was directly between him and the enemy, filling the intervening area with dense clouds of smoke. As Jellicoe had not known whether he would deploy to right or left, it was not until 6:08 that he had ordered his screening destroyers to form into flotillas; this short notice had not permitted them to get out of the line of fire and

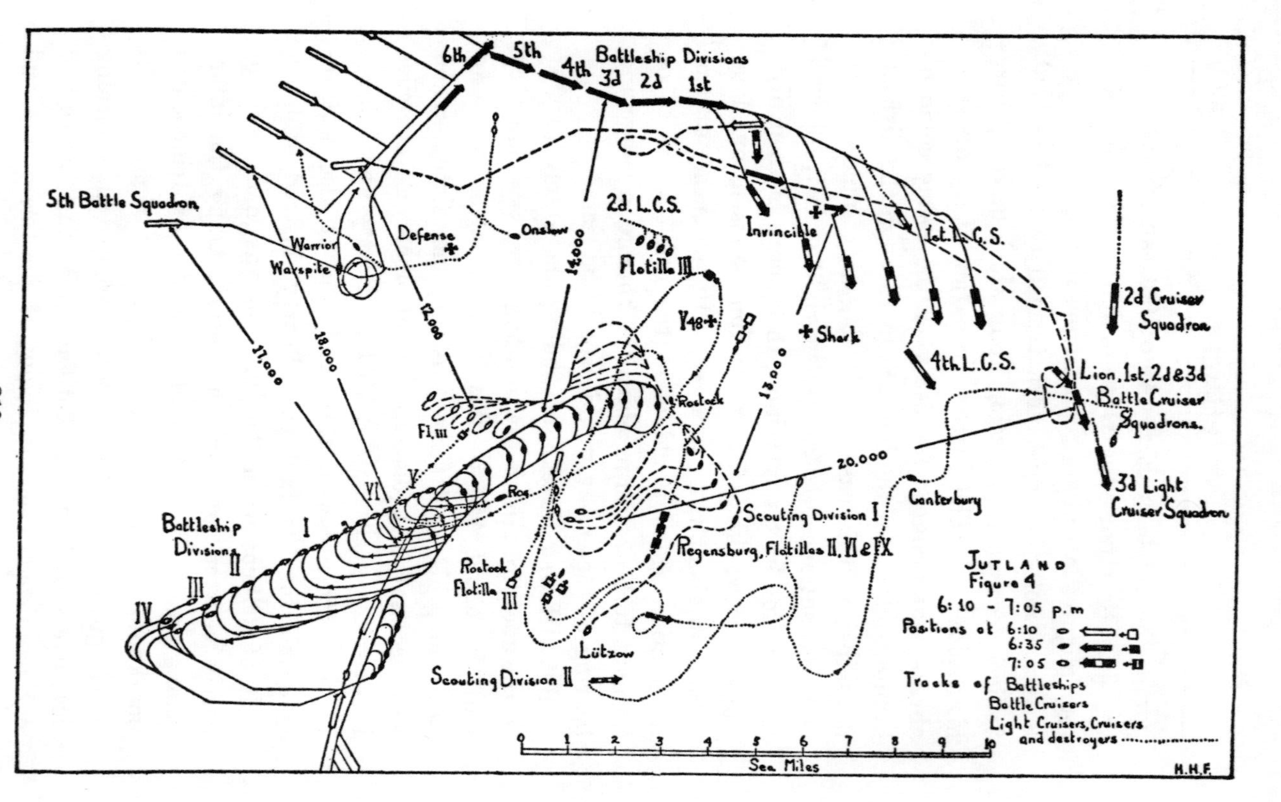

6th
5th
4th
3d
2d
1st
Battleship Divisions
5th Battle Squadron
2d. L.C.S.
Defense
Onslow
Warrior
Warspite
Flotilla III
Invincible
1st. L.C.S.
2d Cruiser Squadron
Y48
Shark
4th L.C.S.
Lion, 1st, 2d & 3d Battle Cruiser Squadrons.
3d Light Cruiser Squadron
17,000
18,000
12,000
14,000
13,000
20,000
Fl. III
Rostock
Ros.
Canterbury
Scouting Division I
Regensburg, Flotillas II, VI & IX
Battleship Divisions
I
II
III
IV
V
VI
Rostock Flotilla III
Lützow
Scouting Division II
JUTLAND
Figure 4
6:10 - 7:05 p.m
Positions at 6:10
6:35
7:05
Tracks of Battleships
Battle Cruisers
Light Cruisers, Cruisers and destroyers
0 1 2 3 4 5 6 7 8 9 10
Sea Miles
H.H.F.

they were mixed up with Beatty's light forces in a wild *mêlée*. "It will never cease to be a source of wonder to me," writes an officer of the *Malaya*, "that so few ships were hit and that there were no collisions. I think it must have been one of the most wonderful displays of seamanship and clear-headedness that ever existed, and as such is very comforting in these days of science and machines."

There were four or five methods of deployment open to Jellicoe, and while to us, looking down on the charts of the battle developed after ten years' work, some may appear better than the one he adopted, this at least was a reasonably good one and its results were generally favorable to the British. It was executed at 6:15 by flags and radio. The left division held its course and led the fleet; the other five divisions simultaneously turned 90° to the left, forming a long column in a northeasterly direction, and then turning in succession to the right after the leading division. As might have been expected, the execution of this manœuver was not particularly good. During the approach the fleet speed had been as high as twenty knots and this was too close to the maximum speed of the slowest ship for ships to maintain their proper positions. Then at 6:26, in order to allow Beatty to clear the range, speed was reduced suddenly to fourteen knots; such a speed reduction often results in the rear ships running up on those ahead; in this case a number of ships had to stop and sheer out of formation. The right division seems to have been a bit late in executing the deployment signal and to have come under a heavy concentration of fire before it could withdraw to the northward to take position in rear of the column. The Fifth Battle Squadron, in taking station in rear of the battle-line, had to make some radical manœuvers which reduced the effectiveness of its gunfire.

At about 6:12 Hipper again turned Scouting Division I to the north and took station about two miles ahead of his battleships, which were turned by Behncke slightly to the left in order to bring the crippled *Wiesbaden* within the German lines.

After dodging the torpedoes fired by the German destroyers, Hood turned to the west toward Beatty and countermarched to take station ahead of him on an easterly course, winning the admiration of his enemies by his "brilliant manœuver." The *Defense* and *Warrior*, in the words of an eye-witness, "pressed forward with great impatience" to attack the crippled *Wiesbaden*, but suddenly found themselves under the concentrated fire of the *Lützow* and four battleships. "From the right to the left," writes Commander Paschen of the *Lützow*, "a ship passed across the field of the periscope. With the first glance I recognized an old English cruiser and gave the necessary orders. Some one grabbed my arm and cried: 'Don't fire, that is the *Rostock*.' But I saw the turrets on the forecastle and the quarter-deck. 'Running fight—armored cruiser, four stacks, port bow—left thirty—range 7600 meters—salvo!' Salvo followed salvo in quick succession and three straddled. Then was repeated the performance of another English ship blowing up before the eyes of both fleets." The *Warrior* limped off with fifteen heavy caliber hits and her engine room flooded. At 6:17, while the Fifth Battle Squadron was manœuvering to take station in rear of the battle-line, the *Warspite's* rudder jammed hard right as a result of a hit from the *Kaiserin.* As the ship swung out toward the German line, she received about fifteen heavy caliber hits which ended her fighting for the day.

At 6:24 the British battle fleet began to enter the action; ship after ship from the rear of the line took up the fire against the battle cruisers and the leading battleship division, while others covered the gallant *Wiesbaden* with a hail of shells. "I particularly admired," Admiral Jellicoe reports with a generosity which does him honor, "the conduct of those on board a disabled German light cruiser which passed down the British line shortly after deployment, under a heavy fire, which was returned by the only gun left in action." It is estimated that the *Wiesbaden* was hit by about thirteen heavy shells. Hood's fire on the German battle cruisers was terribly effective. The admiral hailed the foretop from the bridge: "Your firing is very good, keep at it as quickly as you can, every shot is telling." The *Lützow* was hit by four shells, two of which pierced the forward torpedo room and eventually flooded the entire forward section of the ship. "B" turret was put out of action. "The whole ship gave a tremendous lurch," says Commander Paschen, "the control tower would not stop vibrating and I was thrown head first against its armored wall as I tried to remove one of the slit covers." The *Derfflinger* also was hit.

The Germans could see only the flashes ringed about

their van, and were unable to fire a shot in return until 6:30, when the *Lützow* and *Derfflinger* opened on the *Invincible* at 9000 yards as she momentarily came out of the haze. Both of them hit her heavily, and the *Lützow's* third salvo ripped off the roof of her amidship turret and a terrific explosion tore her literally in two.

By 6:35 the British battleships had hit the *König* three times and the *Markgraf* once; their fire was constantly becoming more effective, and, being unable to make any effective return, Scheer hoisted the flags which indicated "Turn together to starboard to the reverse course." This difficult manœuver was executed superbly, and even the *Markgraf*, which had one engine out of commission, was able to regain her station. During the period from 6:10 to 6:30 the British received about forty-five heavy caliber hits to twenty-two for the Germans.

The badly-damaged battle cruisers followed the battle squadrons in their retirement; the *Seydlitz* had to steer from the steering-engine-room; the *Lützow*, whose speed was reduced to fifteen knots by her twenty heavy caliber hits, was forced to leave the formation; Admiral Hipper, whose splendid leadership had been an outstanding feature of the battle, went aboard the *G-39* to shift his flag; although destroyers quickly covered the *Lützow* with a smoke screen, four more hits crashed into her before she could be disengaged. The *Derfflinger* had to stop to clear away her torpedo nets, which were hanging over the sides; as she went ahead again her commanding officer, Captain Hartog, assumed command of the battle cruisers. He could control their movements only by his example, because signal yards and radio had long since been shot away.

To cover the German retirement Flotilla III, which alone was immediately available, advanced to the attack; being prematurely recalled, only three torpedoes, as far as known, were fired; the *V-48* did not return from the attack; after being hit by both destroyers and battleships, she was later sunk by a division of British destroyers, her brave crew firing until the water rose about them. The captain of the *G-42* on his own initiative laid a smoke screen which relieved the pressure on the battleships. Despite this, however, the German battleships received four more hits before getting clear. Their retirement was facilitated by the fact that the British continued on southeasterly courses, which assisted the Germans in opening the range. A fragment of a shell which hit the *König's* conning-tower wounded Admiral Behncke, but he retained his command over the leading battle squadron. At 6:54 a torpedo, probably fired by the *V-48*, inflicted severe damage on the *Marlborough*. Numerous false reports of submarines, together with this casualty, placed additional mental hazards before the British commander-in-chief. During the twenty-minute period ending at 6:55 the Germans received eight hits, while the British were unhit.

Admiral Scheer, having disengaged his fleet, now came to a Nelsonic resolve: to again throw his whole fleet at the British battle-line, a decision which stamps him as one of the most daring leaders of history. The German battle cruisers resumed their station in the van and the destroyers massed for attack. Three boats of Flotilla III advanced first with orders to save the crew of the *Wiesbaden*, but the hail of projectiles rained upon them forced them back before their objective could be reached. They fired four torpedoes at the British battle-line.

After having lost contact with the Germans, Jellicoe was now coming around gradually to a southern course, but, not knowing the position of the enemy, he could not keep the line of bearing of his division flagships at right angles to their bearing. Consequently, when contact was regained, the situation of 6:35 was practically duplicated, his right divisions being close to the enemy, while the left divisions were almost out of range. Jellicoe endeavored to remedy this condition by holding his course with the Third Division, while the two left divisions eased in ahead of him and the three right divisions endeavored to take station in his rear.

But if Jellicoe's position was not entirely satisfactory, Scheer's soon became even less so, for his long column ran head on into the center of the Grand Fleet. His battle cruisers and leading battleships came under a constantly increasing converging fire, to which the low visibility and his unfavorable tactical position prevented any effective return. The *Derfflinger* was hit four times, one shell wrecking "D" turret and killing its crew. The *König* was hit twice and the *Helgoland* once.

Admiral Scheer, seeing that he could accomplish nothing under these conditions, ordered the repetition of his battle turn to the rear, and to cover it ordered the battle cruisers to turn toward the enemy and attack with their full strength. At 7:18 the battle squadrons executed their very difficult manœuver in good order, while Hartog led the battle cruisers on their "death ride" until they were but 7000 yards from the enemy. The *Derfflinger* had both "B" and "C" turrets wrecked and every gun of her port 6-inch battery except two was out of action. Her conning-tower reeled under the impact of a direct hit, and a 15-inch shell exploded under the bridge. Six hits shook the ship in rapid succession. "I could feel," writes von Hase, "how our fire was soothing the nerves of our crew. If we had not fired at this moment the entire company of the ship would have given way to profound despair, for they realized that if things went on much longer like this we should be lost. But as long as we were firing there must be hope." The *Seydlitz* was hit three times and the *von der Tann* once. The German battleships also suffered: the *Kaiser* was hit once; the *Markgraf* once; the *König* twice; and the *Grosser Kurfürst* four times. Two hits on the *Colossus* was all the Germans could make in return.

When at 7:21 Scheer made the signal "Destroyers attack," the remaining boats of Flotillas VI and IX, under the direction of Commodore Heinrich in the *Regensburg*, were already advancing. The four boats of Flotilla VI pressed in to within 7000 yards from the British battleships, and after two of them had been hit by the terrific fire concentrated upon them they fired eleven torpedoes and retired under cover of a smoke screen. The nine boats of Flotilla IX, coming in a little to the northward of Flotilla VI, made a beautiful attack and fired no less than twenty torpedoes at from 6000 to 7000 yards' range. They paid for their gallantry by the complete loss of the *S-35* with all its crew, the reduction of the *V-28's* speed to eighteen knots and one boiler put out of commission on the *S-51*. Further attacks by Flotillas III and V were made ineffective by the British retirement.

This perfectly executed attack of Flotillas VI and IX, in which but thirteen boats were engaged, had a decisive effect upon the course of the battle which was worth to the Germans all the damage suffered by their battle cruisers and battleships. Not only did it secure the safe withdrawal of these vessels, but for some fifteen minutes it literally drove the British battle fleet before it in considerable disorder, many British units heading directly away. A large number of torpedoes passed through the British line, and although all these were avoided by the excellent seamanship of the British captains, these manœuvers further increased the confusion in the battle-line. Finally—and this was far the most important effect—it undoubtedly confirmed Jellicoe in his determination to play the game absolutely safe, a policy which had received the approval of the Admiralty as early as 1914. "A third consideration," he wrote after the war, "that was present in my mind was the necessity for *not leaving anything to chance in a fleet action, because our fleet was the one and the only factor that was vital to the existence of the British Empire*" (his own italics). From this time Jellicoe

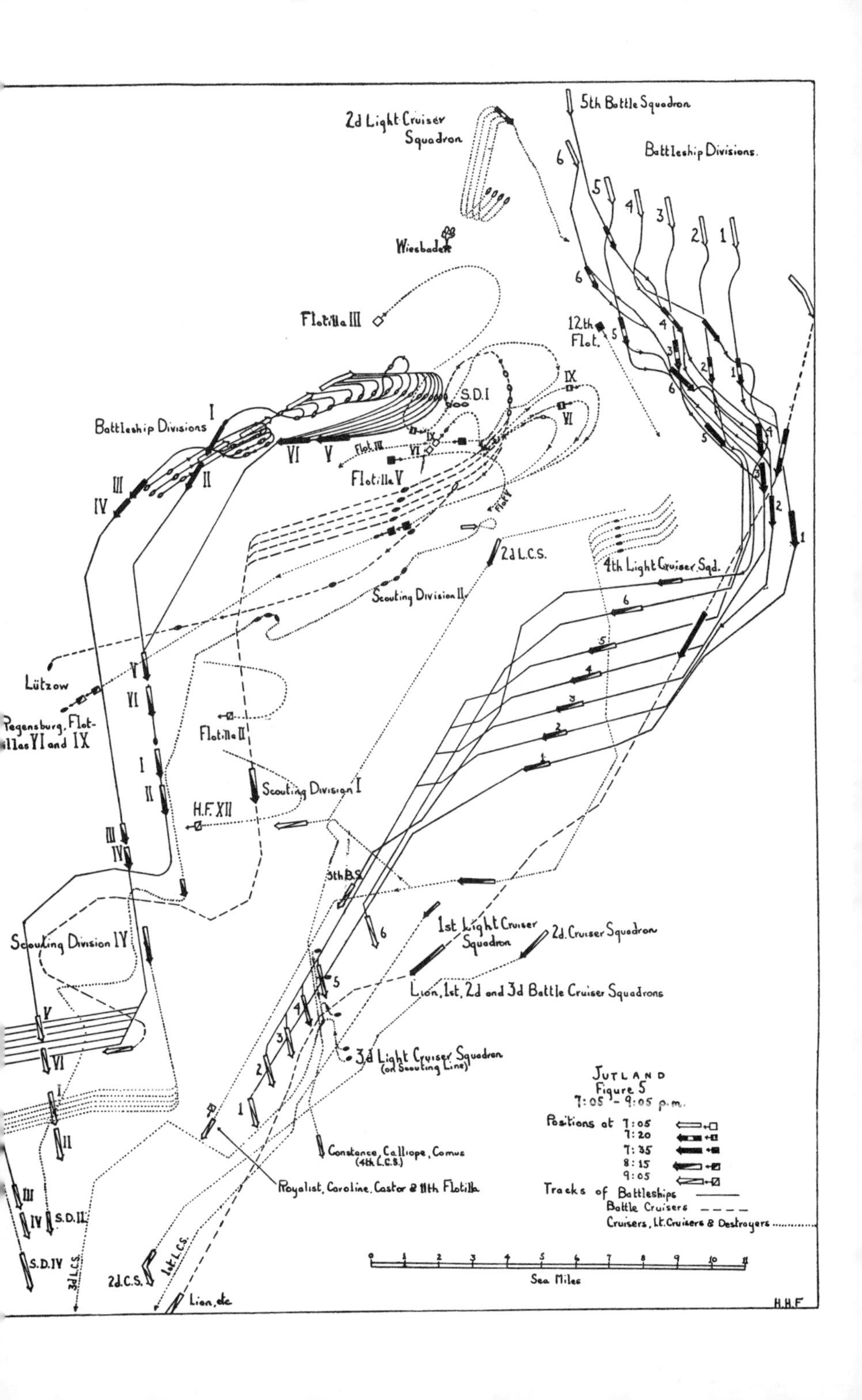
5th Battle Squadron
Battleship Divisions.
2d Light Cruiser Squadron
Wiesbaden
Flotilla III
12th Flot.
Battleship Divisions
S.D.I
Flotilla V
2d L.C.S.
4th Light Cruiser Sqd.
Scouting Division II
Lützow
Regensburg, Flotillas VI and IX
Flotilla II
Scouting Division I
H.F. XII
5th B.S.
1st Light Cruiser Squadron
2d. Cruiser Squadron
Scouting Division IV
Lion, 1st, 2d and 3d Battle Cruiser Squadrons
3d Light Cruiser Squadron (on Scouting Line)
Constance, Calliope, Comus (4th L.C.S.)
Royalist, Caroline, Castor & 11th Flotilla
S.D.II
S.D.IV
3d L.C.S.
1st L.C.S.
2d.C.S.
Lion, etc
JUTLAND
Figure 5
7:05 - 9:05 p.m.
Positions at 7:05
7:20
7:35
8:15
9:05
Tracks of Battleships
Battle Cruisers
Cruisers, Lt. Cruisers & Destroyers
Sea Miles
H.H.F.

a study of literacy in the light of Gresham's law and the law of diminishing returns. Not long ago I looked over a library said to contain a copy of every book published in America down to the year 1800. It bore witness that in those days reading was a fairly serious business; I could find nothing resembling what we should call popular literature on the shelves. The inference was that literacy was not general, and that those who read did so for other purposes than mere pastime, purposes that were pretty strictly non-sensational; and there is every collateral evidence that such was the case.

Mr. Jefferson laid great stress on literacy as an indispensable asset to good citizenship and sound patriotism. He was all for having everybody become literate, and those who have examined his own library (it is preserved intact in the Library of Congress) may easily see why. *Mutatis mutandis,* if everybody read the kind of thing he did, and as he did, he would have been right. But in his laudable wish to make the benefits of literacy accessible to all, Mr. Jefferson did not see that he had the operation of two natural laws dead against him. He seems to have jumped to the conclusion that, because certain qualified persons got a definite benefit out of literacy, anybody could get the same benefit on the same terms; and here he collided with the law of diminishing returns. He seems also to have imagined that a general indiscriminate literacy would be compatible with keeping up something like the proportion that he saw existing between good literature and bad; and here the great and good old man ran hard aground on Gresham's law.

I spent some time last year in Portugal, where the status of literacy and the conditions of the book-market are about what they were in Mr. Jefferson's America. One saw very little "popular literature" on sale, but an astonishingly large assortment of the better kind. I made my observations at the right moment, apparently, because, like all good modern republicans, the Portuguese have lately become infected with Mr. Jefferson's ideas about literacy, and are trying to have everybody taught to read and write; and it interested me to see that they are setting about this quite in our own incurious, hand-over-head fashion, without betraying the faintest notion that anything like a natural law may be a factor in the situation.

Doubtless what has happened elsewhere will happen there. In the first place, the Portuguese are likely to discover that, while no illiterate person can read, it is a mere *non distributio medii* to conclude that any literate person can read. The fact is that relatively few literate persons can read; the proportion appears to be quite small. I do not mean to say that the majority are unable to read intelligently; I mean that they are unable to read at all—unable, that is, to gather from a printed paragraph anything like a correct idea of its content.[1] They can pretty regularly make out the meaning of printed matter which is addressed to mere sensation, like news-

[1] In the interest of accuracy, I submitted these statements to a prominent educator who says that his experience fully bears them out. He carried on experiments over a dozen years with college freshmen—that is to say, with persons who were not only literate but had gone so far as to pass their entrance examinations. He experimented in this way: selecting a paragraph of very simple but non-sensational prose, he asked the freshmen to read it carefully; then to read it carefully again; then to read it aloud to him; then to write down in their own words the gist of what they had read.

matter, statistics, or perhaps an "informative" editorial or article, provided it be dosed out in very short sentences and three-line paragraphs; but this is not reading, and the ability to do it but barely implies the exercise of any faculty that could be called distinctively human. One can almost imagine an intelligent anthropoid trained to do it about as well and to about as good purpose; in fact, I once heard of a horse that was trained to do it in a small way. Reading, as distinguished from this kind of proficiency, implies a use of the reflective faculty, and not many persons have this faculty. According to the newspapers, Mr. Butler, the president of Columbia University, was complaining the other day that the practice of reflective thought had pretty well ceased among us. There is much to be said on this topic, but it is enough to remark here that literacy will not do duty for the power of reflective thought where such does not exist, nor does a state of literacy presuppose its existence.

To cite a rather comical illustration of this truth, a clerical friend lately told me of the troubles that a candidate for confirmation was having with the Nicene Creed. This candidate was a man of more than middle age, completely literate, and of considerable prominence and wealth. The article that he balked at, curiously, was non-

Hardly anyone could do it. He made the interesting remark that the reflective faculty is more easily stirred by speech than by print, because the communication of ideas by hearing is an older racial practice; their communication by sight is something comparatively new, to which the race's capacities are not as yet well adjusted. Therefore, he said, the indiscriminate spread of literacy puts into people's hands an instrument which very few can use, but which everyone supposes himself fully able to use; and this, obviously, is mischievous.

theological and non-metaphysical; it was the one which sets forth that the Saviour "was crucified also for us under Pontius Pilate." He wanted to know why they crucified Pontius Pilate. He knew who Pilate was, and what his rôle was in the great drama, but he had never before heard anything about Pilate's being crucified, and he wondered why the circumstance should be brought in here as one of those things which a Christian should know and believe to his soul's health.

A person of any literary experience, even the slightest, sees such instances time and again, not usually so bizarre perhaps, but essentially quite the same—instances which show beyond peradventure that the persons concerned simply can not read. When confronted with a paragraph requiring the most moderate exercise of reflective thought, they are helpless; and no equipment of sheer literacy can possibly make them less helpless. I have published so little and in such desultory fashion that I can claim nothing for my own experience with the public; yet I regularly get letters from persons who have manifestly gone as far with my writings as literacy will carry them, but who are as manifestly unable to make out correctly the content of English prose as simple and direct as the prose I am writing now.

As for the operation of Gresham's law, one need say little; it is so easily discerned that a glance at the nearest news-stand will show it well enough. The average literate person being devoid of reflective power but capable of sensation, his literacy creates a demand for a large volume of printed matter addressed to sensation; and this form of literature, being the worst in circulation, fixes the value of all the rest and tends to drive it out. In this country, for example, it has been interesting to see the reluctant and gradual submission of some of our few "serious" publications to this inevitable fixing of value. They have brought their aim continually closer to the aim of journalism, addressing themselves more and more to sensation, less and less to reflection, until now their policy favours almost exclusively the kind of thing one would naturally look for in an enterprising Sunday newspaper. Only the other day I came across a market-letter put out by a firm of literary agents, and I observed with interest that "the serious essay, travel, foreign-affairs type of article is unlikely to find a good market, unless by a well-known name."

I had occasion lately to look up something that one of our "quality" magazines published in 1874, and as I went through the two bound volumes I noticed the relative space they gave to material addressed to the power of reflective thought. For curiosity I made a comparison with last year's issues of the same magazine; and I can not suggest a more convincing exercise for any person who doubts the validity of Gresham's law in the premises, nor can I suggest a more substantial basis for generalization.

Gresham's law has, in fact, done far more than revolutionize publishing; it has set up a brand-new business. In the face of this fact, which seems none too well understood, we see publishers and authors occasionally showing something of the splendid intrepidity that one admires in the leader of a forlorn hope, and one thinks of them as perhaps the most public-spirited of all created beings. A little while ago my friend Mr. van Loon, for example, who is a very learned man, brought out a superb book, quite the kind of book that he himself would be glad to read; one need say no more for it than that. He and his publisher must both have known that they could not turn a penny by it; if it paid for itself it would be lucky. The full force of Gresham's law was pressing them instead to put their time and money into another of Mr. Van Loon's ingenious and attractive vulgarizations of history, which would be "sure fire" with a large literate public; yet they went on—went on in the teeth of the fact that under Gresham's law a "good book" must be a book as much as possible like another book that has sold a great number of copies.

What I have been driving at in all this is the suggestion that if we must reëxamine our social theories we should do so with an eye to natural law. Everyone seems a little uneasy about these theories at the moment, and many of our leading publicists say that they must be overhauled; well, if that be so, the practical thing would be to keep on the lee side of natural law while we do it. We have been a little careless about this hitherto, and the consequences are suggestive. Our idea of mass-education, for example, does vast credit to our intentions; like perpetual motion, the thing would be fine if it would work, but the mischief of it is to keep it from colliding with natural law. As results stand now, a graduating class of two, three or five hundred persons is practically nothing but a tableau-display of what the law of diminishing returns can do when it tries. Again, the promotion of mass-literacy is a noble experiment, but apparently there is no way to accommodate our idea of it to the insidious action of Gresham's law. With regard to these and all other aspects of our equalitarian social theory, my only aim is the humble one of suggesting that we bear in mind the disregard that nature has for unintelligent good intentions, and the vixenish severity with which she treats them.

IV

Finally, since various aspects of political theory are much to the fore just now, I suggest that we follow the same procedure with regard to them. Our ideas about the function of government may be very praiseworthy, very creditable, but surely the first thing is to find out whether natural law is with them or against them; and it is in this connexion that I cite the third law which I mentioned at the outset. This law is fundamental to economics, though for some reason our professional economists seldom say much about it; its formula is, *Man tends always to satisfy his needs and desires with the least possible exertion.* Not, it must be understood, that he always *does* so satisfy them, for other considerations—principle, convention, fear, superstition or what not—may supervene; but he always *tends* to satisfy them with the least possible exertion, and, in the absence of a stronger motive, will always do so.

A candid examination will show, I think, that this law is also fundamental to any serious study of politics. So long as the State stands as an impersonal mechanism which can confer an economic advantage at the mere touch of a button, men will seek by all sorts of ways to get at the button, because law-made property is acquired with less exertion than labour-made property. It is easier to push the button and get some form of State-created monopoly like a land-title, a tariff, concession or franchise, and pocket the proceeds, than it is to accumulate the same amount by work. Thus a political theory that admits any positive intervention by the State upon the individual has always this natural law to reckon with.

At the time our government was set up, a century and a half ago, some political thinkers, notably Franklin, had perceived the incidence of this law. Their idea was that it should be no function of the State to intervene upon society's economic life in a positive way, but only negatively as occasion required, to punish fraud and to safeguard the general régime of contract.[2] Aside from this, the State's only function should be that of safeguarding the lives and liberties of its citizens.

Contemporary British liberalism had the same idea; it advocated a rigid policy of State abstention. Liberalism's career was remarkable in presenting a most instructive object-lesson to those who study it in the light of natural law. Its programme missed one point, admitted one exception; and the consequences of this imperfection forced liberalism in the end to turn squarely around on its basic principle, and become godfather to the most elaborate series of positive interventions ever conceived in England.

This imperfect policy of non-intervention, or *laissez-faire,* led straight to a most hideous and dreadful eco-

[2] Franklin wrote, "Perhaps in general it would be better if government meddled no farther with trade than to protect it and let it take its course. Most of the statutes or acts, edicts, *arrêts* and placarts of parliaments, princes and States, for regulating, directing or restraining of trade, have, we think, been either political blunders or jobs obtained by artful men for private advantage, under pretense of public good." *Works,* Vol. II, p. 401.

nomic exploitation; starvation wages, slum-dwelling, killing hours, pauperism, coffin-ships, child-labour—nothing like it had ever been seen in modern times. Mr. Gradgrind, Mr. Bottles and Mr. Plugson of Undershot worked their will unhindered with a fine code of liberalist social philosophy behind them, and the mess they made shortly stank in the nostrils of all Christendom. People began to say, perhaps naturally, if this is what State abstention comes to, let us have some State intervention.

But the State *had* intervened; that was the whole trouble. The State had established one monopoly,—the landlord's monopoly of economic rent,—thereby shutting off great hordes of people from free access to the only source of human subsistence, and driving them into the factories to work for whatever Mr. Gradgrind and Mr. Bottles chose to give them. The land of England, while by no means nearly all *actually* occupied, was all *legally* occupied; and this State-created monopoly enabled landlords to satisfy their needs and desires with little exertion or none, but it also removed the land from competition with industry in the labour-market, thus creating a huge, constant and exigent labour-surplus.

Franklin saw this clearly; he used Turgôt's language almost word for word to show that the "labour-problem," *qua* labour-problem, really does not exist—it is purely a problem of State intervention, State-created monopoly. He said:

> Manufactures are founded in poverty. It is the number of poor without land in a country, and who must work for others at low wages or starve, that enables undertakers [i.e., enterprisers] to carry on a manufacture. . . .

But no man who can have a piece of land of his own, sufficient by his labour to subsist his family in plenty, is poor enough to be a manufacturer and work for a master.

But liberalism did not see this, never saw it; and the consequence was that in the end it was forced by political necessity to sponsor an ever-lengthening, ever-widening programme of regulations, supervisions, exemptions, subsidies, pensions—every measure of positive State interference, almost, that one could think of.

When the State has granted one privilege, its character as a purveyor of privilege is permanently established, and natural law does not permit it to stop with the creation of one privilege, but forces it to go on creating others. Once admit a single positive intervention "to help business," as our euphemism goes, and one class or group after another will accumulate political power in order to command further interventions; and these interventions will persist in force and frequency until they culminate in a policy of pure Statism—a policy which in turn culminates in the decay and disappearance of the society that invokes it.

Such is the grim testimony borne by the history of six civilizations, now vanished, to the validity of the law that *man tends always to satisfy his needs and desires with the least possible exertion*. We ought to be quite clear about this, as a matter of understanding the course of our present governmental policy. Some of us incline to regard the New Deal as something out of the run of our national history and unrelated to it, whereas it is exactly what the run of our history must inevitably have led up to.

One need only shift a switch in the New York Central's yard some three inches to determine whether a train shall go to Boston or to Chicago. We shifted the switch a hundred and fifty years ago, and set the national train going toward the Chicago of hundred-per-cent Statism, with our old friend natural law furnishing abundant steam. The New Deal means merely that we are now somewhere near South Bend, Indiana, and going strong; and if anyone knows how to reverse that train and head it toward Boston without an awful catastrophe, he is just the man that a good many of us would like to see.

The American State at the outset took over the British principle of giving landlords a monopoly of economic rent. That shifted the switch; it established the State's character as a purveyor of privilege. Then financial speculators sought a privilege, and Hamilton, with his "corrupt squadron in Congress," as Mr. Jefferson called them, arranged it. Then bankers, then industrialists; Hamilton also arranged that. Then, as the century went on, innumerable industrial subgroups, and subclasses of special interest, were heard from, and were accommodated. Then farmers, artisans, ex-soldiers, promoters of public utilities, began to accumulate political power with a view to privilege. Now, since the advent of universal suffrage, we are seeing the curious spectacle of the "unemployed" automatically transformed into the strongest kind of pressure-group; their numerical strength and consequent voting-power compelled Mr. Roosevelt to embrace the extraordinary doctrine that the State owes its citizens a living—an expedient little noticed at the time, I believe, but profoundly interesting to the student of historical continuity.

Moreover, as we saw in the case of Mr. Bottles and Mr. Plugson of Undershot, when the State confers a privilege, natural law impels the beneficiary to work it for all it is worth; and therefore the State must at once initiate a whole series of positive interventions to safeguard, control and regulate that privilege. A steady grist of "social" legislation must be ground; bureaus, boards and commissions must be set up, each with its elaborate mechanism; and thus bureaucracy comes into being. As the distribution of privilege goes on, the spawning of these regulative and supervisory agencies also goes on; and the result is a continuous enhancement of State power and a progressive weakening of social power, until, as in Rome after the Antonines, social power is quite extinguished—the individual lives, moves, and has his being only for the governmental machine, and society exists only in the service of the State. Meanwhile, at every step in this process, natural law is pushing interested persons, groups and factions on to get clandestine control of these supervisory agencies and use them for their own advantage; and thus a rapid general corruption sets in, for which no cure has ever yet been found, and from which no recovery has ever yet been made.

V

In a sense, no doubt, it seems officious to write a paper that squints toward a vindication of natural law, because natural law is quite competent and handy at vindicating itself; it needs no help, and has no notion of being any man's debtor. Tiberius Cæsar said in his strong commonsense way that "offenses against the gods are the gods' lookout," and perhaps it would be as well, certainly less thankless, if one should leave in their hands such little matters as those I have been discussing. Indeed, one must do that finally, for one can not hope that criticism based on nothing more pretentious than the plain natural truth of things will be much regarded; so probably as much or as little would be gained by doing it in the first instance.

Yet, in another view, it may be worth while to point out to simple-minded persons like myself, who are perhaps a little confused by the outpourings of publicists and the din of eager innovators, that natural law still exists and is still a respectable force. I have read many words about social reconstruction, industrial reconstruction, political reconstruction; in fact, as I write this paper I am inspired by the latest efforts in the great new enterprise of "economic planning." All these, in their innocent disregard of natural law, remind me of a piece of music I once saw, written for a cornetist. The music was good, but the composer had not put in any rests for the cornetist to take breath; well, as soon as one saw that, one knew that further examination of the piece was pointless. So, in what the journalists call "these hectic days," a suggestion that natural law is still at work, and that there is really not much that one can do about it, may be somewhat of a time-saver and trouble-saver to minds of the simpler sort, like my own; and to such, and such only, I offer it.

New York, February, 1934

17

The Path to the River

NORMALLY, one turns into it at about my age; or perhaps I should say, one discovers that one has turned into it, that one is off the main road. The point of departure must have been most inconspicuous; I did not notice it. All I recall noticing is that of a sudden I began to miss many familiar sights and sounds of traffic. The sensation was odd; it was somewhat like the sensation in one's ears when a locust stops chirring. It brought a certain pleasant ease, a feeling of liberation and expansion of spirit, leading up to an untroubled interest in the rich and quiet beauty of my new surroundings.

The path is winding; one can only guess how long it is, for one can not see its end from any point short of its last turn, apparently. Its declivity, so far, is very gentle; one hardly feels it. One has few companions, latterly almost none, and one is content with that. One or two are willing to go the whole way with me, which troubles me a little, and I hope they will not insist. They are young, and taking this journey just for company would break the continuity of their lives, and be but a tedious business, besides. Then, too, since they will some day be taking it on their own, why should they force themselves to take it twice?

My most astonishing realization is that I have lost a great lot of luggage. I can not imagine what has become of it. I thought I was still carrying almost all I started out with, but as I stop to count it up, a great deal of it is gone. Evidently one begins life like a person on his first trip to Europe, by loading up with things that one has no use for, and that get themselves left behind unnoticed, here and there. I discover that my interest in many matters which I thought were important, and would still say, off-hand, were important, no longer exists; interest in many occupations, theories, opinions; relationships, public and private; desires, habits, pleasures, even pastimes. I can still play good billiards, for instance, and if anyone asked me, I should reply unthinkingly that I enjoy the game; and then it would occur to me that I have not played for months running into years, and that I no longer care—not really—if I never play again. As an item of luggage, billiards has gone by the board, though I do not know when or how; and many matters of apparently greater importance have gone likewise. Other orders of interest, however, remain intact and, for all I can see, as fresh as ever—I think indeed much fresher, though this may be an illusion. At all events, it is only with these that I feel any longer a genuine concern.

Awareness that this process of unconscious sifting and selection has been going on is presumably final evidence that one is off the main road and well on the path to the river. It is called, rather patronizingly, "the acquiescence of age"; but may not that mean no more than an acquiescence in matters which have in the long run proven themselves hardly worth troubling one's head about? "The fashion of this world passeth away," said Goethe, "and I would fain occupy myself with the things that are abiding." If that be the acquiescence of age, make the most of it.

One in my position is expected, I believe, to have a special interest in questions about what, if anything, takes place on the other side of the river, and whether we are likely to have any hand in it. Do we indeed cross the river or do we melt away forever in its depths? I have never had any curiosity about these matters, nor have I any now. Such thought as I have given them has been unaffected, so far as I am aware (and I can not be responsible for what the Freudians might find going on in my *Unbewusstsein*) by any feeling of personal concern. Perhaps this absence of curiosity and concern may go some way towards giving my thoughts a passing interest for others who are likewise incurious and unconcerned, and I, therefore, write them down.

II

As a very small boy with a lively imagination and a budding sense of humour, I used to entertain myself at great length with speculations on what the human world would be like if we all lost our bodies. I made it out as on the whole a rather attractive picture, except that eating had to be counted out; this seemed an appalling calamity. It was more than balanced, however, by other considerations which were all to the good, such as the doing away with clothes and houses and, above all, the abolition of work. Work was inseparably related to food, clothes and shelter; and if there were no need for these, nobody would have to do any work, which suited me admirably.

There appeared to be no difficulty about imagining a distinct human personality existing apart from physical properties, or pervading them, as magnetism—whatever that is—pervades iron. In fact, the most nearly real world I knew, the only one about which I could approach anything like certainty in my own mind, was the world of consciousness. I got at its phenomena directly and was sure of them. I was not so sure of the phenomena of my physical environment, for I got at these indirectly through sense-perception, and my senses were always letting me down in one way or another; I was always having to true up their findings by experience, mostly disappointing, as in the case of plaster-of-Paris fruit or the apparent soundness of tree-limbs. Again, a sense of the most intimate phenomena of consciousness —those associated with music, for instance—was quite incommunicable by physical means; yet I saw that it was somehow communicated to other persons, to my father and mother and certain cronies, for they made responses so appropriate as to leave no doubt.

So sense-perception impressed me early, if vaguely, as a rather poor and fallible interpreter of my environment, and as having little to do with establishing my most interesting approximations to certainty. As I grew older and understood better what stringent limitations our dependence on sense-perception does really impose on us, I began to wonder how our actual present environment would appear if one could get oneself in immediate contact with it, and be no longer dependent on the very incomplete and special reports of five extremely imperfect and special faculties, or "senses"; one so imperfect, indeed, as to be almost useless, and another not much more valuable.

Thus it came about that when at the age of twenty or so I read the observations of Professor Huxley and others on the subject of consciousness, they seemed simple and clear, and not in the least surprising. "The transition from the physics of the brain to the facts of consciousness," said Romanes, "is unthinkable." Just so did it impress Huxley, as not only inexplicable but actually unthinkable. Consciousness exists, and we know it only as existing in association with that which has the properties of matter and force; yet it is clearly not matter or force or any conceivable modification of either; and an interpretation of it in terms of matter and force is simply beyond the power of thought.

By way of illustrating this as simply as possible, Professor Huxley cites the sense of red colour. I am now writing by the aid of a lamp done in red lacquer; I look at it and see that it is red. Trace the whole process of this perception; suppose, says Huxley, that you could watch all the light-waves, nervous reactions, molecular motion in the brain, possible electrical discharges, "as if they were billiard-balls"; at the end you would be as far from the ensuing fact of consciousness, "the feel of redness," as you were at the outset. The phenomena of consciousness can be to some extent controlled by mechanical means or by some appropriate chemical agent like bhang or alcohol, but this throws no light on the nature of consciousness itself. A colour-blind person's testimony about my lamp might not agree with mine, but the content of his consciousness, whatever it may be, is still as unaccountable in terms of matter and force as mine is.

At high noon one day on a crowded street in Berlin, a man behind me hooked his umbrella into my collar, after the manner of Mr. Squeers; and while he was hand-over-handing me in, I recognized him as an old acquaintance who had also recognized me. Just what was it that we recognized? There was not a particle left of the physical structure that either of us had seen before; we had not met in fifteen years, and our former bodies were all worn out and gone. A resemblance persisted, one may say, and he recognized that. True, no doubt, in the first instance; but he also immediately recognized *me;* and in my turn, instantly getting by the accidents of clothes and physique, I also recognized *him.* One may say, again, that our "personalities" overlived these physical changes, and recognized each other. Very well, but just what is personality, and how does it contrive to do all this overliving, and where do matter and force come in? If personality can overlive three, four or half-a-dozen bodies and get along so handsomely without them, might it not manage, on a pinch, to get along without any?

In other words, since we know consciousness only in association with matter and force, must we regard that association as intrinsic and essential? Can consciousness persist dissociated from them, either independently as bare "personality," or in association with some unknown quantity which has not their properties? If someone says flatly that it can not, we must ask him how he knows that. If he says it can, we must ask the same question. The conditions of inquiry being what they are, if he can give a competent answer either way, all we can say is that he is just the man whom a great many people would like to see.

III

Such was the conclusion reached by the best science of the last century, and I have not heard that latter-day science has brought forward anything to invalidate or modify it. One may, therefore, I think, be excused from taking interest in any attempts to reach a "scientific proof" that personality survives death, because these attempts must rest on evidence of the senses; and in the premises, this order of evidence, as we have seen, is inadmissible. For example, if a person says to me, "You will never see me again after I die," it is open to me to reply, "Possibly; but since I never yet saw you and do not see you now, why should I expect to see you then? I see a body and some clothes, but the body is not the same one that I saw a week ago or that I shall see a week hence. I never saw *you,* never shall and never can."

Or, on the other hand, suppose he says, "I can prove objectively that I shall be alive after death," I might reply, "Why, bless you, you can't even prove objectively that you are alive now." Nor can he. Or, suppose he puts it thus, "Personality survives death; and to prove it, I will cause bells to be rung, furniture to be moved around, photographs to be taken, and messages to be written, all by invisible agencies. I will even cause a disembodied spirit to invade my own physical organism and control it, and give you assurance by word of my mouth." I might reply, "Yes, that is all very fine, very good, but it may not prove what you say it does. It may prove only that you are an uncommonly smart man. Moreover, if I admit your evidence, I can admit it only *in limine;* that is, admitting that the disembodied spirit is there and is alive, what does that prove about a future state for you, me, Tom, Dick or Harry? Nothing. If the spirit says it does prove something, who knows but the spirit may be wrong? The assumption that it must be right is clearly gratuitous." The *Santissimo Salvatore* spoke with immense philosophical profundity and soundness when He said that "if they hear not Moses and the prophets, neither will they be persuaded though one rose from the dead." If any conviction on this matter is to be reached, its reasonableness must be established by an entirely different method of approach.

This, apparently, is as it should be. Prince Alfonso of Castile is said to have remarked that if he had been present at the creation of the world he would have suggested some valuable improvements. If man were never to progress beyond the first stages of development, we too might suggest some; we might suggest a world in which there should be no pain, sorrow, labour, bereavement, disappointment, hardship. The trouble is that without these any progress in human development is unimaginable; nobody could ever get on. If there were no such thing as pain, if nothing hurt, the race would not last six months; if there were no sorrow or hardship, it could not elaborate any more character than a jellyfish—and so on. When one thinks these matters through to their logical end, taking careful account of everything, one finds it impossible to imagine human development going on as satisfactorily in any other circumstances than those we are in.

Hence it is probably no bad thing that man is held

down pretty closely to the consideration of one world at a time. Suppose it were otherwise; suppose that by some miracle he were able to get what we call scientific proof that he would, or that he would not, live after death,—cogent, irrefutable proof,—it is easy to imagine the utterly enervating preoccupations that would ensue upon him in either case. One can not say whether they would be more debilitating and retarding in the one case or in the other. The flavour of such preoccupations that one gets from the history of mediæval Christianity is enough to intimate the irreparable misfortune that would be brought upon a world possessed by certainty on this point. It is a great advantage to us that by the ordinary standards of analysis we can know no more than we do; that conviction alone is admissible in the premises, and that the reasonableness of conviction, whether affirmative or negative, can be made out only by an order of evidence which is distinctly subjective.

For my own part, I have an extremely strong conviction that human personality overlives death; so strong and apparently so reasonable that I have long ceased to question it. This is not the same thing as saying I believe that my own personality will survive death, for I can not say that; in fact, I doubt it. I have an instinctive feeling that it will, but when I examine the basis available for rationalizing that feeling, I find it too slight to command confidence. These statements are not inconsistent, as I shall presently show.

IV

There are certain orders or categories of human activity which are useful and indispensable, to which, nevertheless, one can not attach the idea of persistence. As I saw in my childhood's fancies, there is an insurmountable incongruity in such an association; natural truth is all against it. These are what St. Paul calls the ἐπίγεια. The King James Version gives the translation, "earthly things"; that is to say, lines of activity which meet purely physical demands, and which can not be conceived of as going on after these demands have ceased. For example, one can not possibly imagine oneself manufacturing motor-cars "to all eternity," as our phrase goes, or selling bonds, or running a bank. Death would automatically dissociate us from innumerable pursuits such as these, and we can perceive at once that it must do so.

On the other hand, there are categories of activity with respect to which an association with persistence is at least imaginable. Natural truth, if not flatly affirming this association, is at least not flatly against it. In the light of natural truth there is no absolute, violent, even ludicrous incongruity in the suggestion, such as instantly appears when we attempt to contemplate the idea of persistence in the other categories just mentioned. For example, when the Greek mathematician said that God "geometrizes continually," his conception strikes us as not precisely unimaginable or precisely ridiculous. Natural truth goes along with it far enough at least to intimate that despite philology, geometry is not quite one of the ἐπίγεια. It has a differentiating quality. As much may be said of the Aristotelian ποίησις, and of the exercise of certain virtues and affections. Even the clear and lucid perception of the later Greeks saw here no actual collision with natural truth. The last words of Socrates, both to his friends and to his judges, the elegiac lines on

Plato's young and gifted successor, the Master of the Portico, show conviction open either way; natural truth asserts no jurisdiction. It is only in the association of persistence with the practice of love[1] that we first see natural truth legitimized in the parentage of a profound conviction. Heliodorus and Diogeneia, the devoted lovers, died within the same hour; and their friend Apollonides declares that death is no bar to their felicity, but that they are now "as happy lying in the same tomb as they were when lying in the same bed."

As I have already said, I could not possibly prove, even to myself, by the accepted standards of scientific analysis, that I am alive at this moment. *Cogito ergo sum* takes one but a precious little way, as has often been shown. Yet I know I am alive, I have an unshakable conviction about it, built up in this way: In the realm of the ἐπίγεια there are certain disciplines, mostly very rigorous, such as the discipline of hard physical work, the discipline of business and its competitions, the various disciplines prescribed by the social order. Engagement with any of these is attended by a keen sense of *life,* and the closer the engagement the more abounding and exalted the sense becomes; and this sense gives rise to strong conviction and supports it. Our vernacular has terms that reflect this experience. A hard set of tennis, for instance, makes one feel "all alive," and so does a fast bout at commercial competition, or leading a forlorn hope in an attack on sales-resistance. Thus too do we speak of the "live man" or the one who is "alive on his job."

[1] Ἀγάπη; στοργή hardly covers it; certainly not ἔρως.

Conviction on this point, then, appears to be pretty strictly the fruit of experience. Now, leaving the ἐπίγεια and going over into the categories where natural truth is not so peremptory about its findings, one meets with a precise parallel to all this. Here, too, are certain disciplines; the discipline of pure mathematics (to touch again the matter already spoken of), the discipline of the ποίησις, the discipline peculiar to the successful practice of certain virtues and affections, such as the affection of love.[2] Here, too, the occupation with these disciplines is attended by a strong sense of *life,* but life of a different order, corresponding to the order of experience that excites this sense. Here, too, the more one does with these disciplines, the harder one works at them, the stronger this sense becomes; and when it becomes strong enough it leads to conviction—sometimes, as in my own case, impersonal. I am sure as one can be of anything in this highly uncertain world that *some* will survive death, but my own practice of these disciplines has been too weak-willed and fitful to give me any assurance beyond this; it does not assure me that I shall be among them.

The point is that in both sets of categories alike the sense of life and the conviction proceeding from it are matters of experience alone. Conviction is conditioned by experience; it is practically impossible to entertain a conviction that experience does not to some degree back up. Hence it is not to be wondered at that a conviction of the persistence of personality is relatively uncommon at the present time. Both in the realm of thought and action the general tendency is towards an

[2] Ἀγάπη again.

exclusive preoccupation with the ἐπίγεια; take the ἐπίγεια away, and practically the whole of our experience disappears with it; there is nothing left with which we can associate the idea of persistence. It is impossible to make conviction transcend experience; hence the effort to relate persistence to the only kind of life that we have ever experienced results merely in the consciousness of a wholly inadmissible anomaly.

The fifteenth chapter of the First Epistle to the Corinthians is one of the few passages of Scripture that remain at all generally well known; we hear it read at funerals. We may have remarked how impatiently and perfunctorily St. Paul runs off his arguments for persistence, or as he calls it, "immortality," and that in the midst of his arguments he drops in the apparently irrelevant quotation from Menander, that "evil communications corrupt good manners." There is no irrelevance here, however; the quotation conveys the whole point of what he has to say. The civilization of Corinth, like our own, was wholly made up of mundanities; and the gist of the passage is as if he had said, "Here are your arguments, but I might about as well save my breath. You can not take them in, not because they are unsound, but on account of your evil communications; you can not transcend your own experience. The only kind of life you know anything about is not worth being immortal, and you can not help being aware of it."

One may not overpress the point, of course, yet it is worth remarking how persistently the Biblical writers relate the idea of *life* to the practice of special disciplines in the second set of categories that we have been noticing. One such discipline "tendeth to *life*"; in the practice of it "is *life,* and in the pathway thereof there is no death." Another discipline, vividly personified, declares that "whoso findeth me findeth *life.*" Of another it is said, again, that whoso followeth it "findeth *life.*" Of another, that its admonitions "are *life* to those that find them." The great exponent of these disciplines is said to have come that they "might have *life.*" His precepts go forth, "and they that hear *shall live.*" A concordance will show the almost unfailing regularity with which this association occurs; and while, I repeat, too much may not be made of it, one may observe in it, as far as it goes, an interesting correspondence with the suggestions of experience.

V

Unquestionably, too, as one studies the order of nature, one gets certain intimations of purpose. One must speak of these with great caution, for theologians and poets alike have monstrously exaggerated their evidential value. Nevertheless, they are not, I think, to be flatly disregarded; natural truth invests them with a plausibility that is doubtless slight and vague, but is yet sufficiently definite to keep them in view. Nature appears to be very wasteful and to "make for righteousness" by very roundabout ways; yet on closer inspection her most conspicuous wastes turn out to be made in behalf of some highly interesting economies. The most one may say, perhaps, is that under her régime nothing is going to be saved, finally, that is not worth saving. Whether all that is worth saving will be saved is, of course, another question. Still another question is, how far our present estimate of what is and what is not worth saving will be found in the long run to accord with her inscrutable economy.

For my own part, I could not hold it as any count against the order of nature if my own personality did not survive death. On the other hand, my intimations of purpose in nature, vague as they may be, are distinctly affronted by the suggestion that certain other personalities do not survive death. If Socrates, Marcus Aurelius, Dante, Cervantes, Shakespeare and Rabelais do not survive death, then, as all my intimations lead me to see it, the order of nature is a most inglorious fizzle. My intimations bear the same testimony, too, in behalf of equally eminent practitioners, such as we have all seen and revered, who have passed their days in humbler stations and whose eminence, therefore, remains unknown to the world at large.

I see no reason why the great majority of mankind should survive death, because experience and the intimations of purpose in nature alike present the idea of persistence as an achievement, as a matter of diligent and progressive adaptation to environment; and here, too, the analogy with our physical life seems close and orderly. Von Humboldt says that no one could pass from Siberia into Senegal without losing consciousness; one could not expect to survive a sudden change into an environment wholly alien to one's adaptations. To all appearances, then, in respect of adaptation to any other than a purely secular environment, the vast majority are so dead while they live that one may suppose they stay dead when they die. It is quite conceivable that a person's body might outlive his faculty for adaptation; in other words, that his soul—if for convenience one may so designate that faculty—may die before his body does. Quite conceivably his soul might die without his knowing it. Quite conceivably, too, on the other hand, he might have enough vitality of faculty to stand the actual transition into an alien environment, but not enough to enable the process of adaptation to go on; somewhat like a consumptive who has been too dilatory about measures which, taken in time, would enable him to rebuild himself after moving into a favourable climate.

It is thus, then, that I view the matter; and as I have said, as far as I am aware, I view it without prejudice, and certainly with no sense of personal concern. Experience, the intimations of purpose in nature, and the largest available understanding of nature's economies, all, I think, suggest this view as at least permissible; the view that—

> the energy of life may be
> Kept on after the grave, but not begun;
> And he who flagged not in the earthly strife,
> From strength to strength advancing—only he,
> His soul well-knit, and all his battles won,
> Mounts, *and that hardly,* to eternal life.

VI

My adventures on the main road were uncommonly many and diversified. I sought them with ardent curiosity, turned them inside out, and got all kinds of profit from them, except money and fame. Yet I can think of none that I would wish to repeat, nor do I ever find myself looking back upon any of them with any sentiment except that of thankfulness that almost all of them were good. They were good, I have had them, I am sincerely thankful for them, but now that their time is past, I seldom think of them at all, and never desirously or with regret. Nor am I ever tempted to throw any inquiring glances forward into the future, not even upon the fact of death. One rehearses for it so many thousand times on going to bed at night that one is unlikely to get stage-fright over the full-dress performance. The most beautiful figure in all human history, meditating in his encampment "among the Quadi, at the Granua," told himself with hard common sense that "he who fears death either fears the loss of sensation or a different kind of sensation. But if thou shalt have no sensation, neither wilt thou feel any harm; and if thou shalt acquire another kind of sensation, thou wilt be a different kind of living being, and thou wilt not cease to live."

Among the many keen interests of the present there are one or two little undertakings that for my own satisfaction I should like to complete, or at least to carry farther forward. I hope the path will remain peaceful and easy enough to permit me to work at them while I am still able to work. But I am not aware of any anxiety even about this, for these conditions are not in my control, and if they went against me I could find no reason to complain. My state of mind with reference to them, as far as I know it, is that of one who regards himself as

> . . . a citizen of this great state, the world: what difference does it make to thee whether for five years or three? . . . Where is the hardship, then, if no tyrant or unjust judge sends thee away from the state, but nature who brought thee into it? The same as if a prætor who has employed an actor dismisses him from the stage: "But I have not finished the five acts, but only three of them."

Thou sayest well, but in life the three acts are the whole drama; for what shall be a complete drama is determined by him who was once the cause of its composition, and now of its dissolution; but thou art the cause of neither. Depart then satisfied, for he also who releases thee is satisfied.

Brussels, February, 1932